John

EARLY REVIEWS OF *DREAM MAKERS AND DEAL BREAKERS*

"A totally professional presentation of the venture capital market for the novice and older hands who think they know it all. This is a thorough and thoughtful description of the entrepreneurial process, interestingly written and a marvelous guide through the labyrinth."

> **Victor K. Kiam II**
> Chief Executive Officer
> Remington Products, Inc.
> Owner of the New England Patriots

"Congratulations on your very fine book, DREAM MAKERS AND DEAL BREAKERS. Best wishes for every success with your outstanding publication."

> **Sam Walton**
> Chairman of the Board
> Wal-Mart Stores, Inc.

"Our members have called raising venture capital a form of Russian roulette. If you want to increase your chances of having an empty chamber in your gun, read DREAM MAKERS."

> **Joseph R. Mancuso,** founder
> The Center for Entrepreneurial Management
> and The Chief Executive Officers Club
> Author of several best-selling books on entrepreneurship

"You don't have to take a risk to benefit from this good deal. Keith has done it again! Must reading for the entrepreneur."

> **Robert Leeds**
> Former Chairman and
> Chief Executive Officer
> Manhattan Industries

"DREAM MAKERS AND DEAL BREAKERS is absolutely fascinating—an in-depth primer that avoids being pedantic or dull."

Frederick R. Adler
Adler & Shaykin
Adler & Co.

"I found it to be an excellent introduction to the venture capital industry, with a good balance between the basics and the folklore."

James R. Swartz
Accel Partners

"It is really an outstanding piece of work. It should be targeted not only at entrepreneurs but at anyone who needs to understand the venture capital process, including MBA students, policymakers, institutional investors, and novice VCs."

Gordon Baty
Zero Stage Capital

"Well-written, concise and should be read by any entrepreneur before approaching the venture capital industry. I will personally buy at least twelve copies for distribution."

Neill H. Brownstein
Bessemer Venture Partners

"You have made a very complex process straight forward and easy to understand. Perhaps, most importantly, by explaining the process you have helped the entrepreneur gain a sense of timing when to approach the capital markets for financing help."

Howard M. Arnold
President and
Chief Executive Officer
Chartway Technologies

DREAM MAKERS
AND DEAL BREAKERS

Inside the Venture
Capital Industry

W. Keith Schilit

Prentice Hall, Englewood Cliffs, New Jersey 07632

Editorial/production supervision
and interior design: MARY P. ROTTINO
Cover design: LUNDGREN GRAPHICS, LTD.
Manufacturing buyers: KELLY BEHR AND SUSAN BRUNKE
Acquisitions editor: JOHN WILLIG

 Published by Prentice-Hall, Inc.
A Division of Simon & Schuster
Englewood Cliffs, New Jersey 07632

The publisher offers discounts on this book when ordered
in bulk quantities. For more information, write:

Special Sales/College Marketing
College Technical and Reference Division
Prentice-Hall
Englewood Cliffs, New Jersey 07632

Printed in the United States of America
10 9 8 7 6 5 4 3 2 1

ISBN 0-13-934035-1

PRENTICE-HALL INTERNATIONAL (UK) LIMITED, London
PRENTICE-HALL OF AUSTRALIA PTY. LIMITED, Sydney
PRENTICE-HALL CANADA INC., Toronto
PRENTICE-HALL HISPANOAMERICANA, S.A., Mexico
PRENTICE-HALL OF INDIA PRIVATE LIMITED, New Delhi
PRENTICE-HALL OF JAPAN, INC., Tokyo
SIMON & SCHUSTER ASIA, PTE. LTD., Singapore
EDITORA PRENTICE-HALL DO BRASIL, LTDA., Rio de Janeiro

To our newest Dream Maker,
Jordan Michael Schilit

Contents

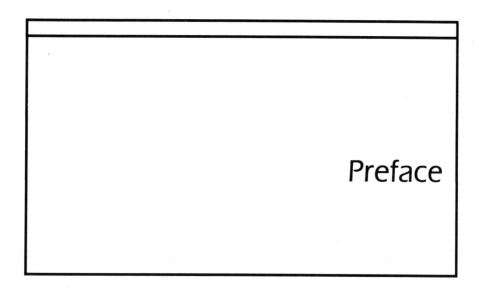

Preface

Several months ago I had the privilege of delivering a keynote address on the topic of strategic planning at a national association annual meeting. As fate would have it, an old friend of mine with whom I had not had contact in more than fifteen years just happened to be at the meeting. It took me a few moments to recognize my friend. After all, he had gone through quite a transformation since the early 1970s; his beard and long hair were replaced by a conservative hairstyle (at least what was left of his hair), and his jeans and tee-shirt were replaced by a traditional "power" suit.

After we talked for a few minutes, it was no surprise to see how we "liberal visionaries" of the 1960s and early 1970s were transformed into the "conservative entrepreneurs" of the 1980s. Since we had last seen each other, we had both spent a good deal of time in the corporate world and had launched business ventures of our own. It soon became obvious that we would be spending more time talking with each other over the next two days of the meeting than we would be attending the other sessions.

I learned that my friend had done quite well for himself. He founded a business about ten years ago and had taken the company from start-up to *Inc.* 500 status.[1] He was now preparing to "take the company public." This would not only make him a multimillionaire, but it would provide his company with the necessary infusion of capital to continue its sensational growth. This was the culmination of a ten-year process that typically included 100-hour work weeks and virtually no vacation time. To him—and to countless others like him—this was the "entrepreneurial dream."

[1]The *Inc.* 500, which is published annually by *Inc.* magazine, is a listing of the fastest growing privately held companies in the United States.

As an outsider, it's easy to focus on the successes that my friend has enjoyed over the years and to ignore the risks and problems that typically confront such high-growth, entrepreneurial companies. To make sure that I didn't come away from the conversation with such a one-sided view of the joys of launching and managing a company whose revenues had been increasing by an average of well over 100% per year, he let me know about the many obstacles that he, like so many other entrepreneurs, faced. In his own words,

> "Entrepreneurship is a roller coaster ride. There are ups and downs every week. There are great rewards, but even greater risks. You never know what to expect next."

He then told me that his greatest concern during his "roller coaster ride" was his attempt to raise capital for his business. To go along with the company's meteoric growth came the need for money to expand operations. He said that this problem was continual. It was puzzling to me why he felt that was such a problem; after all, he was successful in raising two rounds of venture capital from established venture capital firms. He remarked, however, that "making deals" (as he loved to call it) was the only business activity that he has gone through over the past ten years for which, despite his knowledge of his industry and the skills that he had developed in managing his enterprise, he felt, in his own words, "unprepared" and "overmatched."

Nonetheless, my friend felt that the experience was far from unpleasant. In fact, according to him,

> "Aside from my difficulty in dealing with the uncertainty of the situation, it was a rather pleasant experience. It was just so new to me that I didn't know what to anticipate."

It's hard to imagine my friend, who had always taken the Boy Scout slogan, "be prepared," to its upper limits, felt that he was unprepared in *any* situation. However, the venture capital process is not your typical everyday situation. That is, it's *not* your everyday situation if you're an entrepreneur. On the other hand, it *is* your everyday situation if you're a venture capitalist. For that reason, the venture capitalist is usually much better able to anticipate what will take place when an entrepreneur is seeking capital than is the entrepreneur. The result: "dreams come true" for some and "deals gone bust" for others.

Interestingly, I've had this same basic conversation, as the one with my friend, with dozens of entrepreneurs over the years. In most cases, it seems as if the entrepreneur knows very little about the more than *$30 billion* venture capital industry, which, as we will soon see, has been a major force in entrepreneurial growth in this country. Moreover, I have found that many entrepreneurs have (often erroneous) preconceived notions about venture capitalists and about the venture capitalists' relationship with entrepreneurial companies.

Too often, I've heard entrepreneurs speak about this relationship as adversarial. Why? This is largely due to two reasons: (1) the difficulty of the negotiation process (or the structuring of the "deal"), which, as just mentioned, is generally more novel to the entrepreneur than to the investor; and (2) the feeling among entrepreneurs, rightly or wrongly, that the venture capitalist has not lived up to (or will not live up to) his or her expectations. Not surprisingly, I often hear completely different stories about this relationship when I speak to venture capitalists as compared to when I speak to entrepreneurs.

Certainly, there are instances when there are problems in the venture capitalist–entrepreneur relationship (which will be discussed in the next few chapters). However, my experience is that most entrepreneurs that find this relationship adversarial have generally had little or no firsthand contact with *creditable* venture capital firms.[2]

Nonetheless, although there are dozens of high-quality venture capital firms, both large and small, that epitomize the "valued partnership" that can develop between the entrepreneur and the venture capitalist, it is important to note that there is a wide variance in the quality of venture capitalists. The reputable venture capital firms generally have the appropriate professionals to provide significant benefit to the entrepreneurial company. In reality, however, just about *anybody* can be a *venture capitalist* (if we use the term venture capitalist very loosely; we'll define the term as best we can in Chapter 3). For many people, all it takes to enter this profession is some money and/or some contacts. Unfortunately, due to the potential lucrative nature of the profession, the industry has attracted several less than reputable individuals, some of whom are more interested in making a quick deal with a quick payoff than in promoting the growth of emerging ventures. This has resulted in "broken deals" and "shattered dreams." As we'll see later, these "quick-buck artists" certainly do not represent the industry as a whole.

My experience has been that most entrepreneurs who have worked with the more credible venture capitalists generally view this *long-term* relationship, which will generally last five to ten years or more, quite positively. They recognize the value that venture capitalists provide to a company in terms of experience, contacts, long-range planning, management recruitment, and general guidance. To them, venture capital and the entire process that surrounds it have been the *catalyst* to fuel their growth. For that reason, venture capitalists have taken on the role of "venture catalysts," rather than of mere investors, in many growth companies. Consequently, insightful entrepreneurs will usually have one or two capable venture capitalists maintain an active partnership with their company throughout its growth.

---

[2]By creditable, I am referring not only to the giants of the industry (*a few of which* would include such firms as Kleiner Perkins Caufield & Byers, E. M. Warburg, Pincus & Co., Hambrecht & Quist , Burr Egan Deleage & Co., New Enterprise Associates, Mayfield Fund, Brentwood Associates, Sequoia Capital, The Adler Group, and Alan Patricof Associates), but also to the medium-sized firms (*a representative sample* of which would include Accel Partners, Technology Venture Investors, Bessemer Venture Partners, Allsop Ventures, and Allied Capital) and the smaller—and often more specialized—venture capital firms (of which there are *dozens,* including Palmer Partners, DSV Partners, Avalon Ventures, Onset, Phillips-Smith Specialty Retail Group, and Zero Stage Capital) that demonstrate the potential value of the venture capitalist–entrepreneur partnership.

Consider, for example, Compaq Computer, one of the greatest entrepreneurial success stories in recent years. Benjamin Rosen of the venture capital firm Sevin Rosen Management Co., one of the early-stage investors in this high-growth computer manufacturer, is still chairman of Compaq. In addition, numerous other venture capitalists are active members of the boards of directors of some of the other superstar entrepreneurial companies in this country. Obviously, their involvement is far deeper than financial, especially since many of them are still actively involved in these ventures after the companies have gone public and the venture capitalists have cashed out (at least a portion) or their equity position with the company. In all respects, they have served as "venture catalysts" in fostering the development of these ventures and in making these entrepreneurial dreams a reality.

∿∿∿∿∿∿∿∿∿∿∿

The focus of this book is on the role of venture capital (and the venture capital industry) in facilitating the success of entrepreneurial companies and in fostering economic growth. The primary target for this book is the entrepreneur who is seeking to gain knowledge about the nature of venture capital and about the process of securing venture capital. Therefore, the book is both *descriptive,* in providing background information about the industry and its recent trends, and *prescriptive,* in providing practical information for entrepreneurs in their quest for funding. For the entrepreneur, I explore such questions as:

- How is the venture capital industry organized?
- How do venture capitalists make investment decisions?
- How are venture capital deals structured?
- In what kind of companies do venture capitalists invest?
- What is the expected return for a venture capital investment?

Of course, these questions are also of concern to anyone interested in providing financing to entrepreneurial companies.

Although I've presented several suggestions in this book to assist the entrepreneur in his or her quest for venture capital, this book is not presented merely as a "how-to" book.[3] It is a book that should be read by anyone interested in economic development and the free enterprise system. I examine such questions as:

- How have the entrepreneurial "dreams"—like Federal Express, Apple Computer, Compaq Computer, and Sun Microsystems—grown from "seedlings" to multibillion dollar corporations?
- Which companies will be the next wave of entrepreneurial success stories?
- What impact have such companies had on our economy?

[3]If, however, you are specifically looking for an easy-to-follow, "how-to" workbook in the area of raising venture capital, I would encourage you to read my recent book entitled, *The Entrepreneur's Guide to Preparing a Winning Business Plan and Raising Venture Capital,* Prentice Hall, Englewood Cliffs, N.J., 1990.

- What developments are occurring that are likely to lead to a global entrepreneurial economy?

NNNNNNNNNNNNNN

This book is the result of several years of research and experience in the area of venture capital. I explore the issues involved in the venture capital process from the perspectives of the venture capitalists (who have been either "dream makers" or "deal breakers," depending on the situation) and of the entrepreneurs (who have often been referred to as "risk takers"). I, therefore, present both the positive and negative aspects of the venture capital relationship. As we will soon see, there is some justification for viewing this relationship in an adversarial manner: In some cases, venture capitalists do not live up to their expectations; in other cases, entrepreneurs do not live up to their expectations. On balance, however, my experience suggests that, when it is done right, the venture capital partnership has been one of the most powerful ingredients in enhancing the success of entrepreneurial companies. In many regards, this partnership is "the perfect marriage": Both parties depend on one another; both parties grow; both parties benefit.

Acknowledgments

I am extremely grateful to the editorial staff at Prentice Hall for refining this manuscript into its present form. In particular, Jane Bonnell deserves some long overdue credit for her diligent work on my previous book as does Mary Rottino for her efforts with this book. John Willig, executive editor, deserves special thanks for overseeing the entire process from start to finish. In addition, several anonymous reviewers provided keen insight on how to better structure my book.

Over the years, I have benefited greatly from discussions with members of the venture capital community, who have enhanced my understanding of the process surrounding venture capital deals. I will not include all their names here because not only would it take too long to mention all these individuals, but I would certainly inadvertently leave out several of them from the list. However, I would like to recognize a few of the experts in the field who have provided me with specific comments on early drafts of this book. They include Lionel Pincus (E. M. Warburg, Pincus & Co.), Alan Patricof (Alan Patricof Associates), Fred Adler (Adler & Co.; Adler & Shaykin), Don Valentine (Sequoia Capital), Neill Brownstein (Bessemer Venture Partners), Jim Swartz (Accel Partners), Gordon Baty (Zero Stage Capital), and John Shane (Palmer Partners) and Peter McNeish (National Association of Small Business Investment Companies).

I have always believed that the best source of information for reaching a target audience is an entrepreneur who understands the risks and rewards of going through such a process. Several successful entrepreneurs have provided me with some excellent suggestions on how to better reach my target audience. They include: Victor Kiam (chairman of Remington Products and owner of the

New England Patriots, as well as author of a few bestsellers), Sam Walton (founder and chairman of Wal-Mart), Fred Smith (founder and chairman of Federal Express), Bob Leeds (former chairman of Manhattan Industries), Howard Arnold (founder and CEO of Chartway Technologies; founder of Sage Federal Systems and Sage Software), Mitchell Kapor (founder of Lotus Development and ON Technology), A.L. Frank (founder, ONYX Software, Inc.), T. J. Rodgers (founder and CEO of Cypress Semiconductors), Karl H. Vesper (entrepreneur as well as Distinguished Professor, University of Washington, Graduate School of Business Administration), and Joe Mancuso (founder of the Center for Entreprenurial Management; noted author). I also wish to thank the Honorable Sam M. Gibbons (U.S. Congress) for his comments.

I was also fortunate enough to have some of the experts in venture capital in my local community of Tampa provide input on early drafts of this manuscript. I wish to thank Steve Holtzman (partner at the securities law firm Shasteen & Holtzman, Geoff Simon (developer and executive producer of the *Suncoast Business Journal*), and Joel Reedy (who is the creative genius behind the title of this book) for their assistance.

As with most creative works, this project actually happened by chance. Had it not been for a "career-interrupting" knee injury suffered during an "over-the-hill" pick-up basketball game, which sidelined me for several months (in effect, it allowed me to prop my foot up on my desk while I composed the first draft of this manuscript), I would never have had the opportunity to devote the necessary time to write this book. I, therefore, thank my friends at the Harbour Island Athletic Club in Tampa for giving me this opportunity.

Finally, I wish to thank my parents, my brothers, Rob and Howard, my sister Audrey, and my wife, Karen, for their support and wisdom. Karen deserves a special note of thanks, not only for putting up with my schedule during this project, but for bouncing out the newest member of the Schilit family, Jordan Michael, into this world just around the time this book came out of production.

PART I

THE ROLE OF VENTURE CAPITAL IN OUR ECONOMY

Chapter 1

Venture Catalysts and Vulture Capitalists

Having spent several years of my life living in Washington, D.C., one of my most vivid memories of that city is sitting in rush hour traffic on the Beltway, staring at the license plate on the car in front of mine. Something exciting, however, has developed there over the past ten years or so, which has taken my mind off the traffic problem. It seems as though every few months when I return to the nation's capital several new office parks have opened. The suburbs of Maryland and Northern Virginia, such as Rockville, Gaithersburg, Herndon, Manassas, and Fairfax, which were once merely "dots on a map," are now the homes of such successful entrepreneurial companies as Chartway Technologies (which is an outgrowth of Sage Systems), Tempest Technologies, Vanguard Tech International, Iverson Technology, Data Measurement, and some of the countless other businesses that are ranked among the fastest growing emerging businesses in the country. Sure, I still get stuck in rush hour traffic on the Beltway. But I now get to experience the growth of new business activity while I'm driving along a 55 mile per hour road at 5 miles per hour.

The same scenario has unfolded in several other cities across America. A drive along Route 128 near Boston toward some of the suburbs located northwest of the city also reveals one new office building after another. The number of emerging growth ventures has been so much greater than the supply of office and manufacturing space in downtown Boston that the city, very much like Washington, D.C., has expanded in size to keep up with industrial development. Pretty soon, the only landmark to tell you that you are no longer in the Boston area will be a sign that says, "Welcome to New Hampshire."

Similar entrepreneurial growth has been evident in the San Diego–La Jolla area, as well as throughout California. The same is true in Dallas and its neighboring suburbs such as Richardson. Likewise, Atlanta, along with its suburbs of Marietta and Roswell, has experienced and is likely to continue to experience meteoric growth of emerging business ventures. Throughout the country, cities like Portland, Princeton, Minneapolis–St. Paul, Phoenix, Tampa, Orlando, Austin, Memphis, and Raleigh–Durham are becoming major centers of entrepreneurial activity.

AN ENTREPRENEURIAL ECONOMY

What prompted these developments? How has the situation evolved over the last twenty to thirty years? What has been the impact on the economy?

Interestingly, the period immediately following World War II could hardly be called "entrepreneurial." Rather, this period was marked by the unprecedented growth of our largest industrial organizations and by an emphasis among American corporations on diversification and multinationalism. Moreover, the success of such giants as General Motors, Ford, ITT, and Goodyear suggested that what was good for GM was, indeed, good for this country.

Within a few years, however, major corporations such as U.S. Steel, Financial Corporation of America, Continental Illinois, Eastern Airlines, and Braniff were faced with declining profits and employment, restructuring, and, in some cases, failure. The result of this has been the emergence of a new hero in our economy—the *entrepreneur*. Over the past decade or so, we have shifted from a managerial economy to an entrepreneurial economy; concurrently, buzzwords such as "strategic planning" and "competitive strategy," which formed the basis of the private enterprise system from the 1950s through the beginning of the 1980s, have been replaced by such terms as "risk taking," "innovation," and "entrepreneurship."

The Role of the Entrepreneurial Economy in Creating Employment

Although the 1970s through the first part of the 1980s was a period marked by "stagflation" and "deindustrialization," one outcome of the entrepreneurial economy that has developed over the past two decades has been the creation of the largest peacetime economic expansion in American history. While *Fortune* 500[1] companies accounted for most of the jobs created between the mid-1940s and the mid-1960s and small business accounted for most of the jobs *lost* during recessions in that period, the situation has changed dramatically in recent years. Since the mid-1960s, small businesses have become the driving force behind a vibrant economy, creating jobs and profits much faster than have the *Fortune* 500 companies. From the mid-1960s to the mid-1980s, while *Fortune* 500 companies *lost* approximately 5 million jobs, small businesses

[1]The *Fortune* 500 is a listing of the 500 largest industrial corporations based in the United States, as ranked by *Fortune* magazine.

created about 35 million new jobs, most of which resulted from new businesses in such industries as overnight mail delivery, specialty retailing, environmental management, computer electronics, and biotechnology that did not even exist twenty-five years ago.

Since the mid-1960s, small businesses have become the driving force behind a vibrant economy, creating jobs and profits much faster than have the *Fortune* 500 companies.

The creation of jobs has been just one outcome of the entrepreneurial economy. As we will soon see, entrepreneurial companies have created economic and social benefits for communities and have improved quality standards for numerous products and services.

The Entrepreneurial Economy Pervades in High-tech and Low-tech Industries

Some High-tech Success Stories.   Over the past decade, high tech has become fashionable, and high-tech stocks have become the "glamour" initial public offerings (IPOs) that typify the entrepreneurial dream. Apple Computer, which was founded by two "whiz kids," Steven Jobs and Stephen Wozniak, in Cupertino, California, for example, has grown from a start-up company in the mid-1970s to a profitable and highly innovative $5.3 billion company today. Of course, Apple is not alone in this regard. Several other companies, such as Compaq Computer (Houston, Texas), Tandem Computer (Cupertino, California), Sun Microsystems (Mountain View, California), Seagate Technology (Scotts Valley, California), Intel (Santa Clara, California), and Cray Research (Minneapolis, Minnesota), have all grown from start-up to *Fortune* 500 status over the past twenty years. They have also paved the way for newer, smaller start-ups, such as Adobe Systems (Mountain View, California) and Chips & Technologies (San Jose, California), to become the success stories of tomorrow.

The growth of these high-tech companies has been nothing short of sensational. Sun Microsystems, for example, which began in 1982, is now a $2 billion a year company and a leader in technical workstations. Over the last five years, Sun, under the leadership of its founder and CEO, Scott McNealy, has been the leading company in its industry in sales growth, averaging 126% growth per year (versus the industry average of 12%) and the second leading company in its industry in earnings per share (EPS) growth, with an average of 89% per year (versus the industry average of -15%); stated another way, Sun's EPS growth has been more than twice as high as IBM, Hewlett-Packard, and Digital Equipment *combined*, while its sales growth has been about triple the rate of those three giants in the computer industry.

Sun's latest strategy is similar to that of when IBM created the standard design for personal computers with its PC. Sun has created a hardware design, called SPARC, and is inviting other computer companies to build clones. By standardizing the design, it will force the manufacturers to compete on price and performance, which can be advantageous to Sun. This development is likely to result in the continued growth of this $2 billion leader in workstations that has not yet celebrated its tenth birthday.

Compaq Computer's success under its founder and CEO, Rod Canion, is just as remarkable, if not more remarkable, as that of Sun Microsystems. Compaq, which began in 1983 (when it generated an astounding $111 million in sales in its first full year of operation, largely due to the strong relationships it established with its retailer network), became a $2 billion company by the time it was only five years old. Today, its net profit margin exceeds that of its biggest rival, IBM, and its EPS growth is the highest in the industry. Although Compaq is one of the world leaders in personal computers, its sales for 1989 (nearly $3 billion) were only half the level of its other major competitor, Apple Computer, which began only a few years earlier.

In a related industry, Microsoft, of Redmond, Washington, is considered by many to be the leading computer software company in the world. The company was founded in 1975 by William Gates III, along with Paul Allen, who wrote a version of the BASIC programming language to run on early micro-computers. A few years later, the company acquired the disk operating system (referred to as DOS) to be used on IBM personal computers and their compatibles. Microsoft's average annual growth in sales and profits has been approximately 60% over the last 5 years. Consequently, its investors and managers have benefited by the company's success. The most notable individual success is the 34-year-old Gates, the largest single shareholder of Microsoft, whose 45% stake in the company was worth $350 million when Microsoft went public; his stake is now worth over $3 billion—not bad for a college dropout (from Harvard) who taught himself computer programming as a teenager.

Is High Growth Synonymous with High Tech?   From these success stories, we may be seduced into believing that economic development and employment growth have been—and will continue to be—solely in high-tech industries. That is clearly not the case. In fact, according to management guru Peter Drucker, over a two-decade period beginning in the mid-1960s, high-tech companies accounted for only 5 million (out of the total of approximately 35 million) new jobs in this country, or the same number lost by *Fortune* 500 companies over that period.[2]

Of course, high-technology businesses are a vital part of our economic growth. However, perhaps more typical of high-growth companies nationwide is Delta Pride Catfish, Inc., of Indianola, Mississippi. Neither the company nor

[2]See Peter F. Drucker, *Innovation and Entrepreneurship*, Harper & Row, New York, 1985.

its location would suggest anything remotely high tech. Yet, Delta Pride, which was founded in 1981, is a profitable enterprise that generated over $100 million in sales in 1988.

Similarly, consider Carts of Colorado, Inc., of Commerce City, Colorado. The company was founded in 1984 by Stan and Dan Gallery, who are now in their early 30s and is now the leading seller of pushcarts in the United States. The early stages of the company trace back nine years when the Gallery brothers invested $3,600 to buy a couple of hot dog carts in New York City, which they brought to Colorado. They generated $300 to $400 per day per cart at construction sites and $1,200 to $1,500 per day per cart at weekend outdoor events, with food costs equal to approximately 20% of sales. Feeling that they could be more profitable if they built their own carts, they did so at a cost of approximately $750 apiece. Before long, they had a fifteen-cart fleet. Due to problems encountered with the health department of Denver, they were forced to redesign their carts with new cooling units, a high capacity burner, and hot and cold running water. The Gallery brothers were soon approached by one of their customers who wanted to purchase a cart. They priced the cart at $5,200 and, to their surprise, received an order from the gentleman for three carts. Over the next few years, these vendors-turned-manufacturers sold their "mobile vending sites" to such respected corporate clients as Coca Cola, Marriott, Disney, Pizza Hut, and Oscar Mayer. Last year, Carts of Colorado generated $7 million in revenues from the sale of carts.

Anyone who is remotely interested in technology products has to admire the high-tech companies that have not only created products, but have created industries. Yet, to me, it is even more interesting to examine the successful companies that have defied the odds by launching businesses in highly competitive, low-technology industries. Obviously, stores were selling women's clothing before The Limited came into existence, and stores were selling toys long before Toys "R" Us entered the picture. Yet, such specialty retailers have been incredible successes over the last 10 years. So, if you're a high-tech lover, please excuse me for pointing out that the *Inc.* 500[3] lists have included, in addition to the high-tech superstars, businesses that are public relations firms, photographers, printers, photocopying companies, skateboard manufacturers, tobacco distributors, and recreational vehicle (RV) dealers, which have often grown at much faster rates than typical high-tech start-ups in Silicon Valley.

There are countless examples to support the notion that the *real* growth in the economy has come from rather mundane industries, often in "low-tech locations." Some of these would include Blockbuster Entertainment (Fort Lauderdale, Florida), a $400 million operator of video rental stores; Rocking Horse Childcare Centers (Cherry Hill, New Jersey), which generated $25 million in revenues in 1989 operating day care centers; Cash America Investments (Fort Worth, Texas), an $88 million operator of pawnshops; One Price Clothing Stores (Duncan, South Carolina), a $90 million apparel retailer; Rally's (Louisville,

---

[3]The *Inc.* 500 is a listing of the fastest growing *privately* held companies in the United States, as compiled by *Inc.* magazine.

Kentucky), a $30 million operator of drive-through restaurants; Action Staffing (Tampa, Florida), a $130 million provider of employee leasing services; and Catalina Lighting (Miami, Florida), a $55 million distributor of lighting and ceiling fans. Each of the above companies has grown by a compounded annual rate of over 100% over the last five years.

We should keep in mind, however, that high growth does not necessarily translate into success; several of the fastest growing companies in the nation, which would fit very nicely on the above list of high-growth, low-tech superstars have had their share of problems. (I will elaborate on this later in this chapter.) For example, Silk Greenhouse (Tampa, Florida), a retailer of artificial flowers and plants, and WTD Industries (Portland, Oregon), a lumber processing company, are just two examples of high-growth businesses (in low-tech industries) that have recently experienced dramatic declines in their stock prices due to disappointing earnings.

Retailing.   Many high-growth companies have grown dramatically through successful retailer expansion efforts. The classic entrepreneurial success story among retailers is, of course, Wal-Mart, founded by Sam Walton, who is affectionately known as "Mr. Sam." As a result of Wal-Mart's success, Walton and his family are now worth an estimated $8 billion, making them one of the wealthiest families in the world.

Wal-Mart, itself, is certainly not a new idea in retailing. The company is a discount retailer, based (not in one of the nation's high-growth cities, such as San Diego, Tampa, Phoenix, or Austin, but rather) in Bentonville, Arkansas. Wal-Mart generated $26 billion in revenues in 1989, thereby placing it in the number 3 spot of all retailers, behind only Sears and K Mart. Over the past 5 years, Wal-Mart's average growth in sales was 35% (versus 15% for its competitors), its average growth in earnings per share (EPS) was 33% (versus 9% for the industry), and its return on equity (ROE) was 36% (versus 16% for its competitors). If you're a high-tech fan, you may be disheartened to learn that each of those performance measures is comparable to that for Apple Computer, one of the superstar performers in the personal computer industry during the same time period.

Wal-Mart is now considered a "blue-chip" company, having grown well beyond an early-stage venture. There are a few other successes that are not too far behind Wal-Mart. For example, The Limited, Inc. (whose stores include The Limited, The Limited Express, Lane Bryant, Victoria's Secret, and Abercrombie & Fitch), a Columbus, Ohio, based retailer of women's clothing, founded by Leslie Wexner, has had comparably impressive statistics over the past few years. The company, which is now a $4.4 billion per year business, has increased: its sales by an average of 38%, its EPS by an average of 43%, and its ROE by an average of 40% over the past ten years; these are all two to three times the industry average and better than any other major apparel retailer. Moreover (and, again, my apologies to the high-tech fans), these performance measures are superior to those of the two largest computer companies in this country, IBM and Digital Equipment, *combined.*

Similar success stories are indicative of several other entrepreneurial growth companies such as Toys "R" Us, a $4.4 billion retailer of toys and games, based in Paramus, New Jersey; Nordstrom, a $2.6 billion Seattle, Washington, based regional retailer, which has tripled in size since 1983; Circuit City Stores, a $1.9 billion Richmond, Virginia, based retailer of electronics, whose average EPS has grown by nearly 37%—or more than triple the industry average—over the past 5 years; and The Gap, a $1.5 billion San Bruno, California, based apparel retailer, which, despite recent problems with overly optimistic inventory levels, has increased its EPS by an average of 40%—or four times the industry average—over the past 5 years.

Of course, as retailers grow, so do their suppliers, many of which are entrepreneurial success stories in their own right. A good example of a company that has grown with the retailers is Liz Claiborne, a New York based women's clothing company, which has grown from a $230 million business in 1983 to a $1.4 billion company in 1989. Over the last ten years, Liz Claiborne was ranked number 2 among *all* corporations listed in *Forbes'* ranking based on EPS growth, with an average annual rate of 43%, and was ranked number 1 in ROE, with an average annual rate of over 50%.

Two other good examples are in the athletic shoes industry: Reebok International, a Canton, Massachusetts, based company, which has grown from $13 million in 1983 to nearly $2 billion today, and LA Gear, a $600 million Los Angeles based company founded in 1979, which has grown at a 170% compounded annual rate from 1985 to 1989 and (although it had experienced some ups and downs in its stock price in 1990) was one of the leading stock market performers in both 1988 and 1989, having increased in value by 367% and 185%, respectively, in those two years. Although Reebok's most recent performance has been far from exceptional, the company has done quite well over the long term, having experienced average annual increases in sales growth, EPS growth, and ROE of over 200%—more than any other company listed in the *Business Week* 1000 list—from 1984 to 1988, while having an extremely low debt to equity ratio of 2% (versus 26% for the industry).

Membership Warehouse Companies. Arguably, the most phenomenal growth area in retailing (as well as in low-tech industries as a whole, by the way) has come from the newer "niche-oriented" entrepreneurial companies, most of which have only been in existence for the last five to eight years. For example, one of the most significant growth sectors of the retailing industry has been in the membership warehouse companies, which is a $20 billion industry, and is expected to grow at a better than 20% per year level for the next few years. The oldest and largest company in this sector is Price Club, of San Diego, a $5 billion company, founded in 1976, which was ranked number 1 of all corporations in EPS growth (with a ten-year annual average of 49%) in *Forbes'* latest rankings. There are three newer large membership warehouse companies, each of which was founded since 1982 and which generates over $\frac{1}{2}$ billion a year in revenues: Costco Wholesale Corp. (Kirkland, Washington), a $3 billion retailer whose growth rate has exceeded that of Compaq Computer over the last 5 years; Pace Membership Warehouse (Aurora, Colorado), which had a 100% average annual growth rate between 1985 and 1989; and Wholesale Club (Indianapolis, Indiana), whose average annual growth rate over the past five years was 75%. The success of Price Club, Costco, and the others has resulted in a newer entrant in this industry, Sam's Wholesale Club, which is a division of Wal-Mart.

Some suppliers of the membership warehouse companies, such as Jan Bell Marketing (Fort Lauderdale, Florida), an eight-year-old jewelry distributor, whose stock price increased by 250% in 1988 (but has since declined somewhat), and Advanced Marketing Services (San Diego, California), a book distributor, have experienced comparable growth.

More "Niche" Strategies.   Other retailers that have also followed a *niche* strategy of focusing on a clearly defined target market have grown at an equally rapid pace. For example, Office Depot, an office supplies retailer based in Boca Raton, Florida, which began in 1986, generates over $100 million in annual sales. Similarly, Egghead, Inc., an eight-year-old software retailer based in Bothell, Washington (near Microsoft's headquarters), is a $350 million company. Businessland, a $1.2 billion a year San Jose, California, based business, and CompuAdd, a somewhat smaller Austin, Texas, based business, are two microcomputer retailers founded in 1982 that have also achieved early success in a related industry.

Franchising.   The growth of low-tech industries has been enhanced through extensive franchising efforts. Today, franchising is a $200 billion industry, which is larger than the composite size of the entire U.S. food industry, with over 2,000 franchises and 400,000 establishments.

A good example of the growth of franchising is TCBY Enterprises of Little Rock, Arkansas, an entrepreneurial company founded in 1979, which is now the nation's largest frozen yogurt chain. TCBY has been very profitable, while growing at better than a 100% compounded annual rate over the past decade. Similar growth has been characteristic of such other emerging fast-food restaurant franchises, each of which has more than 1,000 franchised units, as Subway (Milford, Connecticut), one of the nation's fastest growing franchisors, which is gearing up to have 5,000 franchise units by 1994; Domino's Pizza (Ann Arbor, Michigan); and Little Caesars Pizza (Farmington Hills, Michigan).

Several other industries have witnessed comparable growth of entrepreneurial companies with franchise operations. These include RE/MAX (Englewood, Colorado) in real estate; Mail Boxes, Etc. (San Diego, California) in business services; Nutri/System Weight Loss Centers (Willow Grove, Pennsylvania) in health and fitness; Sylvan Learning Centers (Montgomery, Alabama) in education; Ugly Duckling Rent-A-Car (Tucson, Arizona) in car rental; Blockbuster Video (Fort Lauderdale, Florida) in video rental; and Precision Tune (Sterling, Virginia) in auto maintenance.

~~~~~~~~~~~~~~~

A strong argument can be made that low-tech service businesses have become the high-growth industries of the 1980s and 1990s. Thus, the growth of businesses and of new jobs has not been restricted to Silicon Valley in California and to Route 128 near Boston, but, rather, occurs in regions throughout the country. In fact, at the top of the list of *Inc.* 500 high-growth, privately held companies for 1988 was American Central Gas (Tulsa, Oklahoma), which gathers, processes, treats, and markets natural gas. The company, started by three Tulsa investors, grew by an incredible *82,168%* (from $113,000 to $93 million in revenues) over the previous five years.

The growth of businesses and of new jobs has not been restricted to Silicon Valley in California and to Route 128 near Boston, but, rather, occurs in regions throughout the country.

Right behind American Central Gas were such high-growth, low-tech companies as West Coast Video (Philadelphia, Pennsylvania), which operates video rental stores; Jenny Craig Weight Loss Centers (Carlsbad, California); Express Services (Oklahoma City, Oklahoma), which franchises personnel offices; H & M Food Systems (Richland Hills, Texas), which manufactures meat-based food products; and CEBCOR (Chicago, Illinois), which provides employee leasing services. Each of these companies has experienced better than *10,000%* five-year growth, while still remaining a privately held company.

THE IMPACT OF ENTREPRENEURIAL GROWTH

Is High Growth Good?

Of course, the extraordinarily high growth—or "hypergrowth"—of the companies to which we have referred in this chapter is just one measure of success. There are several other measures. Specifically, earlier we discussed the impact that entrepreneurial development has had on new job creation. Moreover, to go along with entrepreneurial growth has come economic development, personal success, community success, innovative technologies, and managerial excellence.

Creating Industries. Several entrepreneurial companies have had far-reaching effects on our nation in terms of new product development. Clearly, this is an area in which technology companies have excelled. For example, in recent years, high-tech start-ups have been responsible for the emergence of the minicomputer (by Digital Equipment Corp.), microcomputer (by Apple

Computer), semiconductor (by Intel), and workstation (by Sun Microsystems) industries.

Changing Bureaucracy. Numerous entrepreneurial companies have had a significant enough impact to change the way we live and work. For example, Federal Express, a $6 billion Memphis, Tennessee, based company, has grown at better than a 30% annual rate over the last five years and effectively controls the overnight delivery industry in this country. Federal Express has even *forced* our stuffiest bureaucracy, the U.S. Postal Service, to inaugurate Express Mail, its first real innovation since it started its parcel post service seventy-five years ago. This trend of the private sector getting involved in typically public sector services has been a tremendous opportunity for entrepreneurial companies in transportation services, education, health care, trash removal, street repair, fire protection, vehicle towing, sewer cleaning, graffiti removal, and other areas.

Creating Personal Wealth and Success. High growth has been responsible for the personal financial success of many entrepreneurs as well as the investors in these companies. This has resulted in additional taxes (on earnings, capital gains, and the like), greater philanthropic endeavors, and higher economic status of the communities in which these ventures are located. There has been massive wealth resulting from some of these entrepreneurial companies, with several entrepreneurs being ranked among the wealthiest individuals in the country.

For example, Leslie Wexner borrowed $5,000 from an aunt in 1963 to start a sportswear store. Today, as a result of the expansion of The Limited and its associated stores, Wexner's personal fortune is estimated at approximately $2 billion—and his philanthropic and civic activities are recognized nationally—while the personal fortunes of the investors in The Limited have grown handsomely as well.

Similarly, Bill Hewlett and Dave Packard, founders of the company which bears their names, are billionaires who have established foundations to enable them to share their wealth with those in need of financial resources. And H. Ross Perot, whose net worth is estimated at about $3 billion after he recently sold his company Electronic Data Systems (EDS) to General Motors, has been a strong supporter of educational and other social causes.

On a much smaller scale, Ben Cohen and Jerry Greenfield, founders of Ben & Jerry's Homemade, a gourmet ice cream company based in Waterbury, Vermont, have made their entrepreneurial dream a model for social change. They have participatory management and periodic company-wide employee meetings. Most striking is the compensation scheme employed at the company. The salary earned by the highest-paid employee (who is Mr. Cohen, the chairman, who was paid approximately $80,000 last year) is limited to five times the salary of the lowest paid full-time worker. Compare that to the average compensation of CEOs at major American corporations, which is nearly 100 times the average factory worker's salary. In addition, Ben & Jerry's gives 7.5% of its pretax income to charity, which is about four times the national average and is one of the highest percentage rates of any company in this country.

Enhancing Corporate Reputation.   In addition to promoting personal wealth, the growth of entrepreneurial ventures has often been associated with phenomenal success in terms of reputation, profitability, and innovation. For example, in *Fortune* magazine's annual survey of the most admired corporations in America, Liz Claiborne and Wal-Mart have not only been ranked significantly higher than *any* of their competitors, but they have been ranked consistently in the top ten of all corporations.[4] Liz Claiborne, which was a small, entrepreneurial company just a few years ago, and is now the largest women's apparel company in the world, has increased its sales by an average annual rate of nearly 40% over the past 5 years (versus an industry average of 8%), while its EPS has grown by 37% (versus 17%) and its ROE by 45% (versus 19%). Surprisingly, unlike other companies that have burdened themselves with significant debt to foster their growth, Liz Claiborne has taken on very little debt in the process; it's debt to equity ratio has been less than 4%, as compared to over 40% for the industry average.

Wal-Mart hasn't done too poorly either, as is evidenced by its 40% compounded annual growth over the last 20 years. Certainly, Wal-Mart has been one of the all-time success stories on Wall Street. If you had purchased $1,000 worth of Wal-Mart stock at its initial public offering in 1970, your investment would be worth well over $.5 million today.

And, of course, The Limited has been almost as impressive. One measure of success in retailing is the movement of inventory, which is generally a function of the distribution process. Typical of this industry is the need to place orders six months in advance. Yet The Limited has a response time that is unmatched in its industry. The company tracks customer preferences through point-of-sale computers on a daily basis. It then restocks its inventory by sending orders by satellite to plants in the United States, as well as in South Korea, Hong Kong, Singapore, and Sri Lanka. The goods are then sent back to the company's home base in Columbus, Ohio, four times per week. Within forty-eight hours, the goods are sorted, priced, and prepared for shipment in the company's highly automated distribution center and then shipped out to its more than 3,000 stores. Despite The Limited being able to do something in one week that it takes its competitors six months to accomplish, we can see the hard driving, entrepreneurial attitude of the company's founder, Leslie Wexner, who described this restocking process as "Not fast enough for the 90's."[5]

Like Liz Claiborne, Wal-Mart, and The Limited, other entrepreneurial companies, such as Compaq, Federal Express, Nordstrom, and Apple Computer, have been listed either among the top 5 or top 25 best managed companies

[4]The *Fortune* survey only ranks the ten largest companies in each of a limited number of industries. Many of the companies mentioned throughout this book, however, are not nearly large enough (yet) to be included in the survey. It is likely that they will soon be listed among the elite.

[5]See Jeremy Main, "The Winning Organization," *Fortune*, September 26, 1988, p. 51.

in other surveys.[6] As noted by Daniel Benton, computer analyst for Goldman Sachs,

> "Compaq is a case study in management excellence. It is the only company in the world that has established a brand name better than IBM's."[7]

Incredibly, that comment was made by Benton in 1987, when Compaq was only four years old; its reputation is even stronger today.

Developing Innovative Products and Services.   Emerging growth companies have often had an advantage over their larger counterparts in terms of product quality and innovation. Quality consultant A. Blanton Godfrey, for example, recently referred to Sun Microsystem's line of products as

> "Definitely the best workstations in the world. Even the Japanese use them."[8]

Similarly, Genentech (South San Francisco, California) has developed such innovative new products as t-PA, a clone of one of the body's own enzymes, which dissolves blood clots in the treatment of severe heart attacks. Medtronic (Minneapolis, Minnesota), which has always been at the leading edge of technology, is a world leader in pacemakers. The same is true for Microsoft, in computer software (for example, its Excel spreadsheet) and operating systems (for example, DOS); Tandem, in distributed database management technology; Intel, in microprocessors; Convex Computer, in minisupercomputers; and Cray Research, in supercomputers.

Impacting on Larger Companies.   Often, larger competitors have been forced to shift strategy as a result of the innovative products and services of smaller entrepreneurial companies. For example, IBM has probably become a "better" company, thanks, in part, to the efforts of Apple, Compaq, Sun, and the other successful newcomers in this industry. Of course, the same could be said for low-tech industries. For example, Lipton Tea was forced to alter its product line and strategy as a result of the early success of Celestial Seasonings in introducing new flavors of teas.

Creating Spin-offs and New Start-ups.   Ironically, many of these successful new ventures have given rise to other new ventures, both as spin-offs and as intrapreneurial ventures within the company. These spin-offs have often

---

[6]See, for example, Dun's *Business Month.*
[7]See Dun's *Business Month,* December, 1987, p. 25.
[8]See Christopher Knowlton, "What America Makes Best," *Fortune,* March 28, 1988, p. 42.

been as successful as the companies from which they were formed. For example, Tandem Computer was formed by several executives from Hewlett-Packard, which, itself, is considered one of the greatest entrepreneurial success stories of all time. Similarly, Data General evolved from Digital Equipment Corp. (DEC) and is now one of DEC's leading competitors in selected market segments.

An example of new ventures forming within an entrepreneurial company is seen at Cypress Semiconductor, a $200 million San Jose, California, based company started by T. J. Rodgers in 1982. Although Cypress is an early-stage venture itself, the company creates separate start-up companies within the Cypress umbrella for new product lines. Each of the four companies formed so far is run as a separate entity. There is a president of each company and the employees have stock in their new venture. Apparently, Cypress has benefited by this, as is evidenced by its average growth rate of well over 100% over the last 5 years.

Problems with High Growth

Despite the success stories just cited, we should be cautioned that high growth is not, necessarily, indicative of success. Earlier, I identified Silk Greenhouse and WTD Industries as high-growth companies with declining stock prices. We can add to the list Home Shopping Network (HSN) of Clearwater, Florida, which was founded in 1979 and went public in May 1986 with a market capitalization of $\frac{1}{4}$ billion. HSN's stock price, adjusted for stock splits, was $3 per share at its IPO. The stock, which reached a high of $38 in February 1987, at which time its market capitalization was $3.3 billion, eventually lost 80% of its value. More recently, HSN has faced a host of problems, not the least of which was when the company was ordered to pay GTE of Florida and a subsidiary $100 million for libel and slander in a legal battle. (After an appeal, HSN later settled with GTE for $4.5 million.)

A more extreme high-growth disaster story is Worlds of Wonder, a Freemont, California, based toy manufacturer, which had a market capitalization of over $\frac{1}{2}$ billion in early 1987. Within months, it went bankrupt, after having failed at its attempt to duplicate its earlier success with the Teddy Ruxpin talking teddy bear. In addition to Worlds of Wonder, several other *Inc.* 100[9] companies, including Air Florida Systems, Vector Graphic, Wedtech Corp., Pizza Time Theatre, Xonics, Inc., and Psych Systems, have all gone into bankruptcy.

Why have these failures occurred? Is it due to management? Is it due to the role of the investors in these companies? Probably, it's a result of a combination of factors. I imagine that there were numerous errors and misjudgments that took place over a long period of time prior to the failures described above. As noted by a San Francisco based venture capitalist, in referring to some of these failures,

[9]The *Inc.* 100 is a listing of the fastest growing small *public* corporations in the United States, as compiled by *Inc.* magazine.

"There's been a lack of tough-minded checking out of deals. People get into situations with entrepreneurs or companies that they soon realize aren't going to work out, but once you start, you often find a deal takes on a life of its own."[10]

◆◆◆◆◆◆◆◆◆◆◆◆◆◆

Thus, we recognize that high growth is only one measure of entrepreneurial success. Consequently, we will be examining several factors related to the success of the emerging growth ventures discussed throughout this book.

WHAT FACTORS ACCOUNT FOR ENTREPRENEURIAL GROWTH?

New businesses are being started at the rate of about one million per year, in this country. This is an eight- to ten-fold increase over the business start-up rate of the 1950s and 1960s. The big question, however, is are they successful? Certainly, there is a very high mortality rate; a half-million businesses fail every year. There are statistics that suggest that anywhere between 50% and 90% of new businesses fail.[11] However, there are numerous success stories of emerging growth companies such as Compaq Computer, Sun Microsystems, Liz Claiborne, and Apple, to name just a few, that defy the odds.

◆◆◆◆◆◆◆◆◆◆◆◆◆◆

The primary focus in this book is on what has led to the emergence of this entrepreneurial economy and on what has been responsible for sustaining it. In essence, what has made these entrepreneurial dreams into realities? Moreover, an examination of the factors responsible for shaping our entrepreneurial economy

[10]See Joel Kotkin, "Why Small Companies Are Saying No to Venture Capital," *Inc.*, August 1984, p. 67.

[11]Nobody really knows the actual failure rate of new businesses. The classic statistic that is cited of an 80% failure rate among start-ups over their first five years in business is based on businesses ceasing operation in their existing form. Thus, a sole proprietorship that (1) becomes a partnership, then (2) incorporates, then (3) is acquired by a larger corporation has undergone three changes in form (or three "failures"). Naturally, this would suggest that the failure rate of start-ups is much lower than 80%. However, the statistics also do not take into account businesses that have either (1) registered to conduct business, but have been inactive (that is, have not conducted their operations or generated revenues) for years, or (2) not registered to do business. I would suspect that the "failure" rate among such businesses exceeds 80%.

Numerous research studies have addressed the issue of small business survival. The variances, however, from study to study—due to differences in the nature of the industry, location of the company, date that the study was conducted, period of time from start-up to failure, and the like—are rather large. However, in a representative sample of approximately one dozen studies, contrary to the statistics given above, the reported failure rates were anywhere from less than 10% to more than 60%.

In short, what's the failure rate of small businesses? Your guess is as good as mine. But, based on statistics alone, there are some significant risks associated with entrepreneurship.

has important public policy implications; we are certainly interested in the regulations, policies, incentives, and the social, political, and economic conditions that can ensure that entrepreneurial growth will continue in the future. Let's explore some of these factors that have prompted entrepreneurial growth and development.

Knowledge and Education

Obviously, knowledge and education have played a key role in fostering entrepreneurship, especially in high-tech businesses, such as computers, telecommunications, medicine/health care, and biotechnology. Consequently, scientists from such prestigious universities as MIT, Harvard, Stanford, Cal Tech, the University of California, and the University of Texas have been major forces in the development of our high-tech industries. Thus, it should not be surprising that high-tech centers in this nation, such as Boston, San Francisco, and Austin, are just the locations where these prominent universities are situated.

The University's Role.   MIT has been responsible for the success of over fifty very recent start-ups, including Matritech (Cambridge, Massachusetts), which is involved with new ways to detect cancer; Oculon, Inc. (Seattle, Washington), which has developed a technique to inhibit cataract formation in the eye; and Cirrus Logic, Inc. (Milpitas, California), a manufacturer of high-performance chips. Such ventures have often brought attractive returns to the investors. For example, an early-stage investment of $2.5 million in Cirrus Logic in 1986 by Fred Nazem, a New York based venture capitalist, increased in value by nearly twelvefold in three years.

Technological Growth.   Fifteen years ago, there were no PCs. There were no CDs. There were no VCRs. There were no genetically engineered vaccines. Obviously, knowledge and education have played a significant role in advancing these technology products.

What can we expect over the coming years? It is likely that the growth of technology industries in the 1980s will carry on throughout the 1990s. For example, there are numerous opportunities for growth in business and office automation products. According to Personal Technology Research, fax machine sales will grow from their current level of approximately 2 million units per year to 20 to 25 million units per year over the decade. Similar growth is likely in cellular telephones. According to Booz Allen, over the next five years, this industry will grow by tenfold from its current level of approximately 1 million units per year. And, of course, there is plenty of room for growth in laptop computers.

In home entertainment, we should look forward to the explosive growth of high-definition TVs and VCRs, as well as home satellite dishes. The medical field will have some high-growth sectors, such as outpatient medical facilities, which is likely to become a billion dollar per year industry over the coming years. Similarly, the generic drug industry, according to International Resource Development, is likely to grow from a $300 million industry today to a $25 billion industry by 1997.

More "Future Shock."   One thing is becoming very clear about technological change. Consistent with Alvin Toffler's insightful framework presented in his bestselling book, *Future Shock*, it is likely that change will continue to take place at an increasingly rapid pace in the years to come. As suggested by John Peers, president of Novix, Inc., a communications signal processing company based in Silicon Valley, in speaking about technological change in the year 2000, "We'll see a minimum of ten times as much progress in the next twelve years as we've seen in the past twelve."[12] Peers adds, "I wouldn't want to be a science fiction writer today because reality is leaping ahead of fantasy."

There are two leading technologies on the verge of major breakthroughs—electronics and biotechnology. It takes about ten to twelve years to translate a new technology into a commercially useful product. So the major products that will be available at the turn of the century resulting from these leading technologies are already in the labs at major universities and corporate laboratories today.

Social and Demographic Trends

A second important factor that has created—and will continue to create—abundant opportunities for entrepreneurial companies is the impact of social and demographic trends. This is especially true among service businesses, which have been a major growth sector in this country over the last 20 years. We can expect this trend to be prevalent throughout the foreseeable future.

Aging Population.   Several entrepreneurial companies have taken advantage of the shift in age of our population. As a result of our aging population, such industries as health care management, outpatient care, rehabilitation centers, nursing homes, and home health care have not only grown substantially, but have become some of the fastest *changing* industries in this country. For example, HealthCare Compare (Downers Grove, Illinois), a $30 million, eight-year-old company that implements health care cost management services, and HealthSouth Rehabilitation (Birmingham, Alabama), a $150 million developer and operator of rehabilitation centers founded in 1984, have had compounded annual growth rates of over 100% over the last five years.

Dual-career Households.   Another growth sector is in restaurant chains, as evidenced by Eateries (Oklahoma City, Oklahoma), which develops and manages full service restaurants, and Discus (Bloomington, Minnesota), which develops and operates Fuddruckers, Inc., a chain of hamburger restaurants. The growth of these two restaurant chains, which has been comparable to that of the health care

[12]See Gene Bylinsky, "Technology in the Year 2000," *Fortune*, July 18, 1988, p. 92.

companies just discussed, has been largely a response to the migration of people to high-growth population centers, and the emergence of dual-career households. Today, approximately 50% of all families can be considered dual career. That number is likely to increase to approximately 75% within the next 10 years.

These dual-career households have also been responsible for the explosive growth of such companies as Liz Claiborne, which makes high-quality, but affordable, clothing for professional women, and Kinder-Care Learning Centers, the nation's first day care chain. Furthermore, the fitness craze, which has also been readily seen among young professional couples, resulted in the success of Nike during the late 1970s and early 1980s and, more recently, in the explosive growth of Reebok and LA Gear.

Baby Boomers. Baby boomers have been characterized as proactive "prosumers," rather than as passive "consumers." One industry that has been helped by this market has been the home supplies stores, which target either the do-it-yourselfers or, in the case of the less handy segment of the population that simply want to save on contractors' markups on materials, the "buy-it-yourselfers." Home Depot (Atlanta, Georgia), which generated over $2.5 billion in revenues last year, has been a superstar in this industry. A typical Home Depot store generates more than $20 million in sales annually (that's $400,000 per week), with net profit margins of 3.6%, as compared to some of its competitors, which have 1% to 2% margins. Of course, not every home supplies company will be as successful as Home Depot, as evidenced by the failure of Mr. How, a division of Service Merchandise, which folded in 1986.

Baby Boomers as Entrepreneurs. It's not surprising that the entrepreneurial explosion has coincided with the "baby boom" explosion. Baby boomers, many of whom have distrusted large institutions to begin with—due, in part, to an antibureaucratic value system that prevailed in the 1960s and 1970s, have often found that the corporate hierarchy is extremely clogged and that they are not always "appreciated" by their present employer. Moreover, many baby boomers are now reaching a plateau in their careers. At the same time, they have some vital assets: skills, experience, contacts, and money. Consequently, these have provided many young, ambitious, educated, and talented entrepreneurs the challenge (or opportunity) to start their own ventures. The supply of talented baby boomers is so great that it's likely that this trend will continue for many years.

Venture Catalysts: Providing the Fuel to Generate Growth

A third factor that has contributed significantly to our entrepreneurial economy is our extensively developed, formal and informal venture capital system. Clearly, entrepreneurship has been a major force behind economic growth in this nation. However, venture capital, that is, the funding for the emerging growth business, which generally comes in stages, has been the *catalyst* behind its growth. For that reason, I've used the term *venture catalysts* in this book to refer to the role that venture capitalists have played in entrepreneurial growth and economic development. The analogy is that of the automobile and the fuel necessary to sustain it. The venture is the automobile—that's the true entrepreneurial genius. Venture capital, however, is the fuel to keep it going and to accelerate its movement; no matter how brilliantly the automobile is engineered, it needs the fuel to get anywhere.

The venture is the automobile—that's the true entrepreneurial genius. Venture capital, however, is the fuel to keep it going and to accelerate its movement; no matter how brilliantly the automobile is engineered, it needs the fuel to get anywhere.

How important is this fuel? That is, how vital is adequate funding for a business? As suggested by Alan Shugart, founder of both Seagate Technology and Shugart Associates, "Cash is more important than your mother."

Some entrepreneurs even go to great lengths to thank their investors for the contribution that they have made to foster the company's growth. Herman Miller, Inc., for example, which has been consistently recognized as the most admired company in the furniture industry (and has been recognized as one of the ten most admired corporations of any kind, based on a recent survey in *Fortune* magazine), was not named after the company's founder, D. J. DePree. Rather, it was named after DePree's father-in-law, who provided the start-up capital for the venture in 1923. Today, Herman Miller, Inc., is generating nearly $800 million in revenues annually.

Venture Capital Is More Than Just Capital.   As important as venture capital is in providing the necessary funding for a business, the funding is only one small part of the entire venture capital process. Specifically, it is this *process*, rather than the capital itself, that fuels the growth of the venture and often enables the entrepreneurial dream to become a reality. In essence, the venture capital process makes entrepreneurship better; it is this process that characterizes the importance of the role of *venture catalysts*.

First, the process *forces* entrepreneurs to recruit a management team. For example, in 1988, Barbara Samson was in her mid-twenties when she founded Intermedia Communications, Inc., of Tampa, Florida, a telecommunications company that provides corporate customers with alternative ways to connect to long-distance carriers. Samson hired an experienced executive to run the business. Together, they raised more than $5 million from several venture capital firms, including Alan Patricof Associates (New York, New York) and Prudential Bache Capital Partners (New York, New York). The venture capital firms, which have had significant representation on the board of directors of the company, have played a major role in shaping Intermedia's growth strategy.

Second, the process forces entrepreneurs to be honest with themselves. They might not like the fact that the venture capitalists are asking them some fairly probing and seemingly foolish questions about the company's direction. They may not like the fact that the venture capitalists may be twenty years younger than themselves and may have little knowledge of their industry. They may even get emotional as they go through the process. However, as suggested by Howard Arnold, founder and CEO of Chartway Technologies, who has gone through the venture capital process with Chartway and with his earlier venture, Sage Systems,

> "It's like your mother telling you to eat vegetables. It made us grow up. It forced us to put a process in place to address the important questions about our future."

The process also forces entrepreneurs to prepare a business plan to delineate their objectives and to specify their financial projections. As noted by Nolan Bushnell, founder of Atari and several other ventures, "Every time you prepare a business plan, you become a better entrepreneur."[13]

In addition, as we will see shortly, venture capitalists provide significantly more than capital to the business. They will often assist in strategic planning, recruitment, and other critical areas of need for the entrepreneurial venture. Venture capitalists will usually bring a broad perspective of experience to the venture, thereby strengthening management's existing resources.

Ideally, as a result of the venture capital process, which should be viewed as a *long-term* process, often lasting five to ten years or more, the venture capital firm as well as the entrepreneurial team should benefit. Moreover, the benefit should be significantly more than financial. As we will see in Chapter 3, the venture capital process is structured ideally in a manner that develops better entrepreneurs and better decision-making activity. As such, the entrepreneurs, the venture capitalists, and the economy as a whole benefit. It is such a situation that demonstrates the impact that *venture catalysts* have on our entrepreneurial society, both for the entrepreneurial companies themselves and for our entire economy.

Thus, there *is* a difference between venture capital and conventional financing. Venture capital is more than investing and more than building personal wealth; it is building companies.

"Vulture Capitalists." Unfortunately, there is a fairly commonly held perception that venture capitalists are a group of hungry investors looking for an opportunity to gain control of a young venture. In fact, Lucien Ruby, a well-known venture capitalist, recently recounted a tale of his own entrepreneurial

---

[13]See Jeffry A. Timmons and others, *New Venture Creation*, 2nd ed., Irwin, Homewood, Ill., 1985, p. 432.

pursuits in which he was warned about the "vulture capitalists" and was told by his family, "Don't let those bloodsuckers near your company."[14]

Is there any basis for this? Traditionally, the role of the venture capitalist is to assist in the launching and growth of a business. That role was exceedingly apparent in such classic success stories as Digital Equipment, Federal Express, Apple Computer, Compaq Computer, and Genentech. Unfortunately, however, the traditional venture capital role is not always carried out appropriately. The reason for this is that the venture capital industry is a profession, made up of professionals. As is the case with any professionals, there are good ones (the "dream makers") and there are bad ones (the "deal breakers").

Several years ago, for example, Wayne and Ron Erickson, founders of Microrim, Inc. (Bellevue, Washington), a developer of a database system known as R:base, sought funding and assistance from several venture capital firms in the San Francisco area. Their experience with the venture capital community was far from satisfying. They were met with antagonism, arrogance, and a general feeling that the venture capitalists felt that they knew more about their business than they did. Eventually, they sought a different route to raise capital.

Aside from the problem of the wide variance in the capabilities of the venture capital professionals, another problem with this industry is that it is an industry that involves large investments of money. Anytime that there's money involved, there's always the opportunity for greed to play a powerful role in decisions. Consequently, deals are broken and dreams are shattered.

It has been my experience that the industry, as a whole, has an important mission in terms of promoting the growth of emerging businesses. Overall, the track record has been excellent, as evidenced by the successes of Tandem, Apple Computer, and the countless other examples throughout this book. Moreover, the veteran professionals in this industry, who have committed themselves to the goal of "building companies," have been instrumental in the success of these high-visibility companies as well as the entrepreneurial movement in our country. Yet the industry is not without its share of "professionals" whose contribution to and whose philosophy of building companies is, to put it mildly, questionable.

On balance, I view the current state of the venture capital industry and its professionals quite positively. I would hardly call the industry one of "vulture capitalists" (although there are several with whom I've had contact that certainly belong in this category). Moreover, in many regards, I view investors in small growing privately owned companies just like any other investors; they expect to be compensated (in terms of high returns) for their risks and for the value added that they provide to the venture. However, unlike a mutual fund manager's "passive" investment in a portfolio of publicly held companies, the venture capitalist makes "active" investments in high-risk, privately held ventures.

[14]See G. Kozmetsky, M. D. Gill, Jr., and R. W. Smilor, *Financing and Managing Fast Growth Companies: The Venture Capital Process*, Lexington Books, Lexington, Mass., 1985, p. xi.

Return on Investment Is the Objective. The objective of the venture capitalist is to earn a 40% to 60% annual return on an investment, net of inflation. Although these returns seem high, they are very much in line with the riskiness of such investments. Unlike investors in blue-chip companies who expect a 10% to 20% annual return on less risky companies, which are about as liquid as cash over a ten- or 20-year period, however, venture capitalists expect to realize their returns *only* at the time that they are able to "cash out," hopefully in less than ten years, and preferably in three to seven years. Furthermore, in a typical venture capitalist's portfolio, 10% to 20% of the companies may be considered significantly successful, 30% to 40% may be considered marginally successful, and the remainder may lose money or fail completely.

The objective of the venture capitalist is to earn a 40% to 60% annual return on an investment, net of inflation.

Thus, venture capitalists expect higher than average returns, partly to counterbalance the poor returns realized by many of the other high-risk investments. If they happen to secure a 51% ownership position in the company, it should be reflective of the potential returns necessary to invest in the venture, rather than of the desire to control the company.

Of course, on occasion, venture capitalists will want to exert control over a venture. This can often be justified since not only is the venture capitalist responsible for protecting the interest of the investors, but he or she must contend with the riskiness of the venture. After all, as a result of the high risks associated with entrepreneurial ventures, a large number of companies in which venture capitalists have invested have not performed up to their expectations (see Chapter 13 for a discussion on the performance of venture capital investments).

Sometimes it is very beneficial for the venture capitalist to exert a high degree of control. For example, venture capitalist Fred Adler, founder of Adler & Co., took control of Intersil, Inc., a semiconductor company he had funded a few years earlier, but which had run into difficulty. Adler eventually turned the company around and restored it to profitability.

In other situations, however, venture capitalists will exert *undue* control over some of their investments to the detriment of these companies. For example, I'm familiar with one company that had received early-stage funding from a fairly reputable venture capital firm and was "promised" follow-up funding over the coming years. Unfortunately, the company has not reached its sales objectives for the last two years. Consequently, the venture capital firm has not only withdrawn any offers for additional financing, but has made several significant changes in the makeup of the management team as well as in the direction of the company. When I last spoke to the founder, I learned that the company is a "far different company" today in terms of philosophy, strategy, culture, and even product lines than it was just a few years earlier.

Most venture capitalists with whom I've had contact, however, have no desire to control a venture. The reason they invest in a company is, first and foremost, because they like the management team. Why would they want to take control away from a management team behind whom they've put their faith. Also, venture capitalists are more than passive investors; they are experts in financing companies, in structuring deals, and in advising managers on critical long-term decisions. Certainly, their expertise is not in running the company, especially not on a day-to-day basis. And even if they were capable of running the company, they wouldn't have the time to do it, anyway.

> Most venture capitalists with whom I've had contact, however, have no desire to control a venture. The reason they invest in a company is, first and foremost, because they like the management team.

As noted recently by Benjamin Rosen (of Sevin Rosen Management Co.), one of the most highly respected venture capitalists in the country,

> "We are catalysts in the process of creating new companies, new technologies, new products, new industries. What we try to do is to bring together talented entrepreneurs and technology, mix them together, and make this creative process happen."[15]

So, it must be emphasized that venture capitalists are more than merely investors. (This will be discussed in further detail throughout the book.) The high potential returns for their investments should be viewed as their returns for both taking on an usually high degree of risk and assisting the management of the venture in strategic decisions.

A LOOK AHEAD

Our emphasis throughout this book will be on the *venture catalysts* and on the role of venture capital in the economic development of our nation. As noted previously, although other factors, such as knowledge, education,

[15]Louis Rukeyser, "Venture Capital, an Interview with Ben Rosen," *Wall Street Week*, February 8, 1985.

and demographics, have heavily affected entrepreneurial growth, venture capital has been a significant catalyst for its growth, particularly over the past decade.

One recurring issue throughout this book is that venture capital is *more* than just capital. Thus, unlike traditional passive investments in companies made by mutual fund managers, venture capital represents an active attempt to assist businesses in developing and meeting growth and profitability objectives.

Of course, as noted earlier, we must sometimes draw a distinction between the venture capital industry and the professionals who comprise this industry. Clearly, not all venture capitalists play a positive, active role in their investment activities. I attribute this largely to (1) the loose standards that have historically existed for this "profession" (and by this I mean that there are often significant differences between the "formal" venture capital community and the "informal" investors; see Chapter 4); (2) the influx of less experienced venture capitalists who have not been trained in or exposed to the philosophy of the traditional venture capitalists; and (3) the "greed factor," which can detract from the quality of financially oriented decisions. On balance, however, despite the numerous case examples of selected individual investments that were handled inappropriately, the industry, as a whole, clearly has a philosophy that is extremely supportive of the development of emerging businesses.

We have already mentioned some of the superstar success stories among high-growth entrepreneurial companies. Several of these outstanding companies, such as Apple Computer, Compaq, Sun Microsystems, and Federal Express, have already gone public. We have a great interest in these companies because they serve as the role models of the success stories of tomorrow. Our major focus in this book, however, is on the "Federal Express of tomorrow." Who will be "the next Apple Computer"? How do investors decide on whether to fund "the Compaq of the next decade"? What role does venture capital play in the development of "a future Sun Microsystems"?

In the following chapters, we will examine first the nature of venture capital and its impact on the development of emerging growth ventures. The questions of concern are how did the venture capital industry develop and grow? What is the impact of venture capital on corporate success? What is its impact on economic growth and development?

Following that, we will examine the structure of the venture capital industry. Who are the key players? What are their characteristics? How do they invest?

Then we will explore the nature of the investment process and the performance of venture capital-backed companies. In so doing, we will provide some *prescriptive* guides to assist entrepreneurs in their search for venture financing. Our questions of concern are how do venture capitalists make investment decisions? How do they screen deals? What are their preferred investments? How have their investments performed?

Finally, we will discuss some selected issues in the field. For example, what is the impact of and the outlook for foreign venture capital? What is the impact of public policy and economic issues? Where is the industry headed?

Chapter 2

Great Moments in Venture Capital

How and when did the venture capital industry get started? We can trace back its earliest roots several hundred years. However, venture capital, as we know it in its present form, is a relatively new industry that is still undergoing significant evolution.

This chapter presents a chronology of the emergence and development of the venture capital industry and provides some insight on the philosophy shared by the pioneers of this industry.

EARLY HISTORY

The Early Developments of Venture Capital

The venture capital industry was actually "launched" in Spain at the end of the fifteenth century. The first venture capitalist was Queen Isabella, who was approached by an enthusiastic, young entrepreneur who had an idea. His name: Christopher Columbus. His idea: an adventurous voyage into unknown territory. The risks were high, but so were the potential rewards. (In those days, unlike the recent trend that has been emerging—see Chapter 12—venture capitalists were more active in funding start-ups.) After speaking to Columbus about his new venture, Queen Isabella met with her "board of advisors." The consensus was that the Queen should back Columbus's venture. Being the effective venture capitalist that she was, Isabella not only furnished financial support, but she provided management and recruitment assistance as well. And she went one step further; she allowed Columbus to share in the profits. Thus, the year 1492 marks the beginning of the venture capital industry.

The Emergence of Venture Capital in America

Venture capital was not only vital in the discovering of America, but it was essential in its development. The trading and trapping companies had their financial backers. Years later, investors were responsible for financing the development of several significant new industries, such as steel, petroleum, glass, railroads, automotives, and airlines during the late nineteenth and early twentieth centuries. Some examples are Pierre Du Pont's investment in General Motors in 1919 (which was accompanied by the recruitment of a new president, Alfred Sloan), which resulted from Du Pont's interest to secure the painting and varnishing business of the General Motors cars for his chemical company (Du Pont Chemical), and Laurance Rockefeller's investment in Eastern Airlines in 1938 and in McDonnell Douglas in 1939.

Building a Mega-Corporation

One of the most significant investments in American industry during the first part of the twentieth century was in 1911, when a group of wealthy individuals financed and merged three weak companies—Computing Scale Company, Tabulating Machine Company, and International Time Recording Company—into a single company to manufacture and market office equipment. They named the new company Computing Tabulating and Recording Company. A few years later they recruited Thomas Watson, a young man who had recently been fired by National Cash Register Company, to be the company's president. Ten years later, in 1924, the company's name was changed to International Business Machines (IBM). Today, IBM, a $60 billion a year megacorporation, which is the fourth largest and the most profitable company in the United States, is generally considered one of the most successful and best-managed companies in the world.

Funding from Wealthy Families . . .

Beginning in the early part of the twentieth century, the venture capital industry developed as a means for wealthy families to invest their money. It wasn't until many years later that the process was formalized for such investors with the development of venture capital funds (that is, venture capital partnerships). For example, in 1969, the Venrock fund was established by the Rockefeller family to invest in early-stage, advanced technology companies. Venrock has invested in such industries as computers (with investments in Apple Computer and Apollo Computer), telecommunications (for example, 3 Com Corp.), industrial automation (Mentor Graphics and American Robot), and biotechnology and life sciences (Centocor and Genetics Institute).

Similar funds were established by the Whitneys, the Rothschilds, and the large steel company families—the Hillmans, the Phipps, and the Bessemers. Most of these funds are still very active today in funding emerging growth ventures.

... And from Corporations

Another important trend in the first part of the twentieth century was the emergence of corporate venture capital, that is, an established corporation investing in an emerging growth business. For example, shortly after World War I, three established American companies—General Electric (GE), American Telephone, and Westinghouse—bought out the British interests in American Marconi, whose name was later changed to Radio Corporation of America (RCA). Ironically, when GE purchased RCA a few years ago, it was acquiring a company that it originally helped finance.

POST WORLD WAR II DEVELOPMENTS

The Development of the Formal Venture Capital Industry

Following World War II, the venture capital industry took its modern form as a result of the formation of American Research & Development (ARD) and J. H. Whitney & Co. ARD was organized in 1946 by General Georges Doriot, who can be referred to as "the father of modern day venture capital," along with Ralph Flanders, Karl Compton, Merrill Griswold, and several other investors. This represented one of the first nonfamily-oriented attempts to institutionalize the venture investment process. ARD, which is best known for its investment in Digital Equipment Corporation (DEC; this will be discussed further in the following chapter), was acquired by Textron in 1972, but then spun out as an independent venture capital partnership during the 1980s.

Also, shortly following World War II, John Hay Whitney invested $10 million to form J. H. Whitney & Co., another prototype venture capital firm. Whitney was assisted by Benno C. Schmidt, who, at the time, was actively funding cancer research. The first major investment of the fund was in Spencer Chemical Company, a Kansas-based fertilizer company. In one year, this investment doubled Whitney's capital. Since that time, J. H. Whitney & Co., which is still investing actively today (it invested approximately $40 million in 1988), has invested successfully in such diverse industries as oil, television, land, genetic engineering, and computers.

Investments in Technology

From Haloid to Xerox.   The late 1940s also saw quite a few corporate venture capital investments that were responsible for the growth of several start-up businesses. For example, shortly after World War II, Haloid Corporation, a little known company, funded the commercialization of a new technology developed by Chester Carlson and the Batelle Memorial Institute. The technology, known as xerography, was so successful that Haloid later changed its name to Xerox and became one of the remarkable success stories in American business. It was certainly a success story for its investors. For example, Chemical Fund's $300,000 investment in the convertible preferred stock of Haloid in 1954 grew to over $100 million in a fifteen-year period. Today, Xerox, an $18 billion corporation, is a world leader in copiers and scientific equipment.

Fairchild, Memorex, and Their Offspring.   Following that came an investment in 1957 by Fairchild Camera and Instrument (now owned by Schlumberger) in several technologies that were developed at Shockley Transistor. This venture, known as Fairchild Semiconductor, was headed by Robert N. Noyce (along with Gordon E. Moore and some colleagues), who designed the microchip made out of silicon that has set the standard for the industry. (This is the reason for the region being referred to as Silicon Valley.) A major triumph for Fairchild Semiconductor was when NASA chose them to make the chips for the onboard computers in the Gemini spacecraft.

Within 10 years, Fairchild Semiconductor grew from a start-up to a $130 million company. In 1968, Noyce and Moore left Fairchild and invested $250,000 each (and raised another $2.5 million from venture capitalists) in the formation of a new venture, Intel Corp. Intel, largely as a result of the outstanding leadership of its CEO, Andrew Grove, is now a $3.3 billion leader in the semiconductor industry, with an average ROE of four times the industry average over the last five years.

Fairchild Semiconductor eventually became the "father" or "grandfather" of dozens of Silicon Valley success stories. In addition to Intel, these included Rheem Semiconductor, which was later acquired by Raytheon; General Micro Electronics, which was later acquired by Ford-Philco; National Semiconductor, a $2.5 billion chip company, which has spun off several start-ups of its own; Advanced Micro Devices, a billion dollar chip company that is generally regarded as one of the best companies in America for which to work; and Seeq Technology, which was founded by Gordon Campbell, an Intel alumnus. Thanks largely to the success of Intel, the spin-off companies just mentioned were quite successful in raising venture capital for their own ventures.

Years later, in much the same way that Fairchild spawned the semiconductor industry in California, an engineering group at Memorex Corp. during the 1970s spawned today's disk drive industry. The group was led by Alan Shugart, a former IBMer, who brought several engineers with him in 1969 to set up Memorex's Storage Systems Department. Four years later, Shugart, along with Finis Conner, Herbert Thompson, Don Massaro, Larry Pyle, and others, left the financially weak Memorex to launch Shugart Associates, which manufactured floppy disk drives for most personal computers. In 1979, Shugart got together with Conner, Syed Iftikar, and several other of his engineering associates to start Seagate Technology, a leading maker of Winchester disk drives.

What became of the Memorex group? Conner, after playing a major role in both Shugart Associates and Seagate Technology, later founded Conner Peripherals, a leading maker of $3\frac{1}{2}$ inch disk drives, which generated over $100 million in revenues in its first year of operation (and joined the ranks of the *Fortune* 500 in 1989). Thompson, after cofounding Shugart Associates, joined with two other Memorex alumni, to found Drivetec, a San Jose, California, based maker of floppy disk drives. Massaro took over Shugart Associates upon Shugart's departure, and subsequently sold the company to Xerox, where he became president of the Office Products Division. Later, he founded Metaphor Computer Systems, of Mountain View, California. Pyle also left Shugart Associates and founded Data Management Labs (DML), a manufacturer of equipment that controls disk drives used with Digital Equipment Corp. mainframes. And, Iftikar, after leaving Seagate Technology, founded Syquest, a Fremont, California, based maker of removable hard disk drives.

In all, the Memorex group, which never had more than 100 engineers, resulted in the formation of such companies as Tandon Corp., Miniscribe Corp., Quantum Corp., and over two dozen other ventures over the last two decades. And, like Fairchild's offspring, these companies, as a result of their past association with Memorex, were prime candidates to receive venture capital commitments at early stages of their development.

The implication for any entrepreneur seeking venture capital is that funding becomes more readily available to those people who have had previous management experience with successful entrepreneurial companies. (This is discussed at length in the section on "Management" in Chapter 9.)

The Formation of Small Business Investment Companies (SBICs)

One of the most significant developments in the venture capital industry was the passage of the Small Business Investment Company Act in 1958, which prompted the creation of Small Business Investment Companies (SBICs) to finance small businesses. The act provided tax advantages and government-supported leveraged lending to SBICs, which enhanced significantly the development of the venture capital industry.

American Research and Development (ARD) was actually offered the first SBIC license. General Georges Doriot, the company's president, however, refused the offer since he felt that venture capital investing was too risky an undertaking for taxpayer money.

Within four years, approximately 600 SBIC licenses were approved. However, the industry was soon traumatized by numerous problems, including unrealistic expectations, excessive government regulations, inexperienced management, insufficient private capitalization, and general misunderstanding of the venture investment process and objectives.

The better funded and better managed SBICs nonetheless survived these problems and were primarily responsible for the expansion of the venture capital industry in the late 1960s. The survivors were soon joined by scores of other

SBICs and private venture capital companies, all of whom learned some very valuable lessons from the failure of the many SBICs in their early years.

Another important development for SBICs was the creation of Section 301(d) of the SBIC Act, which allowed for the formation of Minority Enterprise Small Business Investment Companies (MESBICs), which has resulted in the funding of thousands of minority-owned businesses over the years.

RECENT DEVELOPMENTS

More Venture Capital Firms Enter the Picture . . .

By the late 1960s, several new venture capital firms were formed. The newer firms, which were generally formed as limited partnerships, became closely attuned to the potential pitfalls of governmental regulations and private capitalization. Their funding came from wealthy individuals and families and from institutional investors, such as pension and endowment funds, insurance companies, and bank trust departments. The early successes of such investments like Digital Equipment Corporation (DEC) by American Research and Development (ARD) made the industry very attractive to investors. Between the late 1960s and the early 1970s, the industry had raised close to $.5 billion from individual and institutional investors.

. . . But Eventually Fail

Numerous problems arose due to below average portfolio returns, lack of public interest in the stock market, and a severe recession that hurt venture capital commitments in the early to mid-1970s. During that time, several corporate venture capital subsidiaries, both large (for example, Ford, Du Pont, Union Carbide, Singer, and Alcoa) and small (for example, Electronic Memories, Memorex, Mohawk Data, and Applied Magnetics) exited the industry, and SBIC and venture capital activity were at a virtual standstill.

The Resurgence of the Venture Capital Industry

Nonetheless, the venture capital industry began to achieve significant success by the late 1970s, primarily due to the following factors:

- Reduction in the capital gains tax rate (in 1978 and 1981; see Chapter 15 for further discussion of the impact of the capital gains tax)
- Increased liquidity as a result of changes in SEC regulations
- Appealing acquisition prices for small companies, especially ones in technology industries
- Revitalization of the public equity market for emerging growth businesses

For these reasons, venture capital portfolio returns averaged 20% to 40% over the late 1970s and early 1980s. By comparison, the public stock markets remained relatively flat during that time. Consequently, we've seen a significant resurgence of the venture capital industry over the past few years.

A LOOK AHEAD

We've just traced the historical development of the venture capital industry. Within a relatively short period of time, the venture capital industry, while still in its early years itself at this time, has undergone several changes. Notably, as we will see in Chapters 3 and 12, there has been a dramatic shift in investment philosophy to include a balanced portfolio of early- and later-stage companies as well as leveraged buyouts (LBOs).

In the next chapter, we will be introduced to the broad nature of venture capital investments. (This will then be discussed in further detail in Chapter 12.) Then we will examine the impact that venture capital investments have had on the success of the venture capital-backed companies as well as on the economy as a whole.

Chapter 3

Venture Capital and Its Impact

Recently, I was in the New York office of one of the more prominent venture capital firms in this country. No sooner had I sat down to talk to one of the general partners of the firm when he was interrupted with a telephone call from an entrepreneur who was seeking capital to develop a new computer-related product. After about five minutes, he politely said goodbye to the entrepreneur and thanked him for calling. Then he threw up his hands in disgust and said (referring to the entrepreneur who had just called and, I imagine, to the countless similar ones who have contacted him),

> "They just don't understand us. . . . They have no idea what we do. . . .
> I'm amazed how they can expect us to spend so much time researching
> their plans, but they spend so little time doing their homework on us."

To a large extent, it is statements like this that prompted me to write this book in the first place. I, too, am surprised when I hear how little the typical entrepreneur knows about the venture capital industry and about the role of the venture capitalist. There is a commonly held perception that the relationship between the entrepreneur and the venture capitalist is an adversarial one in which the venture capitalist makes a passive investment, gets rich off the entrepreneur's hard work, and then attempts to take control of the business.

True, this does happen on occasion; I know of several instances where investors have acted more like "deal breakers" than "dream makers." For example, I'm quite familiar with a high-tech firm in the Boston area that has virtually been taken over by an individual investor who refers to himself as a "venture capitalist" (although he is certainly not part of the traditional venture capital network in that area, nor is he of the traditional venture capital mold in the sense of "building companies"). The investor knows little about the industry nor about the specific business. He knows quite a bit, however, about money and how to accumulate it. For that reason, he has been able to purchase a controlling interest in the company.

I have found, however, that the above situation tends to be quite atypical of the one that develops when the more reputable venture capitalists are involved. As noted earlier, it is unfortunate that the industry can be tainted by a few professionals whose philosophies and actions differ substantially from the norms of the industry.

****

Two key issues are addressed in this chapter: (1) What is venture capital and how is it used? and (2) What is the impact of venture capital on the company being funded and on the economy as a whole? The reader should come away from this chapter with an appreciation of the active, long-term role that investors play as *venture catalysts*. This has resulted in countless success stories of venture capital-backed companies and has prompted significant economic growth for this nation.

WHAT IS VENTURE CAPITAL?

As suggested earlier, venture capital can be thought of as financing for privately held companies, generally in the form of equity and/or long-term convertible debt. It becomes available when funding from banks or similar financial institutions and the public debt or equity markets is either inappropriate or unavailable.

Venture capital is part of the investment community. It is analogous to commercial banking in that the venture capitalist, like the banker, serves as an intermediary—or conduit—between the investors (or lenders) and the entrepreneurs (or borrowers). Venture capitalists, like mutual fund managers, raise capital from investors in order to manage a portfolio of privately held investments.

The Primary Use of Venture Capital: For Emerging Growth Businesses

Traditionally, venture capital has been and remains, to a large extent, *early-stage* (which, as we will soon see, does not, necessarily, mean start-up) financing for emerging growth, privately held businesses. Such investments differ from investments in publicly held companies in that they are generally:

- For newer companies with little operating history
- For smaller companies in which the venture capital firm and the entrepreneurial company have a high degree of personal involvement

- Illiquid in the short term, that is, until the company goes public or is acquired by another company, a process that generally takes three to seven years
- Difficult to value, as there is no public market for such securities
- Going to require future rounds of financing

A Broader Spectrum of Venture Capital

In recent years, however, the venture capital industry has begun to cover a much broader spectrum of investments, including funding for:

- Established businesses that are in the process of expanding, just prior to going public via an initial public offering (IPO)
- Companies in turnaround situations
- Management teams seeking leveraged buyouts (LBOs), also referred to as management buyouts (MBOs) of their companies

Stages of Financing.   Thus, in a broad sense, we can think of venture capital as funding for businesses in various stages of development, often from the idea stage to just before the company goes public (or is acquired by a larger corporation). The funding generally comes in stages. The first round of financing is generally the most expensive for the entrepreneur, in that the entrepreneur might give up half of his or her equity in the venture.[1] The next round will likely provide a further dilution of equity of perhaps 10% to 20%, as will the following round of financing. Thus, by the time of the IPO, the entrepreneur(s) might own 20% of the company, the venture capitalists and other early stage investors might own 60%, and the public might own 20%.

Multiple Rounds of Financing.   Teradata Corp. is a Los Angeles-based manufacturer of high-performance data-base management systems. The company raised $67 million in venture capital through six rounds of financing between its founding in 1979 and its IPO in 1987. Multiple financing rounds are quite common for high-tech businesses like Teradata, which invest heavily in research and development (R&D). Consequently, the capital raising process becomes a continuous activity for early stage ventures.

Teradata, with 1988 revenues of approximately $100 million, was ranked number 1 on the *Inc.* 100 list of high-growth, small public companies in 1989, due to its 317% compounded annual growth rate over the previous five-year period. (Growth slowed a bit in 1989, with revenues of $140 million.) Yet, it took six years before Teradata had its first profitable quarter. In the case of

---

[1]These are *very* rough, general guidelines. Numerous factors can affect the equity positions of the entrepreneurs and the venture investors, such as past success of the venture, expected returns for investor, proprietary position, quality of management, experience in marketing, and prior investment in the venture by the entrepreneur team. These are all discussed in great detail in Chapter 9.

Teradata, the venture capitalists did quite well. The company's market capitalization at the time of its IPO was nearly $\$\frac{1}{4}$ billion.

Thus, we should view the venture capital process as an activity that can take place over several stages over the life of the venture.

There are three *early stages* of financing, as follows:

1. *Seed financing*: capital provided at the idea stage. The capital, which is usually less than $50,000, generally goes for product development and market research.
2. *Start-up financing*: capital used in product development and initial marketing. This is generally for companies that have been in operation for less than one year but have not sold their product(s) or service(s) commercially.
3. *First-stage financing*: capital provided to initiate commercial manufacturing and sales.

(As we'll see in the section on informal investors in Chapter 4, the formal venture capital industry has financed an extremely small percentage of the seed and start-up situations in this country; this affords the informal investor an attractive opportunity to fund companies at these early stages of development.)

There are also three stages of *expansion financing*, as follows:

1. *Second-stage financing*: capital used for initial expansion of a company that has already been producing and selling a product. The company might not be profitable at this time.
2. *Third-stage financing*: capital provided to fund major expansion, for example, for plant expansion, product improvement, and marketing.
3. *Mezzanine (or bridge) financing*: capital provided for a company that expects to go public within a year or so.

Finally, there are two *special cases* of venture financing, as follows:

1. *Turnaround situations*: capital provided to restructure or revitalize a troubled company that is generally at a more established stage of development.
2. *Leveraged buyouts (LBOs) or management buyouts (MBOs)*: capital provided to fund a management team or a group of outside investors attempting to purchase a company or a subsidiary from a major corporation; in an LBO (which is a type of asset-based lending), the company's assets are generally used as collateral for loans.

Recently, venture capital firms have begun to specialize, either by region, by industry, or by stage of development. (This will be discussed in further detail in Chapter 12.) Several venture capital firms invest solely in start-ups; others only get involved in LBO deals; and so on.

Recently, venture capital firms have begun
to specialize, either by region, by industry,
or by stage of development.

Although LBOs are quite different from traditional venture capital investments, as we'll see later, they are often housed under the same roof. Interestingly,
although venture capital firms have only recently gotten involved in LBOs, the
LBO market has lost much of the luster associated with it during the early to
mid-1980s. Consequently, it is possible that LBOs will be a short-lived type of
investment by venture capital firms.

We recognize that the primary use of venture capital is for emerging growth
ventures; it is generally these investments that most dramatically affect the
economy in terms of employment creation and economic development. Nonetheless, the other types of venture capital investments, which are becoming
increasingly popular, can also enhance economic growth. (This is discussed
further in the next section and in Chapter 12.) Thus, despite our primary emphasis on emerging growth businesses, we will use the term venture capital
fairly broadly throughout this book to refer to all venture capital types of investments. Moreover, we realize that, although the traditional venture capital
firms have really shaped the industry, there are numerous other sources of
investment capital for smaller ventures, which we will discuss in Chapter 5, that
fall under our broad view of venture capital.

THE IMPACT OF VENTURE CAPITAL

What has been the impact of venture capital on entrepreneurial development and growth? We can examine its impact by exploring two important
questions:

1. Does venture capital enhance the likelihood of success of the particular
   entrepreneurial companies receiving such funding?
2. Does venture capital enhance economic development in general?

Venture Capital's Impact on Entrepreneurial Growth and Success

First, does venture capital enhance the success of individual entrepreneurial companies? Earlier, we cited some very dismal statistics regarding the
failure rate of start-ups. One thing is very clear, though. The companies that
receive venture capital or other such financial backing have a much greater
likelihood of succeeding than companies that do not receive such financing.

Several classic research studies showed that there is only a 10% to 20% failure rate for investments in a venture capitalist's portfolio (as compared to, perhaps, a 10% to 20% *success* rate for all new companies). This is based on the findings of Dorsey and of Huntsman & Hoban, who reported failure rates for companies in their first five to seven years of existence of 18% and 16%, respectively, for venture capital investments; in addition, White reported an 8% failure rate among companies funded by a large bank's small business investment company (SBIC).[2]

Venture capital is more than just money.
Venture capitalists do more than merely
fund ventures; they also tend to get involved
in strategic planning, technology
assessment, market analysis, risk and
return assessment, management recruiting

What about for the individual companies in a venture capitalist's portfolio? One of the most significant points that has been made and will continue to be made throughout this book is that there is a difference between venture capital and other investments: Venture capital is more than just money. Venture capitalists do more than merely fund ventures; they also tend to get involved in strategic planning, technology assessment, market analysis, risk and return assessment, management recruiting, and the like, and, therefore, provide a *value added* for the emerging growth company in such nonfinancing activities. Similarly, in the case of corporate venture funding activity, that is, venture capital funding by subsidiaries of large corporations (see Chapter 5), such funding provides the larger corporation with a "window on technology."

The Influence of Georges Doriot.   Perhaps this philosophy of the value added provided by the *venture catalyst* is demonstrated best by General Georges Doriot, an eminent professor at the Harvard University Graduate School of Business Administration during the 1930s and 1940s, as well as an astute investor. In 1946, Doriot founded American Research and Development (ARD) in order to foster the growth of exciting new businesses in the Boston area.

ARD's most significant investment occurred in 1957, when Doriot was contacted by a young engineer named Kenneth Olsen, who had an idea for a

---

[2]For details of these studies, see T. K. Dorsey, "The Measurement and Assessment of Capital Requirements, Investment Liquidity and Risk for the Management of Venture Capital Funds," unpublished doctoral dissertation, University of Texas, Austin, 1977; B. Huntsman and J. P. Hoban, "Investment in New Enterprise: Some Empirical Observations on Risk, Return, and Market Structure," *Financial Management*, Summer 1980, *9*, pp. 44–51; R. White, *The Entrepreneur's Manual*, Chilton, Radnor, Pa., 1977.

device called an interactive computer. This device, which was actually the fore-runner of the minicomputer, would enable the user to communicate directly with the computer via a terminal or keyboard, rather than punch cards.

ARD invested $70,000 in Olsen's start-up company, which was called Digital Equipment Company (DEC). DEC set up its modest headquarters in an old woolen mill in Maynard, Massachusetts, a suburb of Boston.

Over the next 14 years, Doriot worked closely with Olsen, assisting him in establishing a strategic direction for DEC. Over that time, ARD's $70,000 investment grew to $350 million.

Doriot, who sold ARD to Textron in 1972, had other success stories, including Cordis, a pacemaker manufacturer; Cooper Laboratories, a pharmaceutical company; and Teradyne, an electronic test equipment maker. (ARD's overall performance, however, was far from stellar, as we'll see in Chapter 13.)

Doriot's Guidelines. Doriot established a set of guidelines for venture capitalists, which demonstrated his philosophy. The guidelines were as follows:[3]

- Don't try to run the business. You don't know how to do it as a venture capitalist; the entrepreneur knows best.
- Treat the portfolio companies, these little companies you have invested in, like your own children. Kick them every now and then if they need it, but be fair.
- Be a help. Be there when needed. Be an ear, a sounding board, an alter ego, a crying towel.
- Do what is necessary to allow the portfolio company the opportunity to achieve the potential you originally thought you saw was there. In other words, don't pull the plug too soon.
- Be realistic. Don't get swept away. It is very easy to listen to an entrepreneur and start getting fired up. Entrepreneurs are persuasive people. But a venture capitalist can't let himself lose his objectivity.

Many people have criticized Doriot for:

- Having stayed too long with companies in which he invested
- Bending over backward to continue to support companies long after their potential had faded
- Being slow to get into new investments, and
- Being even slower to get out of new investments

Doriot's philosophy of "building men and companies," however, demonstrates the major differences between venture capitalists and other types of portfolio managers. Whereas the portfolio manager often avoids becoming too familiar with the companies in which he invests, because he may have to liquidate his position

---

[3]See G. Kozmetsky and others, *Financing and Managing Fast Growth Companies: The Venture Capital Process*, D. C. Heath, Lexington, Mass., 1985, pp. xii–xiii.

on very short notice in the case of deteriorating market conditions, the venture capitalist must establish a more personal relationship with the entrepreneurs in which he has invested over a much longer duration of time.

Of course, as the industry has evolved and as new professionals have entered the venture capital arena, we can hardly expect that Doriot's guidelines will govern the behavior of *all* venture capital firms or *all* venture capitalists. The concern is probably much greater among the newer entrants in the industry than among the pioneers in this industry.

Enhancing Doriot's Principles.[4]   Doriot's philosophy, both as a teacher (of Thomas Perkins, founder of Kleiner Perkins Caufield & Byers, and numerous others who entered the venture capital business) and as a venture capitalist, has had a powerful impact on the industry over the past twenty years. The creditable venture capitalists recognize their roles as nurturers of emerging growth businesses, rather than merely as passive investors, thereby supporting their roles as *venture catalysts*.

In the mid-1970s, for example, Paul Wythes of Sutter Hill Ventures, a prominent venture capital firm in Palo Alto, reviewed the business plan for Qume, a start-up computer printer manufacturer. When Wythes met with the company's founders, he suggested that Qume refine its focus in order to better meet the market's needs for a faster, more versatile, and higher-quality product. Within two years, Qume was able to capture nearly one-fourth of a very competitive $80 million market.

Jerry Goodwin, a New York-based venture capitalist, sums up the relationship between the venture capitalist and the entrepreneur very well. According to Goodwin,

> "Once one makes an investment in a company you are 'getting into bed' with the other person. You are closely involved with somebody ... for five or six years and there is virtually no way of getting out—you've made your commitment and you'd better make real sure that you like the people that you are involved with.... Otherwise you are going to lose your money in addition to losing a lot of sleep along the way."[5]

Building Management Teams.   In some instances, venture capitalists will even put together management teams with adequate funding in order to start ventures on their own. For example, in 1982, Art Caisse, a vice-president for research at Tymshare, Inc., was approached by a partner at Sutter Hill Ventures. Caisse was offered a loan as well as office space to get started on any computer communications ideas that he felt were viable. Within six months,

---

[4]The examples cited in this section as well as in subsequent sections of this book are based on experiences encountered by the author as well as on cases documented in such leading publications as *Venture, Inc., Forbes, Fortune, Business Week, Nation's Business, Success, Entrepreneur,* and *In Business.*

[5]See Robert C. Perez. *Inside Venture Capital.* New York: Praeger, 1986.

Caisse's new company, Cohesive Network Corp., received $2 million in funding for 50% of his company from Sutter Hill Ventures, along with Bessemer Venture Partners, which has an office in nearby Menlo Park, California.

Similarly, Onset, a venture capital firm in Palo Alto, which invests solely in seed and start-up stage ventures, has served as an "incubator" to several of its investments. For example, in addition to investing $650,000, a typical size of investment for Onset, into Penederm, Inc., a Foster City, California, based skin medication company, Onset provided the start-up with office space at a reduced rent, recruitment assistance, and management guidance. Two of Onset's partners, Terry L. Opdendyk, the former president of (the now defunct) Visicorp, and Robert Kuhing, formerly with Sun Microsystems, are well equipped to provide the necessary guidance to the firm's early-stage investments.

The Experience of Venture Capitalists. Like Opdendyk and Kuhing of Onset, many successful venture capitalists have launched businesses of their own prior to entering the venture capital arena, thereby enabling themselves to help other entrepreneurs do the same. What better way to serve as nurturers of emerging businesses. For example, Eugene Kleiner, a founder of Fairchild Camera & Instrument (which, as was discussed in Chapter 2, later gave rise to Fairchild Semiconductor, which, in turn, practically gave rise to the entire semiconductor industry), and Thomas Perkins, former director of corporate development for Hewlett-Packard, were two of the founders of Kleiner Perkins Caufield & Byers. The venture capital firm, founded in 1972, which is among the ten largest in the nation, is best known for its investments in Genentech, a leading biotechnology company, and Tandem Computer, a manufacturer of mainframe computers with back-up systems (that is, two computers "in tandem").

Similarly, Donald Valentine, a former marketing director of National Semiconductor, is a general partner with Sequoia Capital; Burgess Jamieson, who was chief development engineer of Honeywell's Computer Control Division, is with Sigma Partners.

A Question of Experience. As the venture capital industry has grown and as the financial rewards of venture capitalists have increased, this profession has become a high choice option among top business school graduates. The result has been that the venture capital firms have been able to choose some extremely bright young MBAs from the likes of Harvard, Stanford, M.I.T., Wharton, Columbia, and Northwestern. Unfortunately, many have been lacking in experience. As one entrepreneur recently told me,

> "I have nearly 30 years of experience in the health care industry. Yet, soon after receiving funding from a venture capital firm, I had a 25-year-old kid with an MBA from Harvard acting like he knew more about the health care industry than I did. He wasn't even born when I began developing my client list."

A somewhat related concern is that as the funds have taken on less experienced, although extremely intelligent, associates to assist in investment decisions and in the due diligence process, the entrepreneurs have not necessarily received the expert advice, which is often more valuable than money. The problem is that the pool of available talent has not kept up with the dramatic growth of the venture capital industry itself. Consequently, the venture capital industry has a large number of individuals with less than five years of experience actively involved in the venture capital process. The result is that a junior-level person will often be the contact person with an entrepreneurial company. As noted by John Hines of Continental Illinois Venture Capital,

> "It's like a large law firm. You can say you're with the greatest law firm in the world, but, if a junior person is handling your account, I'd say that's 'baloney.' The question is, Who is your individual lawyer? This is not a profession for a lot of inexperienced, young people in their 20's and 30's."[6]

Entrepreneurs as "Angels."   Several successful entrepreneurs, who have amassed sizable wealth from their own ventures, have entered the venture capital industry on a more informal, yet powerful, basis. For example, several years after Henry Singleton founded Teledyne, he invested in several start-ups, including Steve Jobs' first venture, Apple Computer. H. Ross Perot, founder of Electronic Data Systems (EDS), which was sold to General Motors in 1984 for $2.5 billion, has invested in a few start-ups, most notable of which was a $20 million investment in Steve Jobs' latest venture, NeXT, Inc.

Like Singleton and Perot, several other successful entrepreneurs have entered the "angel network," a loosely structured network of informal investors who fund emerging growth businesses. (This is discussed in further detail in Chapter 4.) Most of these investors invest between $100,000 and $200,000. They have varying levels of involvement.

Some examples of these angels are William Poduska, the classic computer entrepreneur who founded Prime Computer, Apollo Computer, and Stellar Computer; Philip Romano, founder of Fuddruckers, Inc. (discussed in Chapter 1), a chain of hamburger restaurants that he sold in 1985; Robert Darvin, founder of Scandinavian Design, Inc., a $100 million furniture retailer; Mitchell Kapor, founder of Lotus Development, in which he sold his stake in 1986, and of ON Technology, a new software company he started with Peter B. Miller, a former Lotus executive; Warren Avis, founder of Avis, Inc.; and Sophie Collier, founder of American Natural Beverage Corp., which was sold to Seagram Co. for $15 million in 1989.

One note of caution regarding the entrepreneur turned angel. In recent years, many entrepreneurs have accumulated greater and greater wealth and have had numerous opportunities to invest in emerging growth ventures. As informal investors, they represent a tremendous opportunity: for entrepreneurs, for themselves, and for the economy. However, keep in mind that the examples that I've just presented are of the ones who are "doing it right";

---

[6]See Joel Kotkin, "Why Smart Companies Are Saying No to Venture Capital," *Inc.*, August 1984, p. 67.

they're reputable and are quite willing to assume the traditional role of venture capitalists as advocated by Doriot. Unfortunately, as mentioned earlier, there are few restrictions for entering this industry. Consequently, plenty of wealthy informal investors, whether they've accumulated their wealth through entrepreneurial pursuits, investments, real estate ventures, "wheeler-dealer" activities, scams, or any other means (honest *or* dishonest), have taken on the angel title; some of them, however, have played a "devil" role. Although many of these informal investors have provided significant benefits, several have been a discredit to this profession. Yet, as we've already indicated, because their services revolve around something as emotional as money, entrepreneurs have often failed to exert the proper care in dealing with such individuals.

Nonetheless, in most instances, I have found that the hands-on experience and knowledge of these entrepreneurs turned venture capitalists is extremely valuable for the emerging companies in which they invest. For example, in 1980, when Wilf Corrigan had an idea for a company that would make semicustom integrated circuits, he approached Don Valentine, who, with experience in the semiconductor industry, forced Corrigan to better define his ideas for his company, LSI Logic. Earlier, Valentine assisted Altos Computer Systems with its marketing efforts, an area in which he was well versed as a result of his former position as marketing director at National Semiconductor. Valentine also recruited A. C. Markkula for his position with Apple Computer during Apple's early years. These episodes are consistent with Doriot's view of the role of the venture capitalist in building companies and is certainly consistent with our view of the role of *venture catalysts.*

Of course, many venture capitalists have accomplished what Valentine, Kleiner, Perkins, and the other more notable members of this industry have, but on a smaller scale, thereby putting them in an ideal position to assist smaller, younger companies. For example, Kevin Kinsella, who has a management and engineering background from MIT and Johns Hopkins, launched Spectragraphics Corp., a manufacturer of color workstations that operate with IBM software, prior to founding Avalon Ventures, a San Diego-based feeder fund that invests in early-stage technology companies. Recently, Avalon has invested in NeoRx, a Seattle-based biotechnology company; Athena Neurosciences, of San Carlos, California, which is in the health care business; and FASTech, a Waltham, Massachusetts based computer software company.

Venture Capital's Impact on Economic Development

Our second question regarding the impact of venture capital is what role does it play in the economic development of our nation? Several researchers have found that venture capital investments are critical to the economy in terms of capital formation, local development, economic expansion, technological growth and innovation, employment growth, and competitive adaptation in global markets.[7]

Obviously (consistent with what was suggested in Chapter 1), venture capital investments have generated revenues, profits, growth, and jobs. Yet, venture capital investments have also resulted in the development of medical diagnostic and treatment equipment, scientific improvements, and the like. They have resulted in a higher quality of life for the users of such equipment as well as for the employees of the companies that have developed those technologies. Venture capital investments have developed entrepreneurs. They have also contributed to our innovativeness and competitiveness; this is supported by a study by the Commerce Department, which found that small businesses have generated half the major innovations in this country over the last thirty years. Thus, the venture capital process has much more far-reaching effects than the individual venture deal being financed.

The GAO Study.   A study conducted by the U.S. General Accounting Office (GAO) nearly ten years ago, which examined seventy-two venture capital firms established in the 1970s, with a combined paid-in capital (that is, the total money invested to create the venture capital funds) of $209 million, reported that the companies in which those venture capital firms invested were responsible for:[8]

- $6 billion in revenues in 1979 alone
- 130,000 in new jobs
- Nearly $1 billion in exports
- Nearly $$\frac{1}{2}$$ billion in new taxes (corporate plus individual)

Those numbers hardly look startling. However, we should keep in mind that during the 1970s venture capital commitments for the industry as a whole were generally less than $100 million per year (in 1975, venture capital commitments were about $10 million), as compared to about $5 billion today.

Ten Years Later: What Are the Implications?   What does that mean for today? In 1988, there were more than two dozen venture capital firms with paid

[7]For details of these studies, see P. Bearse and D. Konopki. "A Comparative Analysis of State Programs to Promote New Technology Based Enterprises," *New England Journal of Business and Economics*, Spring 1979. W. R. Carleton. "Issues and Questions Involving Venture Capital," in G. Libecap (ed.) *Advances in the Study of Entrepreneurship, Innovation, and Economic Growth*, JAI Press, Greenwich, Conn., 1986, pp. 59–70; J. A. Timmons and W. D. Bygrave, "Venture Capital's Role in Financing Innovation for Economic Growth," *Journal of Business Venturing*, 1986, *1*, pp. 161–176; U.S. Congress, House, Small, High Technology Firms and Innovation Report, Prepared by Subcommittee on Investigations and Oversight of the Committee on Science and Technology, 96th Congress, 2nd Session, 1979; U.S. General Accounting Office (GAO), "Government-Industry Cooperation Can Enhance the Venture Capital Process," GAO/AMFD-83-35, August, 12, 1982.

[8]See U.S. General Accounting Office, "Government–Industry Cooperation Can Enhance the Venture Capital Process," GAO/AMFD-83-35, August 12, 1982.

in capital, individually, of over $200 million (as compared to the total pool of approximately $200 million for the seventy-two venture capital firms in the GAO study), and one firm, E. M. Warburg, Pincus & Co. (New York, New York), which is one of the most highly regarded venture capital firms in the nation, with paid in capital (as of 1988) in excess of $1 billion. (In 1990, the initial committed capital of the funds under management by E. M. Warburg, Pincus & Co. is in excess of $3 billion.) There's more money under management in this one venture capital firm than there was in the entire venture capital pool throughout the 1970s.

Thus, if the venture capital industry has experienced such significant growth over the last decade, so has its economic impact. Although there has not been any follow-up research to the GAO study, it is reasonable to assume that the aggregate economic benefits of venture capital-backed companies today would be well in excess of:

- $100 billion in revenues
- 2 million new jobs
- $50 billion in exports
- $25 billion in new taxes

Stated another way, that would equal the size of the entire computer and office equipment industry[9] in terms of revenues or the combined size of both the entire electronics industry[10] and the entire pharmaceuticals industry[11] in terms of total jobs.

Indirect Effects of Venture Capital Investments.   Of course, the numbers cited in the previous section measure only the direct benefits of venture capital. What about the impact that these early-stage ventures have had on established companies? What about the users and suppliers of the products and services that these companies provide? What about their competitors?

For example, the $20 billion membership warehouse industry (which was discussed in Chapter 1), which includes such players as Price Club, Costco Wholesale Corp., Pace Membership Warehouse, and Wholesale Club, was launched as a result of significant investments of venture capital. More recently, this has prompted Wal-Mart to enter the picture with its Sam's Wholesale Club, as have at least six other smaller warehouse chains across the country. As this

---

[9]That would include such multibillion corporations as IBM, Digital Equipment, Unisys, Hewlett-Packard, NCR, Apple Computer, Control Data, Wang Laboratories, Zenith Electronics, Pitney Bowes, Compaq Computer, Amdahl, and Prime Computer, as well as several dozen smaller companies.

[10]That would include General Electric, Westinghouse Electric, Motorola, Raytheon, Honeywell, TRW, Emerson Electric, Texas Instruments, North American Philips, Whirlpool, Teledyne, Intel, and AMP, plus several other multibillion dollar electronics companies.

[11]That would include Johnson & Johnson, Bristol-Myers, Merck, American Home Products, Pfizer, Abbott Laboratories, Smith Kline Beckman, Eli Lilly, Warner-Lambert, Schering-Plough, Upjohn, Squibb, and the others in that industry.

industry has grown, so have some of its suppliers, which include Jan Bell Marketing and Advanced Marketing Services. Similarly, the growth of such specialty sporting goods retailers as The Sports Authority (Fort Lauderdale, Florida) has coincided with the success of such athletic shoe companies as Reebok and LA Gear.

Another indirect effect of venture capital investments is the impact that entrepreneurial companies have had on the entrepreneurial pursuits of larger established businesses. This entrepreneurial philosophy of small businesses has prompted many larger companies to form *intra*preneurial ventures within the corporate hierarchy. Such ventures have included 3M's Post-It Notes, IBM's personal computer, and Pontiac's Fiero.

Thus, we see that venture capital has had some significant direct as well as indirect benefits on our economy. Venture capital has served as a catalyst for the growth of smaller emerging ventures; moreover, it has supported the growth of suppliers, customers, and competitors of numerous entrepreneurial companies, while it has prompted larger established companies to become more entrepreneurial.

A LOOK AHEAD

As noted earlier, it is entrepreneurship that has been directly responsible for economic growth and development. However, venture capital has been the catalyst for entrepreneurial activity. Moreover, the role of venture capital has not been in merely furnishing financial resources. Rather, venture capitalists, which have been responsible for providing management assistance and strategic guidance to emerging growth ventures, have been very successful in asserting their role as *venture catalysts.*

Venture capital and entrepreneurship have steadily, and positively, affected each other for a number of years. The increase in the availability of venture capital has certainly enhanced new venture activity. At the same time, as the entrepreneurial spirit has increased, there has been more of a need to increase venture capital commitments. As noted by David Brophy, professor of finance at the University of Michigan,

> "In the race for technological growth and development, investors throughout the world are beginning to see the tremendous value that lies in cultivating the partnership of venture capitalists and entrepreneurs."[12]

In the next part of this book, we examine this partnership between venture capitalists and entrepreneurs in greater detail. Who are the key players? What are the demographics of the venture capital industry? What is the role of formal, as well as informal, investments? These questions are all addressed in Chapter 4.

---

[12]See Lee Kravitz, "What Venture Capitalists Want," in *Venture's Guide to International Venture Capital,* Simon & Schuster, New York, 1985, p. 14.

PART II

THE KEY PLAYERS
IN THE VENTURE
CAPITAL INDUSTRY

The Venture Capital Industry

Most of us have heard of such names as Kleiner, Perkins; Hambrecht & Quist; Warburg, Pincus; and Hillman Ventures. Yet, aside from their names, we may know little about these venture capital firms nor about their industry. We know that they invest in some emerging growth ventures. But how actively do they invest? How well capitalized are these firms? What are their typical investments? Are there geographic differences? Do they invest in start-ups? How actively do they invest in leveraged buyouts (LBOs)? Finally, aside from these *formal* venture capital firms, what is the impact of *informal* venture capital investments on entrepreneurial development? Let's explore these issues.

THE FORMAL VENTURE CAPITAL INDUSTRY

Venture Capital Firms

The formal venture capital industry in the United States is characterized by several hundred venture capital firms. These firms, which are also referred to as venture companies, venture firms, venture funds, venture partnerships, and venture capital pools resemble mutual funds, to some extent, in terms of their investment activity, although not in terms of their investment philosophy.

Structure and Fee Arrangement of Venture Capital Firms. The venture capital firms are usually structured as limited partnerships, with a group of investors, called *limited partners*, and a group of managers of the fund, called *general partners*. They share in the profits in ratios disproportionate to their capital contribution. Typically, the general partners, who manage the portfolio,

49

but do not, necessarily invest in the ventures themselves, will usually receive a percentage of the profits, plus an annual management fee. Management fees alone can amount to 20% of the total capital raised over the life of a fund. For example, E. M. Warburg, Pincus & Co. will receive over $200 million in fees alone for managing the $1.2 billion fund it raised in 1986 if the fund is in place for its full lifetime.[1]

Although the fee structure can often be justified due to the tremendous amount of time spent by the general partners in researching their investments and in assisting the entrepreneurial companies on matters related to long-term growth, there is always the fear that as the funds grow larger in size venture capital firms may become driven primarily by management fees, rather than by the potential profits of their investments. Obviously, the size (percentage) of the management fee was very appropriate with funds in the $10 million to $50 million range. However, as the funds have grown so large, into the hundreds of millions of dollars and upward, the limited partners are beginning to question the fee structure.

Venture Capital Firms Versus Mutual Funds. Clearly, the investor–fund manager–investee situation is far different from mutual fund investments in publicly held companies, in which the research demands by the mutual fund manager are far less and the managerial assistance demands are virtually non-existent. Thus, as discussed earlier, venture capital is more than money; the venture capitalist serves as a *resource manager* to the emerging growth businesses by providing them with assistance on such issues as recruitment and planning. As noted by John Pappajohn, president of Pappajohn Capital Resources in Des Moines, Iowa, "I'm really in the business of putting together good ideas and good people with money, of financing companies at start-up and then keeping close tabs on them until they go public."[2]

Although venture capitalists are unlikely to get involved in the day-to-day operations of the business, they will often get involved in strategic planning, marketing, and other long-range issues. Pappajohn, who plays an active role in companies in which he invests, adds, "I call them every day and I make them millions."

Time Demands of Venture Capitalists. Of course, some venture capitalists have a different view of the process; they find themselves devoting more time to raising capital from investors than they do to assisting the ventures in which they invest. This has been more evident among venture capital firms that invest in early-stage ventures, which spend a large portion of their time fund

---

[1]The reader should not be misled by the $200 million figure in management fees for the Warburg, Pincus fund. First, Warburg, Pincus would only receive that amount if the fund is in place for its *full* lifetime of twelve years, which has not occurred for any of its previous funds. In addition, contrary to the practice of many other venture capital firms, Warburg, Pincus doesn't take any investment banking or other transaction fees from its funds.

[2]See Lee Kravitz, "What Venture Capitalists Want," in *Venture's Guide to International Venture Capital*, Simon & Schuster, New York, 1985, p. 11.

raising for subsequent rounds of financing; it becomes even more pronounced during periods of stock market declines, at which time there are fewer IPOs.

∿∿∿∿∿∿∿∿∿∿∿

We have used the term venture capital firms very broadly throughout this book to include not only the traditional venture capital limited partnerships, but also the publicly held venture capital companies, which are called *business development companies* (BDCs); *small business investment companies* (SBICs); venture capital subsidiaries of larger corporations; and others. (These will all be discussed further in Chapter 5.) Any of these managed pools will be referred to as a venture capital firm, a fund, a partnership, or a pool. Furthermore, once the venture capital firm makes an investment in a company, it is the venture capital firm, rather than the limited partners, that is referred to as the *investors.*

The Size of the Venture Capital Industry

A decade ago, the venture capital industry's total capital under management was approximately $3–$4 billion. Today, the pool is approximately ten times that size. It was reported to be a $32 billion industry at the end of 1988.

A decade ago, the venture capital industry's total capital under management was approximately $3–$4 billion. Today, the pool is approximately ten times that size.

Currently, there are over 2,000 professionals in the formal venture capital industry, as compared to about 600 in the late 1970s, who work for more than 600 formal venture capital firms (including SBICs and venture capital subsidiaries of larger corporations).

The Size of the Individual Venture Capital Firms

A decade ago, the largest venture capital firm was about $40 million and the average fund was approximately $15 million. In 1982, the first of the *megafunds* (those with paid in capital of $100 million or more) was created, when Kleiner Perkins Caufield & Byers raised $150 million. Today, the megafunds are commonplace. As noted earlier, there is even one venture capital firm with over $1 billion in paid in capital.

The ten largest venture capital firms in this country, based on paid in capital to the firm (using 1989 figures), are shown in Table 4-1.[3]

[3]See *Venture*, June/July, 1989, pp. 40–50. (*Venture* magazine ceased publication in 1989.)

TABLE 4-1   Largest Venture Capital Firms in the U.S. Based on Amount
Paid in Capital

Name of Firm (Location)[a]	Paid in Capital ($ Millions)	Year Founded
E. M. Warburg, Pincus & Co. (New York)	1,321	1971
Hambrecht & Quist Venture Partners (San Francisco)	650	1968
John Hancock Venture Capital Management (Boston)	533	1982
First Chicago Venture Capital First Capital Corp. of Chicago (SBIC) (Chicago)	507	1961
TA Associates (Boston)	378	1968
Schroder Ventures (New York)	336	1936
Frontenac Co./ Frontenac Capital Corp. (SBIC) (Chicago)	331	1970
Kleiner Perkins Caufield & Byers (Palo Alto, California)	326	1972
Chemical Venture Partners/ Chemical Venture Capital Associates LP (SBIC) (New York)	300	1984
New Enterprise Associates (Baltimore)	285	1978

[a]The location refers to that of the main office; several of these venture capital firms have two or more offices in the United States as well as in other countries.

Venture Capital Firms Are Becoming Even Larger.   More recently, in March 1990, E. M. Warburg, Pincus & Co. completed a $1.8 billion venture capital fund, which not only dwarfs its previous $1.2 billion fund, but is three times the size of any other venture capital partnership. This is indicative of the trend toward larger venture capital funds that has emerged over the past few years.

In recent years, the large venture capital firms have gotten larger, partly because of the larger investments of pension funds. Such investments by pension funds, however, have been very selective; the pension fund managers, in keeping with their fiduciary responsibility and their aversion to risk, have primarily invested in the larger, more diversified, more established venture capital firms.

Of course, the rules of the venture capital game have changed as the stakes have gotten higher and as the funds have increased in size. In some cases, heavy institutional investment has been detrimental for the industry. For example, some of the large institutional investors have put pressure on venture capital firms to take the venture capital-backed companies public too soon. By shortening the time from venture capital funding to IPO funding from five or six years to two or three years, investors can get their money out sooner. However, this often upsets the normal growth pattern of the venture capital-backed company, thereby making it vulnerable in the process. Moreover, this

TABLE 4-2 Amount of Capital Raised by
the Venture Capital Industry

Year	Amount Raised ($ Billions)
1988	3.1
1987	4.9
1986	4.5
1985	3.3
1984	4.0
1983	4.5
1982	1.8

is often in direct conflict to the philosophy of the role of the *venture catalyst* described earlier.

Nonetheless, there have been numerous positive results, as evidenced by the successes of the dozens of venture capital-backed companies mentioned throughout this book. Yet, as is generally the case with the growth of any business, there are sometimes negative effects for the emerging growth company, which have resulted from undue control by its investors.

Amount of Capital Raised by Venture Capital Firms.   One measure of the growth of the venture capital industry is the amount of money raised each year from investors, that is, the limited partners (which include wealthy individuals and families, pension funds, corporate investments, and others; see Chapter 7).

In 1977, the venture capital industry raised a total of $39 million. Since that time, there has been a significant, but fairly steady, increase in funds raised by venture capital firms. According to *Venture Economics*, which tracks such statistics, it reached $$\frac{1}{2}$$ billion in 1979 and then increased to $2 billion in 1982 and to $5 billion in 1987. The amount of capital raised by venture capital firms over the last seven years is shown in Table 4-2. In 1988, note that the total dollars raised by the venture capital industry dropped by over 36%, to $3.1 billion. There were several reasons for this, one of the most important of which was the reaction to the stock market crash of 1987. (This will be discussed in further detail in Chapter 15.)

The Most Active Venture Capital Firms: The Venture Capital 100.   Over the past decade, *Venture* magazine has ranked the 100 most active venture capital firms in the country, based on dollars invested, and has provided statistical data about the firms included in its Venture Capital 100 list.[4] This list probably accounts for 80% of the formal pool of venture capital in this country.

In 1988, the Venture Capital 100 invested $4.5 billion into companies, nearly 60% of which was invested by the twenty largest firms. Investments by the Venture Capital 100 over the past six years are given in Table 4-3. As shown,

[4]See *Venture*, June/July, 1989, pp. 40–50.

TABLE 4-3 Investments by the Venture Capital 100

Year	Amount Invested ($ Billions)	Number of Deals
1988	4.5	4,612
1987	3.7	4,100
1986	3.1	4,421
1985	2.3	3,696
1984	2.3	2,651
1983	2.3	3,119

the $4.5 billion was an increase of 22% over the previous year's $3.7 billion. In terms of number of deals in which they invested, there was a 12.5% increase in 1988, from 4,100 to 4,612. The average size of a deal increased by 7% from $912,000 to $976,000.

Based on total size of investments, the ten largest venture capital firms in this country, which combined invested nearly $2 billion (or over 40% of the total of the Venture Capital 100) in 1988, are given in Table 4-4.

It should be noted that this list does not fully overlap our earlier list of the largest venture capital companies based on amount of paid in capital. Only four venture capital firms, E. M. Warburg, Pincus & Co.; First Chicago Venture Capital; Schroder Ventures; and Chemical Venture Partners, were on both lists. In other words, those venture capital firms with the most money are not necessarily the most active investors. This is, however, partially due to the fact that capital raised in one year may not be invested in the venture capital firm's portfolio until the following year.

Nature of Investments

Where do these investments go? Throughout the 1980s, computer hardware and systems companies have been consistently the largest recipients of these investment dollars. This has been reflected by their relatively large representation (generally 30% to 40%) on the *Inc.* 100 list, which is a listing of the fastest growing, small *publicly* held companies in this country, most of which have gone public within the past few years. This has begun to change somewhat over the last two years or so, since consumer-related businesses have received a greater portion of venture capital funding than the computer and related companies.

We see a similar pattern among the *Inc.* 500 list, which is a listing of the fastest growing, small, *privately* held companies in this country.[5] Over the past three years, three industries—computer related, business services, and consumer goods—have each accounted for approximately 20% of the companies on the *Inc.* 500 list. (This will be discussed in further detail in Chapter 12.)

---

[5]The *Inc.* 500 companies, which are privately held, generally are smaller, earlier-stage ventures than the *Inc.* 100 companies, which are publicly held.

TABLE 4-4 Largest Venture Capital Firms in the U.S. Based on Size of Investments

1988 Rank	1987 Rank	Name of Firm (Location)	1988 Investments[a]		Year Founded
			$ Millions	No. of Deals	
1	1	E. M. Warburg, Pincus & Co. (New York)	644	49	1971
2	3	First Chicago Venture Capital/First Capital Corp. of Chicago (SBIC) (Chicago)	246	49	1961
3	8	Aeneas Venture Corp./ Harvard Management Co. (Boston)	202	68	1973
4	—	Schroder Ventures (New York)	164	63	1936
5	12	BancBoston Capital (Boston)	145	69	1959
6	5	Security Pacific Capital/ First SBIC of California (Costa Mesa, California)	120	76	1960
7	7	Morgan Capital Corp./ Morgan Investment Corp. (SBIC) (Wilmington, Delaware)	100	21	1982
8	13	Clinton Capital Corp. (SBIC)/Columbia Capital Corp. (MESBIC) (New York)	98	284	1980
9	11	Chemical Venture Partners/Chemical Venture Capital Assoc. (SBIC) (New York)	95	40	1984
10	—	Boston Ventures Management/Boston Ventures LP (Boston)	92	6	1983

[a]The investments for 1988 include investments in new situations as well as add-on investments to companies already in the portfolios of these venture capital firms.

Geographic Concentration

As may be expected, venture capital firms are regionally concentrated in this country, with the greatest number located in and around New York City; San Francisco and the Silicon Valley, and Boston. Of the 100 largest venture capital firms in this country, two-thirds are located in just those three areas. The breakdown among the most recent Venture Capital 100 is given in Table 4-5. It is clearly seen that there is a disproportionate distribution of venture capital firms throughout the nation. The three leading states in which venture

TABLE 4-5   Location of the Largest Venture Capital Firms in the U.S.

Geographic Location (includes surrounding area)	Percent of the Largest Venture Capital Firms
New York City/Newark, N.J./Stamford, Conn.	36
San Francisco/Silicon Valley	15
Boston	15
Chicago	6
Washington, D.C./Baltimore	4
Dallas	3
Princeton, N.J.	3
Los Angeles	2
Cleveland	2
Other locations in the Northeast	7
Other locations throughout the United States	7

capital firms are located, New York, California, and Massachusetts, are also the three leading states in which venture capital funds are disbursed, however, not in the same order.

California.   The greatest number and the largest dollar value of venture capital commitments is in California. This should not be surprising, since California has produced the greatest success stories among entrepreneurial companies over the past decade. Specifically, during that time, California has had twenty-one companies, including Sun Microsystems (Mountain View), Businessland (San Jose), AST Research (Irvine), Softsell Computer Products (Inglewood), LSI Logic (Milpitas), Maxtor (San Jose), Everex Systems (Fremont), and 3 Com Corp. (Santa Clara), go from start-up to the $100 million level in revenues in less than ten years; no other state has had more than five.

California venture capital firms have made significant investments in high-tech industries over the past two decades. Hambrecht & Quist (San Francisco), Sierra Ventures (Menlo Park), Sequoia Capital (Menlo Park), and Kleiner Perkins Caufield & Byers (Palo Alto) are some examples of such venture capital firms that have invested heavily in high-tech companies in the Silicon Valley area. There are over two dozen venture capital firms that specialize in high-tech investments in a single location in Menlo Park. They are located in a complex at 3000 Sand Hill Road, which has become known as one of the leading high-tech starter locations in the world.

Over 75% of the venture capital investments by California venture capital firms remain in the state. In addition, entrepreneurial companies located in California receive a substantial amount of venture capital from other states. Thus, California is a *net recipient* of venture capital.

Massachusetts.   After California, Massachusetts companies have been the next biggest recipients of venture capital. Similar to California, there is a high-tech focus among many of the venture capital firms in Massachusetts, especially those located around the famous Route 128 near Boston. Combined, companies in California and Massachusetts receive about 50% of the total dollars invested by venture capital funds in this country.

New York. There are several dozen venture capital companies located in New York, with the majority located in New York City. Many of the New York City-based firms have links with financial institutions, such as commercial banks (for example, Citicorp, Irving Trust, and Chase Manhattan) and investment companies (for example, Merrill Lynch, Salomon Bros., and Donaldson Lufkin Jenrette). New York is a *net provider* of venture capital; more than 80% of the investments of venture capital firms based in New York go to companies located *outside* the state.

Other Regions. In many ways, the venture capital climate in Illinois is similar to New York. Many of the venture capital firms in Illinois are linked to financial institutions (for example, First Chicago Venture Capital Company, First Capital Corp. of Illinois, and Continental Illinois Venture Corp.).

Other regions have been prominent in the venture capital area. Texas has historically funded energy-related companies. This has resulted in problems due to the recent slump in energy prices. Minnesota has had its share of technology investments by venture capital firms located in that state. A good example is the funding of Control Data Corp. (Minneapolis), which spun off from the Sperry UNIVAC project in the 1950s and which later gave rise to Cray Research. Control Data has since become an investor in early growth technologies, as was the case with its acquisition of VTC, Inc. (Bloomington, Michigan), which manufactures high-performance integrated circuits. (More recently, Control Data sold 80% of VTC, which was unprofitable, to privately held Seattle Silicon.)

Locations for Business Growth. The data on the locations of venture capital investments provided should not be surprising, since they parallel somewhat the locations of business growth in this country. Out of the 500 fastest growing, small private companies included in the 1989 *Inc.* 500 list, the greatest number was located in California, which had 83.[6] That was followed by New York (with 34), Massachusetts (29), Michigan (28), Texas (27), and Virginia (27). Those same states have consistently had the greatest number of *Inc.* 500 companies. Over the past four years, there have been only four states with a total of 100 or more *Inc.* 500 representatives: California (with 305), Texas (120), New York (109), and Massachusetts (100).

[6]Similarly, the *Inc.* 100 list of fast growth public companies had 27 representatives from California in 1989; likewise, the *Venture* IPO 100, which is a list of the largest small public corporations, compiled by *Venture* magazine, had 40 representatives from California in 1909.

TABLE 4-6 Venture Capital Investments Based on Stage of Development

Stage	1988 (% of total)	1987 (% of total)	Percent of Change of $
Seed/start-up	$557 million (12.4%)	$550 million (14.7%)	1.3
Later stage (first stage; second stage)	$1.40 billion (31.1%)	$1.00 billion (26.7%)	40.0
Follow-on (third stage; mezzanine)	$1.24 billion (27.6%)	$1.15 billion (30.7%)	7.8
Leveraged buyouts (LBOs)	$1.32 billion (29.3%)	$1.05 billion (28.1%)	25.7

Investments Based on Stage of Development

Out of the $4.5 billion invested by the 100 largest venture capital firms in this country in 1988, the breakdown, based on stage of development, was as shown in Table 4-6.[7]

Changes in Investment Philosophy.   As illustrated in Table 4-6, from 1987 to 1988 there was a decrease in the relative level of investment in early-stage ventures, with a corresponding increase in the level of investment in later-stage ventures and LBOs. Although the differences in percentages are not that great, this is a continuation of a trend that has taken place throughout the decade. For example, in 1983, start-up ventures represented 27% of the investments of the Venture Capital 100, or more than double their current amount, and LBOs represented 14% of their investments, or less than half of their current amount.

From 1983 to 1988, venture capital investments by the Venture Capital 100 nearly doubled, from $2.3 billion to $4.5 billion. If we compare the investments in seed and start-up ventures in 1983 to 1988, we find that there was actually a slight *decrease*, from $571 million in 1983 to $557 million in 1988. The change in LBO investments during that time is quite dramatic—a nearly fivefold increase, from $280 million in 1983 to $1.32 billion in 1988. These are rather significant changes to the makeup of venture capital portfolios in a period of just five years.

What Prompted This Change in Investment Philosophy?   One reason for this change in investment philosophy is the size of the venture capital funds. As several of the funds have increased in size to the hundreds of millions of dollars in paid in capital, the trend has been away from start-ups in favor of more established companies.

This should certainly not imply that *all* large venture firms have abandoned

---

[7]These data, taken from *Venture* magazine, vary somewhat from the data provided by *Venture Economics*. This is due to the differences in the samples selected by the two sources and in the definitions used to describe the various stages of development.

start-ups. For example, E. M. Warburg, Pincus & Co., whose $3.4 billion in paid in capital easily makes it the largest venture capital firm in this country, has *always* made its investments in three distinct types of situations: undervalued assets, developing and expanding companies, and start-ups. The company uses the following framework to balance the risk/reward levels of these three types of investments:

1. Undervalued assets, which represent 50% of the fund's dollars of capital but only 20% of the number of deals
2. Developing and expanding companies: 35% in terms of dollars and 30% in terms of number of deals
3. Start-ups: 10% in terms of dollars and 50% in terms of number of deals

Certainly, Warburg, Pincus has not abandoned start-ups, as evidenced by the $180 million it invested in fifty-one start-up situations over the past decade. The result of this investment philosophy has been quite appealing to the limited partners of Warburg, Pincus. The firm had a 25% compounded annual return for its investment portfolio over a twenty-year period from the time it was formed in 1971 through the end of the decade of the 1980s.

Thus, the trend away from start-up investments has been more evidenced by the *dollars invested* than by the *number of deals* funded by the venture capital firms. As noted by Frederick M. Haney, of 3i Ventures in Newport Beach, California,

> "When you have that much money, the tendency is to put it out in large chunks. Very little is likely to go to early-stage companies."[8]

Nonetheless, many of the larger venture capital companies are investing more actively in later-stage investments, and particularly in LBOs, and less actively in start-ups. Many "purists" in this industry are quite upset by this evolution in investment philosophy. Certainly, a strong case can be made in support of LBOs, as evidenced by the creation of jobs, economic gains through increased taxes, and the like (this will be discussed at length in Chapter 12). However, the typical argument against funding LBOs, and often rightly so, is that the process has resulted in many venture capitalists becoming strictly investors, rather than investors and advisors, which clearly runs counter to Doriot's principles of building companies.

Seed and Start-Up Investments. Of the approximately $.5 billion invested in the seed and start-up stages in 1988, the leading investors were as given in Table 4-7.

LBO Investments. Venture capital firms, even the traditional venture capital firms, are investing increasingly larger percentages of their portfolios in LBOs. Bain Capital of Boston, for example, which is well known for its early-

---

[8]See Udayan Gupta, "Venture Capital Funds Grow Larger and Larger," *Wall Street Journal*, September 7, 1989, p. C2.

TABLE 4-7   Largest Seed and Start-up Investments by Venture Capital Firms

Name of Firm (Location)	Seed and Start-up Investment ($ Million)	Percentage Change, 1987–1988	Percent of Total Investment in Seed and Start-up
Warburg, Pincus (New York)	55.0	7	9
Aeneas Venture (Boston)	48.5	137	24
Clinton Capital (New York)	31.4	322	32
3i Corp. (Boston)	13.9	163	35
Merrill, Pickard, Anderson & Eyre (Palo Alto, Calif.)	13.4	111	47
New Enterprise Associates (Baltimore)	13.4	−46	24
Edwards Capital (New York)	13.2	−53	100
Hillman Ventures (Menlo Park, Calif.)	13.2	51	18
Allied Capital (D.C.)	12.8	−38	34
Healthcare Investment Corp. (Edison, N.J.)	12.5	na	55

TABLE 4-8   Largest LBO Investments by Venture Capital Firms

Name of Firm (Location)	LBO Investment ($ Million)	Percent of Change, 1987–1988	Percent of Total Investment
First Chicago Venture Capital (Chicago)	169.5	1	69
BancBoston Capital (Boston)	124.7	129	86
Schroder Ventures (New York)	123.9	na	75
Security Pacific Capital (Costa Mesa, Calif.)	75.2	6	62
Manufacturers Hanover Venture Capital (New York)	75.0	67	89
Aeneas Venture (Boston)	71.7	56	35
Chemical Venture Partners (New York)	60.5	9	64
Frontenac Co. (Chicago)	58.7	na	84
TA Communications (Boston)	37.7	na	44
Hillman Ventures (Menlo Park, Calif.)	36.4	7	49

stage investment in Staples, a Newton, Massachusetts, based retailer of office supplies, has earmarked more than 75% of its recent investments for buyouts. Several other venture capital firms, which were formed with the intent of funding early-stage ventures, invest either primarily or exclusively in LBOs. (This is discussed in further detail in Chapter 12.) Of the $1.3 billion invested in LBOs in 1988, the leading investors were as shown in Table 4-8.

It should be noted that, even though venture capital firms are investing more in buyouts, they will often assist management in the same way as they do for early-stage ventures; in that way, they *are* building companies. For example, Hambro International, a New York-based venture capital firm, recently invested $3.6 million in the buyout of Building Technologies Corp., a manufacturer of metal building systems, from Southwestern General Corp. (Cincinnati, Ohio). Hambro also raised another $40 million in a combination of straight debt and subordinated debt. It is Hambro's plan to work with management over the next few years to streamline the company and to expand its markets.

Of course, in some cases, venture capital firms have virtually ignored the newer, smaller companies in their portfolios, which can become even more prominent as selected investments in LBOs and later-stage ventures become even larger. For example, I'm familiar with one early-stage high-tech manufacturing company in New England that was able to raise nearly $1 million from a leading venture capital firm located just a few miles from the company. Unfortunately, the amount raised represents less than 1% of the venture capital firm's paid in capital, with the vast majority of its investments being targeted to later-stage ventures and LBOs. Despite the fact that the venture capital firm is represented on the company's board, the company claims that it has received very little from the venture capitalists other than a "large check to help scale up production."

THE INFORMAL VENTURE CAPITAL INDUSTRY

"Angels"

The structure of the formal venture capital industry, which includes the major venture capital firms, which raise money from investors and invest in growth-oriented companies, is fairly well defined. However, recently, many entrepreneurs have sought funding from *angels*, wealthy individual investors who are most interested in providing capital to start-up businesses.

The notion of angels is nothing new. After all, in 1903, Henry Ford's automobile company was started partly as a result of five angels who invested $40,000 in the venture. The idea is commonplace today. Countless ventures get their start through the funding by such angels. For example, when Ben Bush of St. Petersburg, Florida, recently launched Brass Letters & Logos, Inc., he relied on personal contacts (as well as self-funding) for the necessary start-up capital. The company has used the capital to enhance its manufacturing process and to expand the distribution network for its merchandise.

Angel Networks.   Angels, which are also referred to as *adventure capitalists*, can be found in private clubs throughout the nation. Joseph Mancuso, director of the Center for Entrepreneurial Management in New York, has organized angel chapters in several large cities. In addition, William Wetzel, professor at the University of New Hampshire has developed the Venture Capital Network, a computerized database to link entrepreneurs with investors.

The Impact of Informal Investors

According to Prof. Wetzel, who is the leading researcher in this country on informal investors, if institutional venture capitalists finance less than 1,000 start-ups annually, where do the other 24,000 (give or take a few thousand) find their equity capital?[9] Wetzel suggests that informal investors probably fund twenty times more ventures than do established venture capital companies. Frank Swain, chief counsel for advocacy of the Small Business Administration (SBA), suggests that self-funding and informal investments account for 75% of all equity investments in small business.[10]

A Large Pool Available for Start-Up Capital.   Prof. Wetzel indicates that there may be as many as 250,000 informal investors (as compared to the approximately 2,000 formal venture capitalists) in this country who are responsible for a $50 billion pool of venture capital (as compared to the $32 billion pool of formal investors). Moreover, as suggested by Robert Gaston, who was commissioned to do a study for the Small Business Administration (SBA), informal investors are the major sources of start-up capital, investing approximately $27 billion per year primarily in start-up deals.[11]

As indicated earlier, established venture capital companies have been devoting a larger portion of their portfolios to later-stage investments at the expense of start-ups. This has made informal investors prime candidates for the funding of early-stage ventures; in fact, the informal investors tend to favor the early-stage investments over later-stage ones, as they feel they can get involved in the growth of the company as early as possible. Informal investors, who are often the financial backers of technology start-ups, are often interested in funding ventures:

- That are seeking approximately $20,000 to $50,000 in start-up capital
- That are in close proximity to where they live
- In which they can also play an active consulting role
- That are appealing in terms of product features and potential returns

ⵖⵖⵖⵖⵖⵖⵖⵖⵖⵖⵖ

Although a large portion of this book is devoted to the formal venture capital industry, we should not lose sight of the impact that informal investors have on the venture capital process, especially in the case of early stage ventures.

---

[9]See William E. Wetzel, "Informal Risk Capital," in D. L. Sexton and R. W. Smilor (eds.), *The Art and Science of Entrepreneurship*, Ballinger Publishing Co., Cambridge, Mass., 1986, pp. 85–117.

[10]See *Journal of Accountancy*, December 1988, p. 17.

[11]See Robert Gaston, *Finding Private Venture Capital for Your Firm*, Wiley, New York, 1989.

A LOOK AHEAD

In this chapter, we examined the nature of the formal venture capital industry, an industry that raises and invests over $4 billion annually. When combined with the informal venture capital industry, we can see the tremendous impact that venture investments have had on the development and growth of entrepreneurial companies.

Up to this point, we have not made a distinction between the different types of venture capital firms and the other similar investment companies. That will be the subject of the following chapter.

Chapter 5

Venture Capital Firms and Other Investors

We often use the terms venture capital and venture capital firm very loosely to describe any type of funding for privately held businesses. Actually, venture capital firms are just one source of such financing. There are several other sources, including government- and university-supported programs that provide investment capital as well as management assistance. The purpose of this chapter is to draw distinctions among the different types of investors and to discuss the recent developments affecting their investment practices.

STRUCTURE OF THE VENTURE CAPITAL INDUSTRY

The venture capital industry[1] can be broken down into the following groups:

- Private independent venture capital partnerships
- Private Small Business Investment Companies (SBICs)
- Public venture capital companies
- Venture capital subsidiaries of large corporations
- State venture capital funds
- University-related incubators

[1]In this chapter, (1) we're using the term venture capital very broadly to describe not only the investments of a traditional venture capital limited partnership, but to describe similar types of investments in private companies; and (2) we're referring to the formal venture capital industry, rather than to the informal investors discussed in the previous chapter.

- Private sector incubators
- Investment banking firms

Let's explore these in detail.

Private Independent Venture Capital Partnerships[2]

Private venture capital partnerships are either traditional partnerships established by wealthy families to aggressively manage a portion of their funds (for example, Venrock Associates, which is the fund established by the Rockefeller family) or professionally managed pools that are funded by institutional investors (such as Hambrecht & Quist, Kleiner Perkins Caufield & Byers, and E. M. Warburg, Pincus & Co.). Such partnerships represent the predominant type of venture investors in this country.

Some venture capital partnerships provide seed capital for start-up businesses. Others invest in turnaround or LBO situations. However, the majority of venture capital partnerships invest in growth companies. Investments are usually in the range of $.5 million to $2 million.

Venture capital firms are generally organized as limited partnerships for tax purposes (to avoid corporate income tax) and other legal reasons. As discussed earlier, these partnerships have a general partner, which is usually the venture capital firm that manages the partnership's investment portfolio. The limited partners of the fund are the investors, who are usually passive, who each would typically invest a *minimum* of $1 million and often much more in the larger funds. The investors will include pension funds, foreign investors, corporations, banks, insurance companies, and wealthy individuals. Since a typical investment by a venture capital firm has a time horizon of three to seven years, most partnership funds establish an eight- to ten-year lifetime, whereby the general partner holds the option to extend this lifetime for up to three years. This ensures the orderly dissolution of investments by a fund.

Venture capital firms are generally organized as limited partnerships for tax purposes (to avoid corporate income tax) and other legal reasons.

The general partner is usually paid a management fee of approximately 2.5% of the committed capital plus an incentive bonus of 20% of the fund's realized net gains. The limited partners (the investors) would receive the remainder.

[2]The trade association of the venture capital industry is the National Venture Capital Association (NVCA), located in Arlington, Virginia.

Private Small Business Investment Companies (SBICs)[3]

Small Business Investment Companies (SBICs), which were created by an act of Congress in 1958 (see Chapter 2), are licensed and regulated by the Small Business Administration (SBA). These government-backed (but privately owned) investment companies (which include such companies as Citicorp Venture Capital, Allied Investment Corp., and Clinton Capital) may provide management assistance as well as venture financing to emerging businesses.

In recent years, SBICs have provided financing for such entrepreneurial successes as Apple Computer, Cray Research, Intel Corp., ROLM Corp., and Federal Express. SBICs have also enabled several unprofitable or marginally profitable ventures to become profitable businesses. Typical success stories include American Frozen Foods, Inc., of Bridgeport, Connecticut; NBI, a Boulder, Colorado, based manufacturer of word-processing systems; Ault, Inc., a manufacturing company in Minneapolis; Lifeline Systems of Waltham, Massachusetts, a manufacturer of emergency response systems for the elderly and handicapped; and Pandick Press of New York.

Due to SBA regulations, the investment policies for SBICs are much more restrictive than those for traditional venture capital firms. SBICs must uphold guidelines related to the size of the companies in which they invest and the portion of their portfolios that are invested in any particular company.

There are nearly 300 SBICs in this country, with total capital resources of $2.6 billion. Combined, they invested about $600 million in over 2,000 small ventures in 1989. Most of the SBICs are found in the states where entrepreneurial growth is highest: New York, California, Massachusetts, Connecticut, and Texas.

There are nearly 300 SBICs in this country, with total capital resources of $2.6 billion. Combined, they invested about $600 million in over 2,000 small ventures in 1989.

Some SBICs are primarily interested in equity positions in their investments; others serve as lenders. American Commercial Capital Corp. of New York, for example, lends money on a secured basis. (Thus, there is less risk and, consequently, less potential return for the investor.) The company's clients, therefore, tend to be low-technology companies with fixed assets, rather than high-technology companies with merely ideas. If the borrower does not succeed, American Commercial will take ownership of the secured assets.

[3]The trade association for SBICs is the National Association of Small Business Investment Companies (NASBIC), located in Washington, D.C.

Like many venture capital firms, some SBICs specialize in specific industry groups (for example, high technology or health care), whereas others provide funding for all types of ventures. Although a few SBICs, most notably, Clinton Capital Corp. (New York, New York), Edwards Capital Co. (New York, New York), Allied Capital Corp. (Washington, D.C.), Medallion Funding Corp. (New York, New York), and Transportation Capital Corp. (New York, New York), are actively involved in funding start-ups, most of the SBICs engage in later-stage investments.

SBICs are initially capitalized from private sources. They then become eligible to obtain loans at attractive interest rates from the government (or guaranteed by the government), thereby enabling the SBICs to leverage themselves by three times and, in the case of SBICs that fund minority-owned businesses (these are called Minority Enterprise Small Business Investment Companies [MESBIC's]; see below), four times their paid in capital. This financing ability allows SBICs to either make long-term loans or equity investments to emerging growth companies.

SBICs can be either private individuals, publicly held corporations, or subsidiaries of larger companies. Many SBICs, such as Citicorp Venture Capital (New York, New York), First Chicago Venture Capital (Chicago), Chemical Venture Partners (New York, New York), Chase Manhattan Capital Corp. (New York, New York), Manufacturers Hanover Venture Capital Corp. (New York, New York), are subsidiaries of commercial banks whose capital comes from clients of the bank.

Minority Enterprise Small Business Investment Companies (MESBICs).[4] In addition to SBICs, there are over 100 Minority Enterprise Small Business Investment Companies (MESBICs) that provide funding to businesses owned by racial minorities. They operate in a manner similar to other venture capital companies and, therefore, will evaluate proposals based on the owner's previous experience and on the company's business plan. Some of the larger MESBICs in the country (in addition to Medallion Funding Corp. and Transportation Capital Corp., which were just mentioned as SBICs that invest heavily in start-ups) include Columbia Capital Corp. (which is affiliated with Clinton Capital Corp.) (New York, New York), Allied Financial Corp. (which is affiliated with Allied Capital Corp.) (Washington, D.C.), Fulcrum Venture Capital Corp. (which is affiliated with Syndicated Communications, Inc., and Syncom Capital Corp.) (Washington, D.C.), and Pro-Med Investment Corp. (which is affiliated with Pro-Med Capital and Western Financial Capital Corp.) (North Miami Beach, Florida).

One current controversial issue is a federal regulation that prohibits MESBICs from having controlling interest in a minority business. According to some MESBIC investors, this has limited the returns to the MESBICs.

---

[4]The trade association for MESBICs is the National Association of Investment Companies (NAIC), located in Washington, D.C.

Public Venture Capital Companies

Several of the large venture capital firms (as well as SBICs) in this country are publicly held corporations and are referred to as business development companies (BDCs). They have similar investment orientations to privately held venture capital firms. However, because they are public corporations, they differ from private venture capital firms in terms of regulations placed on them by the Securities and Exchange Commission (SEC), tax laws that may affect their investment activity, and the expectations from their investors. For example, unlike private venture capital limited partnerships, a BDC does not liquidate itself after a set period of time. In addition, because BDCs are public corporations, management must be concerned with the stock price of the corporation.

Some of the larger publicly held venture capital companies are Allied Capital Corp. (Washington, D.C.), Capital Southwest Corp. (Dallas, Texas), and Rand Capital (Buffalo, New York). Publicly held SBICs include First Connecticut SBIC (Bridgeport, Connecticut) and Greater Washington Investors (Chevy Chase, Maryland).

Venture Capital Subsidiaries of Large Corporations

Large corporations often invest in smaller companies to supplement their R&D programs as well as to keep abreast of technological and other innovations. This can be done by investing in private venture capital limited partnerships (discussed earlier in this chapter). It can also be done by a direct investment in a smaller corporation. Furthermore, it can be accomplished by the formation of an internal venture within the company, that is, an *intrapreneurial* venture. Or this process can be formalized through the creation of a *venture capital subsidiary* (which operates like a trust department in a bank or a separate wholly owned company) of the large corporation. Some examples of the latter include Xerox Venture Capital (Stamford, Connecticut), Amoco Venture Capital (Chicago), Lubrizol Enterprises (Wickliffe, Ohio), Hewlett-Packard Co. Corporate Investments (Palo Alto, California), Sears Investment Management Co. (Chicago), and Caterpillar Venture Capital (Peoria, Illinois). Such venture capital subsidiaries are often attractive sources of capital for entrepreneurial companies because they can invest $10 million to $20 million in some ventures.

Today, this multibillion segment has about 100 nonfinancial corporations with venture capital subsidiaries, with many more doing some sort of ad hoc investing. These corporate subsidiaries not only have large pools of capital available for direct investments, but the parent corporations and their pension plans invest as limited partners of other venture capital partnerships. In addition, unlike typical venture capital funds, they have "deep pockets"; they can generally get additional capital resources from the parent company if attractive opportunities develop.

Benefits to the Corporate Venture Capital Subsidiary.   There are several reasons why corporations have established venture capital subsidiaries:

- To derive attractive financial returns
- To develop technology licenses, manufacturing rights, and marketing and supplier agreements
- To control supplier uncertainty
- To identify flourishing (or fading) industries
- To identify and assess acquisition candidates
- To spin off businesses
- To generate new products
- To learn the dynamics of a particular marketplace
- To gain exposure to new markets and technologies

Product Marketing Rights.   Because large corporations can provide marketing and distribution systems, small ventures are often happy to have larger companies sell their products. For example, NCR and Burroughs secured marketing rights for Convergent Technology's products, which are manufactured for them on an OEM basis. Similarly, in the biotechnology area, several large pharmaceutical companies (in the United States, Europe, and Japan) have secured marketing rights to various products developed by Genentech in return for development funds.

Acquisition Candidates.   A few years ago, General Electric made a direct investment in Applicon, Inc., a computer-aided design, computer-aided manufacturing (CAD/CAM) company. Eventually, GE attempted to acquire Applicon. However, it was unsuccessful in its bid. Nonetheless, armed with the knowledge of the CAD/CAM industry, GE bid successfully for Calma, another company in that industry. Similarly, Lubrizol recently acquired Agrigenetics, thanks in part to its venture capital involvement in related companies.

A Window on Technology.   Perhaps the most notable benefit that large corporations have derived from their investments in entrepreneurial companies is that they have gained a "window" on new technological developments without having to get directly involved with technologies that may deviate somewhat from their existing business mission. For example, when supercomputer genius Steve Chen, a 45-year-old native of Taiwan, left Cray Research (which was, itself, formed by managers from Control Data Corp.) to start his own company, Supercomputer Systems, Inc. (Eau Claire, Wisconsin), IBM immediately invested in the new venture.

The desire to keep pace with technological developments has certainly been a driving force behind the emergence of corporate venture capital subsidiaries. This is evidenced by the fact that all the ten largest electronics companies in the United States, as well as several prominent foreign corporations, have made direct venture investments over the last decade.

Numerous fledgling companies have derived the benefits of such investments by venture capital subsidiaries. Recent examples of technology companies that have received corporate venture capital include:

- *Artificial intelligence*: Carnegie Group, Interference, Lisp Machines, Symbolics, Syntelligence, Teknowledge
- *Biotechnology*: Advanced Genetic Systems, Amgen, Biogen, Calgene, Centocor, Cetus, Collaborative Research, Cytogen, DNA Plant, Genentech, Genex, Genzyme, Hana, Ingene, Liposome, Molecular Genetics, Oncogene, Synergen, Syntro
- *Computers*: Amdahl, Altos, Apple, Cray, Fortune Systems, Stratus, Sun Microsystems, Tandem, Trilogy, Wang
- *Instruments*: Analog Devices, Nicolet, Waters Associates
- *Medical Electronics*: ADAC, Cordis, Kolff Medical, Orien Research
- *Peripherals*: Centronics, Computer Memories, Decision Data, Seagate, Zitel
- *Robotics*: Adept Technology, Advanced Robotics, Automatix, Robotic Vision Systems, Synthetic Vision Systems, View Engineering
- *Semiconductors*: Cypress, Intel, LSI Logic, Micron, Siliconix, VLSI Technology, Xicor, Zymos
- *Software*: Adobe, Comserve, Interleaf, Seattle Silicon, Synektron, Synercom
- *Telecommunications*: Comdial, Intercom, MCI, Network Systems, Paradyne, Quotron, Rolm, Ungermann-Bass, VMX, Vodavi, Ztel
- *Terminals*: Datapointe, Esprit, Lee Data, Ramtek, Syntrex, Wyse
- *Others*: Businessland, Data Card, Federal Express, Fibronics, Key Pharmaceutical, Siltec, Xidex

You will, no doubt, recognize many of the names above as companies that have recently gone public and have generated outstanding returns for their investors.

Benefits to the Emerging Growth Company.   There are numerous benefits that corporate venture subsidiaries bring to companies in which they invest. In addition to the typical financial, resource, and strategic benefits that most venture capital firms provide, corporate venture subsidiaries have been able to provide:

- Established customer base
- Credibility with customers and suppliers
- Credibility with bankers and other financial sources
- General assistance in managing the business
- Merger partner
- Additional capital
- Flexible financing package

Investing in Employees.   One way in which large corporations have funded emerging growth ventures has been through their own employees who wish to start companies of their own. For example, Tektronix provided financial support to Jim Hurd, a former manager of solid-state engineering with the company, in order to form Planar Systems in exchange for 49.5% of the equity of the new business. Similarly, Campbell Soup provided William Sharp, a research director of the company, with the necessary financial, marketing, R&D, and personnel assistance (including a $5 million research laboratory) in return for a 30% equity position in the new venture. By providing employees with the necessary support to begin new ventures of their own, both the established companies and the new ventures have benefited tremendously.

Collaborative Arrangements.   Another way in which corporations have invested in smaller companies has been through collaborative arrangements. For example, Immunex Corp., a genetic engineering start-up in Seattle, signed a collaborative research contract whereby Hoffman LaRoche paid Immunex $500,000 up front (plus subsequent sales royalties) as well as monthly research payments so that it could manufacture and market Immunex drugs, pending regulatory approval.

Several other biotechnology companies have entered into similar arrangements with larger corporations. This has been due to the scarcity of venture capital dollars and the high costs of developing and testing new products. For example, Collaborative Research, Inc., of Boston, entered into an arrangement with American Hospital Supply Corp. for the funds needed to test and market its immunological products; Cetus Corp. received funding from Nabisco, Shell Oil, and Weyerhauser; Genetic Systems Corp. had assistance from Cutter Laboratories; and California Biotechnology, Inc., of Mountain View, California, created an alliance with Pfizer, Inc., to develop cures for diabetes and obesity.

Some Problems Associated with Corporate Venture Capital.   Despite the positive features noted, corporate venture capital programs have had their problems, generally arising from such reasons as the following:

- Contradictory investment goals of the corporate venture subsidiary and the parent corporation (or division)
- Unwillingness on the part of the corporate venture subsidiary to invest the seven to ten years necessary for venture capital commitments
- Conflicts of interests and legal problems, such as those involving fiduciary responsibility of the investing company
- Lack of skilled professionals
- Inconsistent goals of the corporation (the corporate venture subsidiary) and the entrepreneur

A recent study reported in the *Harvard Business Review* reinforces some of the limitations of corporate venture capital.[5] The authors found that, although there are positive features of corporate venture capital, such efforts have gen-

[5]See G. Felda Hardyman, Mark J. DeNino, and Malcolm S. Salter, "When Corporate Venture Capital Doesn't Work," *Harvard Business Review*, May–June 1983, pp. 114–120.

erally not been successful in promoting corporate diversification, primarily due to:

- Limited investment opportunities
- Difficulty of acquiring the funded company
- Complications involved in obtaining technology from the funded company
- Irreconcilable differences between organizational requirements for running a diversification program and those for building a healthy portfolio of investments

Moreover, such ventures have not always worked out well for the entrepreneur. As noted by one entrepreneur,

> "If the venture works out well, you can bet the corporation will end up owning it. And that is a contradiction to what entrepreneuring is all about."[6]

This may be the reason why, although approximately 30% of the *Fortune* 500 companies established venture groups during the 1960s and early 1970s, many of those are no longer in existence today. Consequently, such corporations as GTE, 3M, and Corning, which had traditionally invested directly in ventures, are now investing as limited partners through more traditional venture capital partnerships.

Keys to Successful Corporate Venture Capital Programs.   What makes corporate venture capital programs successful? It has been shown that, for corporate venture capital programs to succeed, the key elements of the corporation's operating environment and organizational structure should be adapted to its special characteristics.[7] This would include:

- Establishing appropriate, realistic goals
- Establishing a reasonable purpose for making such an investment, which should not, necessarily, be to eventually acquire the company being funded
- If a technology venture, selecting an investment in which the corporation can gain access to a new technology
- Providing a system of control and evaluation
- Selecting the appropriate professional personnel

Thus, there are mixed feelings regarding the advantages of organizing and maintaining venture capital subsidiaries of established companies. Some efforts, such as the ones at Tektronix and Campbell Soup, have been successful; others have not fared as well. It is safe to conclude, however, that it is the manner in which such a program is implemented that is the best predictor of its success.

---

[6]"Why Corporations Back Entrepreneurs," *Venture*, May 1980, p. 38.

[7]See Richard P. Greenthal and John A. Larson, "Venturing into Venture Capital," *Business Horizons*, September–October 1982, pp. 18–23.

State Venture Capital Funds

In 1975, Massachusetts and Connecticut established government-sponsored venture capital funds to provide financial assistance to emerging growth businesses. They were called, respectively, the Massachusetts Community Development Finance Corporation (CDFC) and the Connecticut Product Development Program. Since that time, several other states, including Georgia, Indiana, Michigan, Minnesota, New York, and Wyoming, have established similar programs, and Massachusetts has developed a second program, called the Massachusetts Technology Development Corp. (MTDC).

A Comparison of the Programs.   Although the purposes of each program are essentially the same, the programs differ with regard to the sources of funding, investment parameters, and investment preferences. Specifically, funding for state-supported programs may come from either state sources exclusively (which is the case in Connecticut, New Mexico, and Utah), a combination of state and federal sources (for example, Massachusetts and New York), private sources exclusively (for example, Minnesota and Wyoming), or a combination of state and private sources (for example, Georgia and Michigan). Furthermore, investments can be targeted primarily for early-stage ventures (which is the case in Georgia, Iowa, and Minnesota), for product development (for example, Connecticut), or for high-tech businesses (for example, Utah and New York). In addition, the funding can be in the form of royalty payments (which is the case in Connecticut), debt (for example, New Mexico), equity (for example, Utah, Georgia, Indiana, Iowa, Michigan, and Minnesota), or a combination of debt and equity (for example, Massachusetts, New York, and Wyoming).

The Impact of State-Supported Programs.   What has been the impact of these programs on economic development? In Massachusetts, where the program was initiated, the results have been very positive. Massachusetts Community Development Finance Corp. (CDFC) has invested in such companies as Automated Assemblies Corp., a systems integrator for industrial robots, and Runtal North America, which markets and distributes hydronic radiators. The other state-supported program in Massachusetts, the Massachusetts Technology Development Corp. (MTDC), has limited its funding to technology businesses, such as Access Technology, a developer of business software, and Zoom Telephonics, a telecommunications company.

Other state programs have had similar success stories. The Corporation for Innovation Development (of Indiana) has invested in such companies as Stratojac, a manufacturer of men's overcoats, and The Wholesale Club, which operates a chain of warehouse membership clubs. The Corporation for Innovation Development (of New York), which, like MTDC, has geared its investments to technology start-ups, has invested in Applied Robotics, Inc., a manufacturer of robotic systems, and Xertronix, a semiconductor processing equipment company.

The Enterprise Fund (of Nebraska) has invested in ICR Research Associates, which provides contract chemical analysis services, and Addax, Inc., which manufactures advanced composite material components for industrial use. The New Mexico R&D Institute has invested in RhoMed, a biotechnology company, and Bacchus Industries, which manufactures energy-efficient residential cooling units.

Tax Incentives.   Some states (for example, Indiana, Iowa, Minnesota, and Wyoming) provide tax incentives to private investors who fund their state venture capital pools. In addition, aside from venture capital pools, states have found other ways to support small business efforts. For example, investors who fund companies in Maine with annual sales of up to $200,000 can receive a tax credit on their Maine income tax of up to 30% of the amount invested.

University-Related Incubators

A recent development, especially for technology-oriented ventures, has been the emergence of the *incubator*, a structure that enables entrepreneurs to develop their business skills in an environment conducive to fostering technical creativity. Incubators, which are often university related, generally provide low-cost laboratory and office space, state-of-the-art technical thinking and equipment, administrative support, computer and library facilities, consultants, and contacts with bankers, venture capitalists, government officials, and the like, to selected entrepreneurs for a nominal fee. Since the entrepreneurs are surrounded by others like themselves, there is often a sharing of ideas and contacts, thereby enhancing entrepreneurial growth. In addition, these incubators enhance public-private-industry-university relations, which often results in economic benefits for all parties involved.

Incubators, themselves, have been a growth industry. In 1984, there were 40 incubators nationwide. Today, there are more than 300, with the greatest number found in Pennsylvania, Illinois, and New York.

The prototype university-related incubator and research center is the University City Science Center (UCSC) in Philadelphia. UCSC, which is affiliated with twenty-eight universities, colleges, and medical schools in the Philadelphia area (including the University of Pennsylvania, the Philadelphia General Hospital, the Philadelphia College of Pharmacy and Science, the Presbyterian University of Philadelphia Medical Center, Drexel University, and Villanova University), is the only entirely urban research part in the country. UCSC has the capacity to house nearly 100 companies in its 1 million square foot facility. Most of its current tenants are in high-tech industries.

Other similar, but much smaller, university-related programs include Western Pennsylvania Advanced Technology Center, in Pittsburgh, sponsored by the University of Pittsburgh and Carnegie-Mellon University; Georgia Advanced Technology Program in Atlanta; Rensselear Polytechnic Institute (RPI), in Troy, New York; Utah Innovation Center (UIC), in Salt Lake City, which has had a relationship with the University of Utah; and Institute for Ventures in Technology INVENT), which is sponsored by Texas A&M University.

The Role of Private Venture Capital in University Research Efforts.   A somewhat related structure is the Dallas Biomedical Corporation, a $12 million venture capital firm that limits its investments to research projects at the University of Texas Southwestern Medical Center that have the potential for commercialization. The firm, started in 1986, serves as a bridge between other private venture capital firms and university research efforts. Dallas Biomedical invests only the interest on its capital (investments will, therefore, be in the range of $50,000 to $250,000) and returns any profits plus the original principal to the outside investors in five years in return for half the interest in the technology; the other half is split between the university and the scientist. The firm, which is managed by Devon Giacalone, who was formerly with Biogen, the Cambridge, Massachusetts, based biotechnology company, has established a low-risk, socially oriented concept that could serve as a prototype for public-private-university relationships. Similar to this program is BCM Technologies, Inc. (BCMT), a for-profit business development arm of Baylor College of Medicine, which establishes new commercial entities based on inventions from researchers at the college. In its first five years of operation, BCMT developed five companies in such fields as blood salvage in open heart surgery and cancer diagnostics. The funding for these projects comes from outside venture capital companies, rather than from the college or the university system.

Private Sector Incubators

Private sector incubators, like university-related incubators, provide office space, administrative support, and an entrepreneurial atmosphere to entrepreneurs. However, they differ from university-related centers in that (1) the funding is strictly from private, rather than public, sources, and (2) the primary goal is profit; job creation and community economic development are not nearly as important as the profit motive.

Incubators are generally ideal for early-stage ventures, that is, preseed or seed stage. Some examples of private incubators include The Technology Center (Montgomeryville, Pennsylvania) and The Rubicon Group (Austin, Texas).

Investment Banking Firms

Investment banking firms are usually involved in more established companies, but occasionally form investor syndicates for venture proposals. These firms are in business to arrange financing and structure deals for emerging growth businesses. Many sophisticated entrepreneurs consider the use of investment bankers as the rule, rather than the exception, for raising capital, as they can do so more quickly and efficiently than can the managers of the venture themselves. Some of the larger investment banking firms in this country are ABS Ventures Limited Partnership (Baltimore, Maryland), Salomon Brothers (New York, New York), Morgan Stanley & Co. (New York, New York), and Montgomery Securities (New York, New York).

Boutiques.   Similar to the investment banking firms, but on a much smaller scale, are the "boutiques," which raise cash from banks, finance companies, and private individuals.[8] Like investment banking firms, they will sometimes invest their own capital. Their clientele is generally local or regional, and they can usually arrange financing for companies in the $1 million to $10 million range.

The boutiques will generally charge .5% to 3% of the capital raised to arrange for a debt placement and 2% to 8% to arrange for an equity placement. A commonly used fee arrangement in equity transactions is the "Lehman formula" of 5–4–3–2–1%, which translates into 5% of the first million dollars of capital raised, 4% of the next million, and so on. Thus, for a $3 million deal, the fees would be equal to $120,000, or 4% of the total capital raised:

$$\underset{\substack{\text{(5\% of the}\\\text{first million)}}}{\$50,000} + \underset{\substack{\text{(4\% of the}\\\text{next million)}}}{\$40,000} + \underset{\substack{\text{(3\% of the}\\\text{next million)}}}{\$30,000} = \$120,000$$

SYNDICATION

To satisfy the risk and return concerns of venture capitalists, most venture capital firms coinvest or *syndicate* with one another. For example, Sierra Ventures, a technology-oriented venture capital firm based in Menlo Park, California, was the lead investor in StrataCom, Inc., a manufacturer of high-speed telecommunications equipment. However, in addition to Sierra Ventures's $1.4 million investment in this Silicon Valley start-up, Sierra arranged for an additional $3 million in funding from Venrock Associates, U.S. Venture Partners, and International Technology Ventures.

As noted by George Middlemas, formerly with Citicorp Venture Capital, and now a partner with Inco Venture Capital Management,

> "Venture capital firms prefer syndicating most deals for a simple reason— it means they have a chance to check out their thinking against other knowledgeable sources. If two or three other funds whose thinking you respect agree to go along, that is a double-check to your own thinking as well as diversifying out the risk over several funds. However, syndication does not mean that you defer to the judgment of others."[9]

According to a recent study, between 75% and 90% of the deals of

---

[8]An extensive listing of private deal makers has appeared in the September issue of *Venture* magazine over the past few years.

[9]See Robert C. Perez, *Inside Venture Capital*, Praeger Publishers, New York, 1986, p. 53.

independent and corporate venture capital firms were syndicated. The study also found that only about one-third of the venture capital deals of SBICs were syndicated.[10]

A LOOK AHEAD

In the past two chapters, we discussed the nature of venture capital firms and other similar investors. Earlier, we indicated that the role of the venture capital firm is to raise capital from investors (the limited partners) and to use those funds to invest in emerging growth businesses. From where do the venture capitalists raise the money? Who are the limited partners? These questions are the focus of Chapter 6.

[10]1985 JEC Survey, p. 29.

Investors in Venture Capital Funds

The venture capital process is generally as follows: Pension funds and other investors invest gradually in a venture capital limited partnership. These investors add to the limited partnership as the venture capital firm doles out money to the emerging growth companies as it is needed, rather than all at once. When the partnership closes, the partners receive their share of the payback, which, as noted earlier, is usually split approximately 80% for the limited partners (the original investors) and 20% for the general partners (the venture capital firm).[1] It is often difficult to calculate the return on investment since the size and value of the investment have varied over the life of the partnership.

SOURCES OF FUNDING

Who are the limited partners in venture capital partnerships? Although they vary from one venture capital fund to another, there are some major similarities. Over the past few years, the funding for venture capital firms has come mostly from institutional investors, primarily from pension funds, endowment funds, insurance companies, and the like. As an example, Technology Venture Investors (TVI), a technology-oriented venture capital firm based in Menlo Park, California, has raised money from insurance companies (for example, The Kemper Group, Mutual Life Insurance Company of New York, New England Mutual Life Insurance Company, Penn Mutual Life Insurance Company, and Phoenix Mutual Life Insurance Company), endowments and foundations

---

[1]In addition, as mentioned earlier, the general partners typically receive an annual management fee of 2% to 3% of the paid in capital.

(for example, University of California, Stanford University, and Ford Foundation), and pension funds (for example, Dow Chemical Employees Retirement Plan Trust, General Electric Pension Trust, and Hewlett-Packard Co. Pension Plan).

Similarly, the limited investors in Oak Investment Partners, a Westport, Connecticut-based venture capital firm that has funded primarily computer and electronics (and related) companies, such as Sage Software, Triad Systems, Daisy Systems, and Compaq Computer, have been corporations and financial and insurance companies (such as Citibank, Equitable Life, The Kemper Group, Travelers Insurance, and 3M Corp.); universities and foundations (such as Harvard, MIT, Yale, and Ford Foundation); and pension funds (Amoco, Atlantic Richfield, CBS, Corning Glass Works, General Electric, and IBM).

Foreign investors have been limited partners in many venture capital funds. For example, most of the limited partners of Harvest Ventures, a New York-based venture capital firm with approximately $100 million under management, are Western European banks and other companies. These include Alfa-Laval, a Swedish manufacturing company; Nixdorf Computer of West Germany; VMF N.V., a Dutch manufacturing company; Procordia, a diversified Swedish company; Amro Bank of The Netherlands; and Deutsch Bank of West Germany.

Often, venture capital firms will serve as limited partners for other venture capital partnerships. For example, the limited partners of the Pittsburgh Seed Fund, a venture capital firm that invests primarily in early-stage companies in the Pittsburgh area, include (in addition to the major corporations, universities, and individual investors) The Hillman Co., Fostin Capital Corp., VenWest, Inc., and PNC Venture Corp.

Pension Funds

In his 1976 book, *The Unseen Revolution: How Pension Fund Socialism Came to America*, Peter Drucker noted:

> "We are organizing a capital market totally unequipped to supply entrepreneurial capital needs . . . the problems of the small but growing business are dissimilar from those of the established big or fair-sized businesses. They require a different investment policy, different relationships to management, and a different understanding of business economics, management, and dynamics."

Drucker suggested, at that time, in describing the role of pension funds, that

> "What is needed, therefore, are new capital market institutions specifically provided to give these new, young, growing businesses the capital (and the management guidance) they need; and which, at the same time, can act as investment vehicles suited for the fiduciary, the asset manager trustee."

Apparently, pension funds have heeded Drucker's advice. Today, pension funds account for approximately half of the funding for venture capital firms, as compared to approximately one-third of the funding from the late 1970s to the mid-1980s.

The Increase in Pension Fund Investments.   Up until the late 1970s, several provisions of the Internal Revenue Code of 1954, the Welfare and Pension Plan Disclosure Act of 1958 (the 1958 Act), and certain state trust laws precluded pension fund managers from investing in smaller, lesser known companies. Moreover, the Employment Retirement Income Security Act (ERISA) of 1974, which was intended to provide a flexible definition for "prudent" investments by pension funds, actually created tougher standards for investments, in stating that fiduciaries must act "with the (same) care, skill, prudence and diligence of . . . a prudent man acting in a like capacity. . . ."

One shortcoming of ERISA was whether "prudence" would be based on individual investments or on an entire portfolio of investments. The venture capital industry received a tremendous boost in 1979 when the Department of Labor ruled that pension fund managers could participate in venture capital activity without violating the "prudent man" rule, which served as a prime deterrent to such investments since 1974. That enabled pension fund managers, in an attempt to increase their returns for the investors, to divert a small percentage of their (at that time) $800 billion in pension fund assets to venture investments, as well as investments in office buildings, shopping centers, and acquisitions.

Today, there are 870,000 private U.S. pension plans with 76 million participants. These pension funds have accounted for approximately half of the venture capital funds raised over the last few years (but less than 50% of the total pool of $32 billion).

Over the past decade, pension fund assets in this country have more than doubled to about $2 trillion. That is approximately twice as much as the total of federally insured deposits held by S&Ls in this country. Stated another way, the total pension fund pool in the United States is larger than the real gross national product (in current U.S. dollars) of Japan.

Today, there are 870,000 private U.S. pension plans with 76 million participants. These pension funds have accounted for approximately half of the venture capital funds raised over the last few years (but less than 50% of the total pool of $32 billion). Yet, as large as those numbers seem, that amount is less than 2% of the total pension fund pool in this country.

As noted earlier, there are positive and negative features of such pension fund investments. Clearly, pension funds have been responsible for the major growth in size of the venture capital funds. However, in some instances, as their investments have increased, so has their desire to exert control over the venture capital firms and, ultimately, over the entrepreneurial companies receiving the funding. This, of course, could adversely affect the venture capital industry.

Direct Loans by Pension Funds. Recently, another trend has developed in the pension fund area—direct loans to smaller ventures. For example, the Massachusetts Industrial Financial Agency, a state agency that assists small businesses, helps companies to apply for letters of credit from local banks and then issues bonds to cover the borrowed amounts. Similarly, the New York City pension fund agreed to set aside $50 million for lending to small businesses, with the loans guaranteed by the Small Business Administration (SBA).

If this trend continues, it may be indicative of increased venture capital investments by pension funds in the coming years.

᠁᠁᠁᠁᠁

Aside from pension fund investments, venture capital firms receive approximately 15% to 20% of their capital from foreign investments and approximately 10% to 15% each from wealthy individuals or families, corporations, and insurance companies. Endowments also provide a substantial amount of capital.

Foreign Investments

In recent years, foreign investors have played an increasingly significant role in venture capital activity in the United States. They have invested directly in businesses (for example, Mitsubishi's investment in Suprex Corp., a Pittsburgh-based instrument company) and have invested in traditional venture capital limited partnerships, for example, the Japanese banks and trading companies that have invested in Hambro and other similar venture capital firms. (An extensive discussion of foreign venture capital investments is presented in Chapter 14.)

Corporate Investments

Although corporate investments represent a sizable portion of venture capital pools, such investments have declined somewhat in recent years from their annual levels of nearly $.5 billion in 1983 and 1984. These statistics, however, are a bit misleading. One reason for the seemingly declining level of corporate investments is that, as discussed in Chapter 5, corporations have emerged as major players in the venture capital industry and have invested directly themselves (through their corporate venture capital subsidiaries), therefore bypassing the venture funds, or have invested through corporate pension funds.

An attractive feature of direct corporate investments is that they provide companies a chance to "cash out" without going through initial public offerings (IPOs). The entrepreneurial companies benefit in that they will often get an attractive valuation; the large corporate investors benefit in that such investments are generally cheaper than developing the venture on their own from scratch.

A good example is Federal Filings, Inc. (Washington, D.C.), which was recently acquired by Dow Jones. Federal Filings, which provides time-sensitive reports on recent SEC filings to institutional investors, fits in very neatly with Dow Jones's basic mission. To start up such a service and to bring it to the level of Federal Filings today would have taken years. Yet, by acquiring the company, Dow Jones acquired the knowledge and existing customer base of Federal Filings immediately. Of course, Federal Filings benefited in that it could expand its existing customer base under the prestigious Dow Jones name.

A LOOK AHEAD

Part II of this book has examined the key players in the venture capital process: the venture capital firms, which act as general partners in venture capital deals; the private and public investors, such as pension funds, wealthy individuals, and corporations, which are the limited partners; and the entrepreneurial companies, which are the recipients of their investment dollars.

In Part III we examine in depth the process by which venture capitalists make investment decisions. In so doing, we provide prescriptive guidelines to assist entrepreneurs in their search for venture capital. Questions of concern include the following: How do venture capitalists screen investment opportunities? How do they select suitable companies in which to invest? As *venture catalysts,* what role do they play after making an investment? These questions are addressed in the following chapters.

PART III

THE VENTURE CAPITAL PROCESS

Chapter 7

An Introduction to the Venture Capital Process

A few years ago, I met with a general partner of one of the more established venture capital firms in the Boston area. My most vivid image of my meeting was seeing the dozens of business plans (or venture proposals from entrepreneurs in search of funding) stacked neatly in orderly piles on his desk. When I asked him how long it took to accumulate that many plans, he told me that those piles were from the weekend mail; they often receive forty or fifty plans in a given week. In his words, "they just keep coming ... and coming ... and coming."[1]

Everyday, one of his associates separates the plans based on the industry and the stage of development. Then the associate briefly scans the business plans and categorizes them to allow for further review by one of the general partners; they are categorized as (1) "clear losers," (2) "possibilities," or (3) "extremely promising." The general partner subsequently goes through the piles to better assess the investment potential of the proposals.

▸▸▸▸▸▸▸▸▸▸▸▸

Venture capital funding involves a decision process, such as the one just described, in which some proposals are judged acceptable, while the vast majority are not evaluated positively. There are five chapters in this part of the book, which *prescribe* guidelines for entrepreneurs to follow to increase their likelihood of their obtaining venture capital and of their working effectively with the venture capitalist. These guidelines, although they are pre-

---

[1] My executive editor at Prentice Hall recently reminded me that he has used essentially the same quote to refer to how frequently he receives manuscripts.

scriptions for success, are presented in a case-oriented format throughout Part III of this book.

This chapter is designed merely to serve as an introduction to the other four chapters in this part.

HOW DO VENTURE CAPITALISTS MAKE INVESTMENT DECISIONS?

Venture capitalists tend to make decisions regarding their investments in a systematic, orderly process. Some researchers have attempted to model the process by describing the following sequential process of venture capital investment activity:[2]

- *Deal origination*: by which deals enter into consideration as investment prospects, some of which, particularly technology ventures, are actively sought by investors, but most of which enter into contention via the referral process
- *Deal screening*: in which prospects, which are likely to number over 1,000 per year for an established venture capital company, are narrowed down in a series of stages to a few for in-depth evaluation
- *Deal evaluation*: in which prospects are evaluated based on their relative levels of perceived risk and expected return
- *Deal structuring*: which describes the negotiation for equity position
- *Postinvestment activities*: which includes management recruitment, strategic planning, location expansion financing, assistance in the cash-out, and so on; the expectation is that such ventures that go through the formal venture capital process will either go public, merge, or be acquired

In the next four chapters, we will discuss in detail the process described above. Chapter 8 will examine how deals originate. Chapter 9 will be concerned with how deals are screened and evaluated. In Chapter 10, we will discuss the structure of venture deals. Finally, Chapter 11 will examine postinvestment activity.

[2]See T. T. Tyebjee and A. V. Bruno, "A Model of Venture Capitalist Investment Activity," *Management Science*, 1984, *30*, pp. 1051–1066.

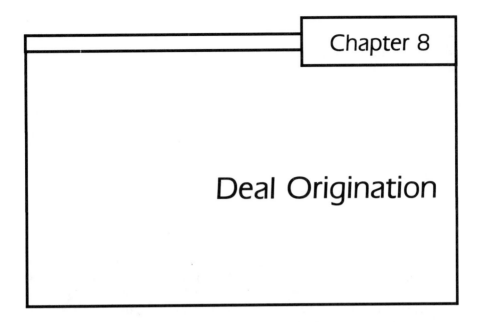

Chapter 8

Deal Origination

A few months ago I spoke to a young man who had recently received his bachelor's degree from one of the most prestigious engineering programs in the country. Over the previous two years, he had teamed up with two of his classmates to begin to develop a high-tech device to be used by telecommunications companies. As is typical of such entrepreneurs, they needed about $\frac{1}{4}$ million in venture capital just to develop a prototype and would need several million dollars more to scale up production after completing the prototype.

These three engineering students turned entrepreneurs had the makings of a potential success story. They had a viable product. Although they lacked experience, they had the perseverance and the intellectual capability to turn their idea into a useful product. They had the beginnings of a management team and were actively recruiting someone with marketing experience to strengthen their team. They even had a high-quality business plan. Unfortunately, however, after sending their business plan out to about two dozen venture capital firms, they soon felt like, in their words, "A couple of C+ students applying to Harvard ... we sent out twenty-five plans and received twenty-five rejections."

A few of the comments from the venture capitalists who reviewed their plan helped them better define their business. Things seemed to be going in the right direction for them, despite their lack of funds, when they learned of another company with a similar product—but with a management team that had broken off from a *Fortune* 500 company—that received $2 million in venture capital to scale up production of its product. In contrast to their own company, their "competitor" was flooded with inquiries from investors willing to fund their product.

That was a very frustrating episode for the young entrepreneurs (who, by the way, have since abandoned their entrepreneurial pursuits). It's quite a contrast; one company can have no success in raising capital, let alone in meeting with a potential investor, while another company with the same product can have investors "banging down their door" to fund them.

In this chapter, we explore this contrast by examining how venture capital proposals get into the hands of investors. This is the first step of the venture capital process, which we refer to as *deal origination.*

LEADS TO VENTURE CAPITALISTS

Venture capital deals enter into consideration in a variety of manners. Of course, entrepreneurs can make cold calls to venture capital firms. The conventional thinking has been that the likelihood of getting funded in this manner is not too great. As noted by Harvey Mallement, managing director of Harvest Ventures of New York, "We've never done a deal from a cold call."[1]

This would suggest that entrepreneurs who are referred to venture capitalists are in a better position to get funded. As noted by Joseph A. Bartlett, an attorney with the New York-based law firm, Gaston & Snow, and a noted writer on the subject of venture capital,

> "Unless the plan is accompanied by an introduction from someone who carries great weight, the odds against acceptance of a humdrum document are about equivalent to the odds against Mrs. Onassis responding to an unsolicited dinner invitation."[2]

It should be pointed out, however, that as venture capital firms have become more specialized, they are becoming increasingly receptive to entrepreneurs who approach them with niche-oriented products and services, even if it is done via a cold call.

Zeroing in on the Right Investor

One reason that so many proposals for funding are rejected by venture capitalists is that they are sent out indiscriminately to investors who do not fund such ventures. For example, if a venture capital firm invests solely in land development businesses, it would be foolish to send a business plan for a high-tech venture to such a firm. Similarly, a start-up business is unlikely to get funded by a venture capital firm that provides only second- or third-stage financing. Incredibly, so many entrepreneurs spend months preparing a business plan and then spend just a few minutes haphazardly sending out those plans

---

[1]See Jon Levine, "Money for the Asking," in *Venture's Guide to International Venture Capital,* New York: Simon & Schuster, 1985, p. 16.

[2]See Joseph A. Bartlett, *Venture Capital: Law, Business Strategies, and Investment Planning.* New York: John Wiley & Sons, p. 20.

to twenty or thirty venture capital firms without regard to the investment priorities (type of business or industry, stage of financing) of those firms. Thus, the first step in the deal origination process is for the entrepreneur to "prospect" for the investors who might be interested in funding such a venture.

Establishing Appropriate Linkages

Interestingly, a majority of a venture capital firm's leads comes from the entrepreneurial companies in which the firm has invested. Therefore, one of the best linkages for an entrepreneurial company to establish is with entrepreneurs already in a venture capitalist's portfolio. Other linkages, although not nearly as valuable, are through:

- Other venture capitalists or other similar investors
- Individual investors in a venture capitalist's portfolio
- Friends or associates of an investor
- Other business associates, such as lawyers, accountants, bankers, consultants, and small business owners

Venture Capital Fairs

Recently, some entrepreneurs have made contact with venture capitalists at venture capital fairs. The fairs, which are conducted throughout the nation (but especially in areas where there is high growth in new ventures such as San Francisco, Boston, New York, and Washington, D.C.), enable owners of fledgling companies to make proposals to investors. The most notable fair is the one sponsored by the American Electronics Association in Monterey, California. There is a screening process for this fair whereby only the most qualified new ventures are invited to attend.

Proactive Attempts by Venture Capitalists

Some venture capital firms are becoming more active in seeking out deals. Two-thirds of the investments of the Boston-based TA Associates, one of the largest venture capital firms in the country, are from proactive methods.

Examples of Proactive Methods.   This proactive practice is nothing new. For example, in 1973, Thomas Perkins, of the prominent San Francisco-based venture capital firm Kleiner Perkins Caufield & Byers, recruited Jim Treybig to examine business plans of other entrepreneurs in order to formulate one of his own. Treybig, who had a bachelor's degree in electrical engineering and an MBA from Stanford University, had been working as a marketing manager with Hewlett-Packard for the previous five years. After reviewing the business plans, Treybig came up with an idea for a pressing need for businesses: a double-fail safe computer. So, in 1974, he recruited several of his colleagues from Hewlett-

Packard to help him launch Tandem Computer (that is, two computers "in tandem" with one another). Within ten years, the company was generating over $1 billion a year in revenues.

A more recent example of a proactive attempt to fund an emerging business was, in 1983, when Kevin Kinsella of Avalon Ventures (San Diego) placed an ad in the *Wall Street Journal*, looking for someone to bring a start-up venture to "world class" status. The ad interested Robert T. Abbott, who was then a senior manager with Oncogen, a cancer research company. Abbott, who holds a Ph.D. in pathology and an MBA, didn't want the job. However, in the process, he was able to get Kinsella to back his own idea. The result was the formation of NeoRx Corp. (Seattle), a biotechnology company founded to develop monoclonal antibodies for cancer detection and treatment. The company, which raised close to $40 million from corporate backers (including Eastman Kodak) and venture capital firms (including Technology Venture Investors and Wind Point Partners), went public in 1988, four years after it was founded, with a market capitalization of nearly $100 million, while still in its developmental stage.

A LOOK AHEAD

We just examined the first step in the venture capital process: deal origination. The next two steps deal with the screening and evaluation of venture proposals, which are addressed in the following chapter.

Chapter 9

Deal Screening and Evaluation

Securing leads requires that the entrepreneurial team and/or the venture capital firm play an active role in getting the venture proposal in the hands of the venture capitalist. After securing leads comes the screening and evaluation of venture deals. At that point, the venture capital firm plays the active role in determining whether a given proposal is worthy of investment.

Let's now explore the nature of the venture proposal screening process and examine what factors are considered most important by the venture capitalist in making such investment decisions.

THE VENTURE PROPOSAL SCREENING PROCESS[1]

How Venture Capitalists Screen Proposals

Due to the riskiness of the venture business—only a limited number of investments provide adequate returns—investors set rigorous standards in evaluating venture opportunities. A large majority of them are rejected, either due to the nature of the product or service, the quality of the business, or the capabilities of management.

In just about every case, the entrepreneur submits a venture proposal, or

[1]A more detailed discussion of the venture proposal screening process, with an emphasis on how to prepare a business plan from the perspective of the potential investor, is provided in my recent book entitled *The Entrepreneur's Guide to Preparing a Winning Business Plan and Raising Venture Capital* (© 1990, pp. 4–17, adapted by permission of Prentice-Hall, Inc., Englewood Cliffs, N.J.). The book is organized as a workbook and includes checklists and worksheets to guide the entrepreneur through this process. There is also a three-ring binder format version of the book that includes a computer software program to assist the entrepreneur in generating financial projections for a venture.

a business plan, to the venture capitalist in order that the feasibility of the project can be evaluated. Numerous deals are rejected solely due to the quality of the business plan itself.

Venture capitalists screen proposals in stages, as follows:

- A large majority, perhaps over 80%, of the preliminary proposals (executive summaries of the business plan) are rejected shortly after the venture capitalists receive them.
- After this initial screening process, the formal written business plan is evaluated by the venture capitalist. A large portion of these plans are also rejected.
- Further rejections are made on the basis of an oral presentation of the plan by the entrepreneurial team.
- A final evaluation is generally made one to four months following the oral presentation, after the venture capitalists have conducted background checks on the management team and have discussed the business with experts in the field. This process is called *due diligence.*

Although the statistics will vary somewhat from firm to firm, a typical medium- to large-size venture capital firm will receive anywhere from 500 to 2,500 venture proposals per year and is likely to fund between five and fifty companies.

Evaluating the Venture Capital Firm

It is also important to recognize that the venture capital process is a two-way process. Not only does the venture capital firm choose to invest in an entrepreneurial company, but the entrepreneurial company must choose to develop the linkage with the venture capital firm. Entrepreneurial companies must carefully research the past performance and the investment philosophy of the venture capital firm in order to guarantee that a proper fit exists. Choosing the *right* venture capital firm is a vitally important decision for entrepreneurs to make.

What Is the Likelihood of Receiving Venture Capital Funding?

Consistent with the popular notion of the difficulty of obtaining venture funding, several researchers have found that less than 5% of the proposals received by formal venture capital firms were funded.[2] Therefore, we would

---

[2]For details of these studies, see J. B. Maier and D. A. Walker, "The Role of Venture Capital in Financing Small Business," *Journal of Business Venturing,* 1987, *2,* pp. 207–214; J. A. Timmons, "Venture Capital Investors in the U.S.: A Survey of the Most Active Investors," *Frontiers of Entrepreneurship Research, 1982.* Babson College, Wellesley, Mass., 1981, pp. 199–216; and J. A. Timmons and D. Gumpert, "Discard Many Old Rules about Getting Venture Capital," *Harvard Business Review,* January–February 1982, *60,* pp. 273–280. In addition to the above research articles, similar results were reported in a survey given to the Venture Capital 100; see *Venture,* June 1988, pp. 36–42.

expect that entrepreneurs would have to look elsewhere for funding. This is supported by a recent study conducted by the National Federation of Independent Businesses (NFIB), which found that 72% of new businesses get at least part of their financing from friends and relatives.[3] This also supports the vital role that informal investors, or "angels" (see Chapter 4), play in funding early-stage ventures.

What Factors Do Venture Capitalists Consider When Making Investment Decisions?

In examining the factors considered in funding entrepreneurial ventures, researchers found that venture capitalists make decisions regarding funding of such ventures based on product market attractiveness, product differentiation, management capabilities, resistance to environmental threats, and cash-out potential.[4]

Researchers have also suggested that the quality of management is often the key factor in determining whether or not a venture proposal receives funding by a venture capital firm.[5] Similar conclusions were reached for corporate venture capitalists.[6]

TURN ONS AND TURN OFFS

Up to this point, we've pointed out several differences—in terms of investment philosophy, involvement activity, time perspective, and the like—among venture capitalists. Essentially, they have different attitudes about their investments *after* they've committed to funding them. Fortunately, however, there is a very strong level of agreement on the important characteristics of *potential* recipients of funding; that is, they usually agree on the criteria, (the characteristics of management, financial attractiveness, and the like) with which to judge investment opportunities. (That's part of the reason that syndication is becoming so commonplace.)

The Investor's Perspective

Investors generally agree that an effectively prepared business plan is a requisite for obtaining funding for any business, whether it is a new business seeking start-up capital or an existing business seeking financing for expansion,

[3]See S. Bartlett, "It Will Get a Bit Easier to Find Startup Cash." *Business Week*, November 3, 1986, pp. 100, 104.

[4]For details of these studies, see L. N. Goslin and B. Barge, "Entrepreneurial Qualities Considered in Venture Capital Support," *Proceedings: Babson Research Conference*, 1986, pp. 366–379; I. C. MacMillan and others, "Criteria Used by Venture Capitalists to Evaluate New Venture Proposals," *Journal of Business Venturing*, 1985, *1*, pp. 119–128; I. C. MacMillan and P. N. Subbanarasimha, "Characteristics Distinguishing Funded and Unfunded Business Plans Evaluated by Venture Capitalists," *Strategic Management Journal*, 1987, *8*, pp. 579–585.

[5]Refer especially to the MacMillan and others (1985) reference cited in the previous footnote.

[6]See Coopers and Lybrand, "Charting a Course for Corporate Venture Capital," 1988.

new business activity, or a turnaround situation. It is this plan that forms the basis of the evaluation process. As a first step in preparing a business plan, it is crucial that the entrepreneur understand how the plan is read and evaluated by the investor. The entrepreneur must be concerned with how to turn on the investor and how to avoid turning off the investor. In short, what is the basis of the investor's evaluation?

A Matter of A's, B's, and C's.   Most entrepreneurs and other business owners can prepare a B or a B+ business plan without too much trouble. That would be fine if investors would fund B or B+ plans. Investors, however, only fund A or A+ plans. In essence, a B business plan is no better than a C or D plan because none of them is likely to get funded. Thus, the real skill is in turning a B business plan into one that warrants an A+.

An A+ business plan might be only a 10% or 20% improvement over a B or B+ plan in the eyes of the entrepreneur; it might also take 80% more effort on the part of the entrepreneur to gain a 20% improvement. Yet that 20% improvement will seem like a 100% improvement in the eyes of the person that matters the most, the investor, and will therefore increase the likelihood of getting funded by close to 100%.

What differentiates a B plan from an A+ plan? In general, the key difference is that an A+ plan is written *from the perspective of the investor!* The A+ plan gets the investor to believe in the product or service, the target market, the management team, and so on, while it addresses the problems or the key concerns of the business. In addition, the A+ plan demonstrates that something is unique about the particular deal—something that distinguishes this investment opportunity from perhaps the over one hundred other ones that are brought before the investor every week. The real indicator of an A+ plan is that it is one for which the entrepreneur has to turn away money.

What differentiates a B plan from an A+ plan? In general, the key difference is that an A+ plan is written *from the perspective of the investor!*

Turning Venture Capitalists on

There are several specific guidelines that successful entrepreneurs follow in order to develop a convincing business plan for venture capitalists. For a plan to receive a favorable review by an investor, it must generally demonstrate the following four features:

1. Clear definition of the business
2. Evidence of marketing capabilities
3. Evidence of management capabilities
4. Attractive financial arrangement

Let's examine each of these.

Definition of the Business.   There are three basic questions regarding the business that, when answered, provide a working understanding of the definition of the business, also known as the mission or scope of operations of the business (that is, what business are you in?):

1. What is the product or service?
2. What is the industry?
3. What is the target market?

These three questions underlie the basic strategy (or direction) of the firm.

No small business venture can be "all things to all people." Thus, in the earliest stages of a business it is critical that the company develop a logical, somewhat stable business definition or strategy and avoid any dramatic changes to it. Any alteration of one or more of these three features—the product or service, the industry, or the target market—results in a new and riskier strategy for the company. Of course, as the business expands, the only way to accomplish significant growth will be to alter its current business definition, whether by expanding the product line, entering a new industry, or seeking a new market for a given product or service. Investors, however, will want to see some initial stability in the company's strategy or business definition.

Let's explore these three components of a company's strategy.

What Is the Product or Service?   Venture capitalists are always looking for that "something extra" in a product or service that will provide the company with a decided advantage over its competitors. This may include a new product feature, a cost advantage, technical competence, or something else that will be a significant benefit to the customer.

A great way to win the favor of a venture capitalist is to have a unique product that is of a proprietary nature, either by copyright, trademark, patent, or some other exclusive arrangement. Two classic examples of companies benefiting from their proprietary positions are Polaroid, with their instant printing process, and Xerox, with their "xerography" or photocopying process.

More recently, Apple Computer had a tremendous advantage over others with its proprietary technology. The company made numerous errors in its early stages, but was able to succeed because the market was so forgiving for a company with such a technology edge.

Apple Computer is a classic case of the traditional route of venture capital investments. The two founders, Steven Jobs and Stephen Wozniak, were college dropouts who built their first computer in Jobs's garage when they were in their early twenties. Earlier, Wozniak tried to interest his employer, Hewlett-Packard, with his idea, but when he met with resistance, he decided to form his own venture with Jobs. The prototype that Jobs and Wozniak developed was the predecessor of the Apple.

Demand for the original Apple was too great for Jobs and Wozniak to handle by themselves. So they sought the help of two more experienced individuals with backgrounds in marketing and manufacturing: A. C. Markkula, former vice-president of marketing at Intel, and Michael M. Scott, formerly in charge of production at National Semiconductor. (We'll discuss the importance of developing an experienced management team later in this chapter.) Scott took a 50% pay cut to join Apple; Markkula invested over $90,000 of his own money in the venture.

The new entrepreneurial team then raised $600,000 from such notable venture capital sources as Arthur Rock, Hambrecht and Quist, Henry Singleton (a founder of Teledyne), and Venrock Associates. In 1980, when Apple went public at $22 per share, the company raised $110 million, the largest initial public offering (IPO) since Comsat raised $200 million 15 years earlier. In the immediate after-market, Apple's stock traded at $34 per share; by June 1983, the stock had reached a high of $63 per share.

In the three years prior to Apple's IPO, earnings had grown by 700%. This allowed the underwriter, Morgan Stanley, to price the stock at a premium to other similar high-growth technology companies such as ROLM, Paradyne, and Tandem, which were selling at approximately eighteen times their anticipated 1981 earnings. Apple's total valuation at the time of the company's IPO was in excess of $1 billion—not bad for a company that earned a "mere" $11.7 million the previous year. When Apple went public, Steve Jobs's shares were worth $165 million. The early investors did quite well, too. For example, Arthur Rock's $57,600 investment in 1977 grew to $14 million in 3 years.

Keeping it simple.   Although the product or service idea should be unique, it should also be kept simple. Any idea that cannot be described in a sentence or two is too complex. Many entrepreneurs who have developed technology products fail to attract funding because they do not describe their product in such a manner that nontechnical persons understand it; they become more infatuated with the product than with the market for the product.

Another problem is one of overdiversification of products or services in the earliest stages of a venture; one or two product or service lines should be sufficient until the company has generated annual revenues of at least $1 million.

What Is the Industry?   The industry should be clearly defined and should have growth potential. Venture capitalists prefer to fund businesses in industries that have at least a 25%—and preferably a much higher—growth rate. High growth is much more important than high tech, as evidenced by venture capitalists giving greater attention to specialty retailers than to technology companies in recent years (see Chapter 12).

Opening up industries.   Many venture capitalists are particularly at-tracted to companies that have the ability to open up whole new industries, as was the case of McDonald's in fast food, Federal Express in overnight delivery, Head in ski equipment, Apple in personal computers, and Digital Equipment in minicomputers. An excellent example of an entrepreneur opening up new markets is the case of Thomas Bata, who grew up in Czechoslovakia where his father was the owner of a shoe company. After his father's death in 1932, the younger Bata assumed control of the company. When it became apparent that Czechoslovakia might fall to Hitler, he fled his country and opened up a factory in Canada. Today, the Bata Shoe Company sells a quarter-billion pairs of shoes a year (one out of three pairs sold in the noncommunist world). A famous story told by Thomas Bata summarizes his philosophy of opening up new markets: "two shoe salesmen were sent to a poverty-stricken country. One wired back, 'Returning home immediately. No one wears shoes here.' The other cabled, 'Unlimited possibilities. Millions still without shoes.' "[7]

Riding the growth curve.   Some venture capitalists prefer to fund busi-nesses in the electronics industry. Others prefer biotechnology companies. Still others prefer to invest in companies involved in real estate development. As a rule, however, venture capitalists prefer innovative product-oriented companies in industries that are just beginning to approach their growth stage. The venture capitalists realize their greatest returns as they "ride the growth curve."

Venture capitalists shy away from revolutionary products in industries that have not yet been developed. Although such developments as the light bulb, telephone, television, camera, and automobile have had a dramatic effect on all of our lives, they would not have been prime investment opportunities for most venture capitalists today because their development time was extremely long and there was no evidence of consumer acceptance of these products until their development was completed.

What Is the Target Market?   Entrepreneurs must be able to identify a specific target market for their product or service, recognizing, nonetheless, that the market is substantial enough to provide adequate revenues; yet, capital requirements make it impossible to reach everyone, thereby necessitating a clearly defined or focused target market, discussed next.

Marketing Capabilities.   Four features demonstrate a company's mar-keting capabilities:

1. Benefit to the user
2. Evidence of marketability or past success
3. Widespread appeal
4. Selling ability

[7]See E. Severeid, *Enterprise*, McGraw-Hill, New York, 1983, p. 13.

Benefit to the User.   Perhaps the best indicator of a company's marketing capabilities is the ability to demonstrate user benefit: how will the customer profit, gain, or otherwise benefit from buying the company's product or service? Demonstrating user benefit will necessarily strengthen the entrepreneur's contention that the company can generate sales and will, therefore, be an attractive investment opportunity.

Benefits to the user vary considerably from product to product. However, there are a few guiding questions to demonstrate this characteristic:

- Will the product save the customer money?
- Will it save time?
- Will it provide status?
- Will it enhance the customer's life-style?
- How long will it take to pay for itself?

Quantifying User Benefit.   The entrepreneur can strengthen his or her arguments of user benefit by quantifying the benefits to the user. For example, a certain breakthrough patented genetic engineering process developed by a team of scientists was able to increase yields by more than 200% while it reduced costs to biotechnology companies (the users) by over 50%.

On a mass appeal level, a residential energy-saving device, which reduced energy consumption by 40% on average, paid for itself within one year. This can be contrasted to an alternative residential energy-saving device with which I'm familiar that sells for over $10,000 and results in a 10% to 20% savings in energy. Based on an average monthly energy bill of $250, the device wouldn't pay for itself for nearly 20 years, thereby making its user benefit extremely questionable.

Thus, the benefit to the user can be quantified by describing the cost savings to the customer, which are generally measured in terms of:

- Lowered reject rate
- Lowered warranty costs
- Reduced labor costs
- Lowered storage costs
- Lowered inventory costs
- Reduced downtime
- Greater convenience
- Amount of time before the product pays for itself

Similarly, user benefits can be expressed in terms of increased earnings to the customer (for example, through increased productivity) or in terms of various nonmonetary benefits (for example, better health).

To catch a venture capitalist's eye, many entrepreneurs have explained what will happen to potential customers who don't buy the product. Insurance companies have used such an approach in their advertising campaigns for many years.

Evidence of Marketability and Past Success.   Even if the product has benefit to the user, a critical question is whether enough customers will buy it. A well-recognized market can certainly enhance the likelihood of obtaining funding.

Venture capitalists generally want to see some indication that customers or clients have used the product or service, even if only on a trial basis (for example, a prototype), and are happy with it. Obviously, the best indicator of whether there will be customers in the future is if there have been customers in the past. Moreover, existing customers will be able to provide the company with feedback to alter the product design or service features if necessary.

As a general rule, most venture capitalists prefer to fund companies with some operating history (this provides some assurance of success), although it is not necessary that the venture be operating profitably.

Stated another way, venture capitalists would prefer to have their money used for production and selling, rather than for product development and market research, thereby reducing the risk and accelerating the time span for profits to be generated. This explains the recent trend in funding expansion efforts more so than funding start-up efforts (refer to Chapter 12 for a complete discussion).

Widespread Appeal.   The growth potential of a business is often related to the widespread market appeal of a product or service. As a rule, venture capitalists shy away from businesses whose basic product or service must be specially designed for each customer. In most such situations, costs are high due to specialized labor requirements, profits are low due to an inability to achieve advantages from economies of scale, and growth is slow.

For example, I'm familiar with a biotechnology laboratory that was planning to develop a diagnostic test for laboratory technicians exposed to a specific strain of woodchuck virus. Their interest in developing this diagnostic test resulted from their chief immunologist's research interests while in graduate school. Unfortunately, however, only ten or twelve laboratories in the country conduct research on woodchuck virus, thereby limiting the marketability of this product. A company developing a diagnostic test or a treatment for AIDS or herpes, which would have a very wide market appeal, would be seen as a more attractive investment opportunity than would a company developing a test for detection of woodchuck virus.

Of course, even if there is a large potential market, there can be significant impediments for a company. For example, probably the biggest obstacle to Cambridge BioScience Corp., a Worcester, Massachusetts, based company that is developing a test for AIDS, has been government regulation. The Food and Drug Administration (FDA) has approved the company's "5 minute AIDS test." However, approval on its second AIDS test, based on recombinant proteins, has been a much longer wait. This is a luxury that early-stage ventures can ill afford. Aside from regulators, there are other obstacles, among which is the constant threat of competition from larger, more established pharmaceutical companies.

Selling Ability.   Even if the product or service has user benefit and has a demonstrated market available, it is still crucial that the company have the capabilities to sell and support it. For example, I recently encountered a young engineer–entrepreneur whose company developed a unique audio speaker system to reduce sound distortion. The company consisted of the engineer, who was responsible for designing the product, and three employees who manufactured the product. Although he had a fairly sound business plan with carefully researched market projections, he was at a loss for words when a potential investor asked him, "Who's going to sell the product?"

Thus, it must be shown how the product will move "from the shop floor to the customer's floor." This demonstrates a market-driven, rather than a product-driven attitude, which is critical for the success of any venture. If I had to describe one essential characteristic of a successful entrepreneur (or a successful entrepreneurial company), it would be the ability to sell. You could have the most impressive product imaginable and could be extremely well capitalized; yet, without sales, the business cannot succeed. Numerous entrepreneurs have risen through the ranks in established companies in sales capacities prior to launching their own successful ventures. Victor Kiam, for example, was a top salesperson at Playtex before purchasing Remington Products and leading it through one of the most dramatic turnarounds in recent business history. Similarly, H. Ross Perot was a star salesperson at IBM—he would generally reach his annual sales quota for the *year* in January—prior to starting Electronic Data Services (EDS). When EDS was recently purchased by General Motors, Perot's net worth was in excess of $2 billion.

Management Capabilities.   Most venture capitalists feel that management is the key factor in securing funding for a venture. For example, Aryeh Finegold, who is credited with Daisy Systems Corp.'s early success, recently joined Ready Systems, a Palo Alto, California, based developer of real-time operating system software. Finegold was largely responsible for the company, which was then generating about $6 million in sales, raising $6.75 million in second-round financing from several major venture capital companies, including Adler & Co., Accel Partners, Venrock Associates, and Warburg, Pincus. According to Jim Swartz, managing partner of Accel Partners, "There's one major reason why we did the deal and that's Aryeh Finegold."[8] Consistent with Swartz's view, Ramon v. Reyes of Nazem & Co., a venture capital firm in New York, recently suggested that "More than ever, the name of the game is management. If you find a company with the right horses, you back it to the hilt. Otherwise, you think twice."[9]

[8]See *Venture*, May 1987, p. 96

[9]See Lee Kravitz, "What Venture Capitalists Want," in *Venture's Guide to International Venture Capital,* Simon & Schuster, New York, 1985, p. 14.

Venture capitalists invest in management, rather than in products. As noted by Arthur Rock, principal of Arthur Rock & Co., a San Francisco-based venture capital company that has funded such companies as Fairchild Semiconductor, Scientific Data Systems, Teledyne, Intel, Diasonics, and Apple Computer,

> "Over the past 30 years, I estimate that I've looked at an average of one business plan per day, or about 300 per year, in addition to the large numbers of phone calls and business plans that simply are not appropriate. Of the 300 likely plans, I may invest in only one or two a year, and even among those carefully chosen few, I'd say that a good half fail to perform up to expectations. The problem with those companies (and with the ventures I choose *not* to take part in) is rarely one of strategy. Good ideas and good products are a dime a dozen. Good execution and good management—in a word, good *people*—are rare."[10]

One prominent member of the venture capital community goes as far as suggesting that

> "It's really the people who are important. The plan just gives the investor the opportunity to meet people and see what kind of people they are, to learn their visions, their philosophies, and see what kind of intelligence went into the plan."

There are three features that demonstrate the company's attention to the importance of management:

1. The management team
2. Experienced managers
3. The board of directors

Venture capitalists would much rather fund an experienced management team, especially if their experience is in the same industry as the venture needing the funding, than sole entrepreneurs. The management team should have a demonstrated track record and competences in each of the critical functional areas: marketing, finance, product design and production, control, and personnel. Furthermore, the board of directors should enhance the capabilities of the management team.

Let's explore these three features of capable management in greater detail.

The Management Team.   In 1982, Sevin Rosen Management Co., a venture capital firm in Dallas, invested $2.5 million in a start-up company that was then called Gateway Technology, Inc. Gateway's plan was to manufacture an IBM-compatible computer. Ben Rosen, general partner of Sevin Rosen and

---

[10]See Arthur Rock, "Strategy vs. Tactics from a Venture Capitalist," *Harvard Business Review*, November–December 1987, p. 63

a seasoned venture capitalist, had trouble believing Gateway's sales projections of $35 million in its first year and $198 million in the second year. Nonetheless, Rosen saw a capable management team in which to invest. Gateway later changed its name to Compaq Computer Corp. and sold $111 million in its first year—a record, at that time, for a start-up—and $329 million in its second year. Sevin Rosen's investment grew by over fifteenfold to $38 million at the time of Compaq's initial public offering (IPO). Furthermore, since that time, Compaq, which is now generating more than $2 billion per year in revenues, has been one of the leading stocks on Wall Street.

Another important point related to Compaq is that, although it is a fairly new venture itself, it has been largely responsible for the growth of several other ventures that supply products to it. One, for example, is Conner Peripherals, a company started by Finis Conner, who had earlier been with Alan Shugart at Shugart Associates and Seagate Technology. Conner Peripherals supplies $3\frac{1}{2}$ inch hard disk drives to Compaq as well as to other computer manufacturers. Conner Peripherals, which was started in 1986 and amassed first year sales of $113 million—topping Compaq's previous record—actually received $12 million in seed funding from Compaq itself for 40% of the ownership of the start-up. Conner Peripherals went public in 1988 and is now a $700 million company (it has attained *Fortune* 500 status in a remarkable four years; not surprisingly, the only other company to have matched this feat was Compaq), with perhaps half of its sales going to its investor and customer Compaq.

The effective use of management teams is becoming very evident in today's growth companies. In addition to Compaq, companies such as Linear Technology, AST Research, and Quantum Corp. have each avoided the "one-man show" and have assembled top management teams that are able to look beyond the narrow confines of specific functional areas to the broad concerns of the company as a whole. Consequently, the VP of finance or controller is an extremely important member of the management team as he or she speaks the language of the investor. Furthermore, the VP or director of marketing is vital in that sales is, perhaps, the most important function of small, growth-oriented businesses.

Venture capitalists will almost always prefer a first-rate management team with a second-rate product over a first-rate product with a second-rate management team.

Venture capitalists will almost always prefer a first-rate management team with a second-rate product over a first-rate product with a second-rate management team. Perhaps the most attractive arrangement for an investor would be to fund a venture managed by a previously successful entrepreneurial team. If they've succeeded before, then they will be likely to succeed again.

For example, Tandem Computer was founded in 1974 by Jim Treybig, along with one dozen other experienced managers, primarily from Hewlett-Packard. It is not surprising that Kleiner Perkins Caufield & Byers, the Mayfield Fund, and some of the other leading venture capital firms in the country invested in this start-up firm. Over the next ten years, it returned nearly forty times its original investment in the company. Tandem has already had some of its managers leave to form their own ventures. Perhaps the best known is Stratus Computer.

One of the more interesting management teams to be formed in recent years is that of Echelon, Inc., of Los Gatos, California. The founders include M. Kenneth Oshman, formerly CEO of ROLM (the "O" in ROLM is for Oshman), and A.C. Markkula, formerly with Apple. Echelon has been quite successful in raising venture capital, due largely to its prominent management team. The company is developing an integrated home control system, whereby all electrically powered devices are operated through a central controller that can be accessed through a phone line or a remote controller.

Assistance from venture capitalists.   One of the biggest problems faced by less experienced entrepreneurs is that they have gaps in their management team. For such entrepreneurs, venture capitalists can be valuable in assisting the start-ups in "filling in the gaps" by providing introductions to marketing or finance executives.

In some cases, venture capitalists will want to take on very active roles with the company that they are funding. For example, in addition to the venture capital firm of Kleiner Perkins Caufield and Byers providing Genentech with the necessary capital to support its early levels of growth (their $200,000 investment in 1976 increased by 800-fold in five years), they also provided Genentech with a chief executive officer, thereby enabling Genentech's scientist-executives to return to their research labs to develop new biotechnology products. That decision has been primarily responsible for Genentech's remarkable success since its inception.

Of course, not all venture capitalists will take on such an active role in the selection of management. Worse yet, some venture capitalists will exert extreme control in their choice of managers, to the point of hurting the company. For example, I'm familiar with a five-year old company on the West Coast where the venture capital firm brought in several outsiders to manage the company. This ultimately resulted in a dramatic change in the culture of the company and to a total loss of entrepreneurial zeal. The founders of the company, who wound up becoming minority shareholders, have since left the company to launch a new venture.

Experienced Managers.   In recent years, we've seen numerous experienced managers with excellent track records at established companies, such as Digital Equipment, General Electric, Honeywell, IBM, and Hewlett-Packard, become very successful in starting their own businesses. For example, Ed De Castro, who was unable to get Digital Equipment Corp. (DEC) to back his revolutionary new computer, left to form Data General, which became one of

DEC's leading competitors; Richard Blackmer founded Oxygen Enrichment Company after spending 25 years as an engineer with General Electric; and Dean Scheff started CPT Corp. after having worked for Univac and Honeywell.

Although many outsiders view IBM as a bureaucratic organization where employees typically spend their entire career with "Big Blue," it is interesting to note that IBM has one of the best track records of turning out entrepreneurs. Gene Amdahl, for example, left IBM to launch a computer company sporting his name, while Richard Greene left IBM to start Data Switch Corp. Former IBMers have also become part of the management teams of such companies as Computerland (Edward Faber) and Tandon (Don Wilkie).

Of course, such a career path will not guarantee success. For example, Edward Esber, who left IBM to run Ashton Tate (the developer of the DBase software package), recently resigned his position as chairman and CEO of the software company amid slumping sales of the company. A more extreme example is that of Jesse Aweida, who left IBM to launch Storage Technology, one of the supergrowth companies of the early 1980s. Revenues had increased steadily to almost $1 billion by 1983. However, earnings had declined at a faster rate than sales growth, forcing the company to file for bankruptcy in 1984.

Once is not enough.   Similarly, "repeat entrepreneurs" such as Nolan Bushnell (Atari & Pizza Time Theatre), Steven Jobs (Apple and NeXT), William Poduska (Prime Computer and Apollo Computer), Alan Shugart (Shugart Associates and Seagate Technology), Phillippe Villers (Computervision and Automatix), Mitchell Kapor (Lotus Development and ON Technology), and Irwin Selinger (Surgicot and Patient Technology, Inc.) have found that securing funding from venture capitalists becomes increasingly easy with experience. Venture capitalists invariably invest in the experience of the entrepreneur or the entrepreneurial team more so than in the growth potential of a given product or service idea.

It's OK to fail.   Often, venture capitalists prefer to invest in repeat entrepreneurs who have launched businesses that eventually did not materialize than to invest in unknown entities. For example, although Osborne Computer Corp. went bankrupt in 1984, its founder, Adam Osborne, started a new software company within a year with $2.2 million in funding from venture investors. Similarly, after Robert McNulty's failed attempt in SportsClub, a discount sports retailer, he was able to raise funds for H Q Office Supplies Warehouse (Long Beach, California), a chain of discount office products, and A G Automotive Warehouses, Inc., a chain of warehouse stores selling automotive parts. Of course, McNulty's earlier successful venture, the Fullerton, California, based HomeClub, which quadrupled his investors' money when it was sold to Zayre for $151 million in 1986, three years after it was founded, gave him the credibility to raise capital for his two most recent ventures.

Bouncing back.   One of the real success stories of an entrepreneur "bouncing back" is of Wilfred Corrigan, who left Fairchild Camera and Instrument following its acquisition by Schlumberger in 1979, after the company had been transformed into a state of technological mediocrity. Shortly thereafter, thanks in part to a $6 million infusion from Sequoia Capital and other investors, Corrigan took LSI Logic from start-up to its initial public offering in 1982. At that time, the Milpitas, California, based semiconductor company was valued at $½ billion.

We tend to see acceptance of this notion of an entrepreneur bouncing back from failure quite often in high-tech companies, especially in Silicon Valley, where there seems to be more freedom to fail than in other parts of the country. As noted by Jean Deleage, managing partner of the San Francisco office of Burr, Egan, Deleage & Co., "It is as if there had been a 27th amendment to the American Constitution in Silicon Valley—one saying that to have failed is not an ineradicable black mark against you."[11]

Such failure can be very positive for our economic development. As noted by Robert D. Hormats, vice-chairman of Goldman Sachs International,

> "An entrepreneur who has gone bankrupt with one idea can come back and get the venture capitalist to start another idea. In a period of low savings rates, high government spending, and other economic problems, this stands out as a big advantage."[12]

The Board of Directors. Venture capitalists are also very sensitive to the qualifications and experience of the members of the board of directors. In many instances, an experienced board will partially offset some of the gaps in the management team. At a minimum, such a board will enhance the capabilities and experience of any management team in the eyes of the investor.

The purpose of the board of directors is to aid, challenge, and replace (if necessary) the officers of the company. Thus, a passive unquestioning board (which is often the case if the board is composed primarily of either inside managers or friends and relatives) can have a disastrous impact on the business. Just as in the case of your top management team, selectivity is critical in choosing members of the board. Successful entrepreneurial ventures will generally have two or three outsiders (that is, not members of the organization; for example, a banker, an attorney, or a supplier) serve on the board to assist in making decisions and in monitoring the environment. There are numerous competent directors available who would welcome the opportunity to work with a small growth venture and who will accept a minor token payment of cash and/or equity for their services.

For example, Chester Kirk, founder, chairman, and CEO of Amtrol, Inc., a very successful privately owned manufacturing company in West Warwick, Rhode Island, has made extensive and effective use of outside directors over the past few years. Kirk has acknowledged that outsiders often possess expertise in areas where his own management team may be lacking. Outside directors

---

[11]See Cheryll Aimee Barron, "Silicon Valley Phoenixes," *Fortune*, November 23, 1987, p. 129.

[12]Ibid., p. 129.

with backgrounds in finance and international business were especially helpful in making recommendations related to selecting inventory accounting methods, choosing a computer system, developing an employee ownership plan, and making general decisions on the long-term growth of Amtrol.

Similarly, Alejandro Zaffaroni, a Ph.D. chemist who was executive vice-president of Syntex, invested $2 million of his own money to launch another pharmaceuticals company, ALZA (which is named after him), in Palo Alto, California. Zaffaroni also recruited a prominent board of directors, who were instrumental in giving the company the credibility to raise a total of $50 million (in multiple rounds of financing) while its products were still under development. ALZA, now an $80 million innovative pharmaceuticals company, has experienced an average increase in revenues of 29% per year over the last five years, with an average increase in EPS of 69% over that time.

More recently, Vipont Pharmaceuticals, of Fort Collins, Colorado, which develops and markets oral hygiene products, has an internationally recognized board of directors, who have given the company an international name and have provided them with credibility and contacts. The company, founded in 1968 and growing at a compounded annual rate of over 100% from 1984 to 1988, has a board that includes Bruce Merrifield, a Nobel laureate in chemistry; Jere Goyan, a former FDA commissioner; and Barry Goldwater, the former senator from Arizona.

Just as impressive as Vipont is the management team and board of directors of Nova Pharmaceuticals, an early-stage biotechnology venture founded in 1982, based in Baltimore, Maryland. They include Chairman John Lloyd Huck, former president of Merck; Solomon Snyder, a neuroscientist from Johns Hopkins Medical, who is chairman of Nova's Scientific Advisory Council; Henry Wendt, CEO of SmithKline Beckman, a company that has invested $70 million in this venture; Ralph Gomory, recently retired chief scientist of IBM; Edward Hennessy, chairman of Allied-Signal; and Gerald Ford, former president of the United States. Apparently, these credentials have been vital in enabling the company to secure funding. Aside from SmithKline Beckman, Nova received early-stage funding from Eastman Kodak, Marion Laboratories, and Celanese. Moreover, the company was able to go public in 1983 without even a lab. Up until recently, the company had still not yet marketed a product, although several of its products were in clinical or preclinical studies.

Assistance from venture capitalists.   Venture capitalists will often make suggestions regarding potential members of the board of directors. In most cases, the venture capitalists will want to be represented on the board personally in order to remain involved in critical strategic decisions. This is highly advisable as most venture capitalists can provide experience and important contacts— in essence, their advice can be as valuable as their money.

Of course, venture capitalists can also hurt the company in terms of decisions regarding the board of directors. I recently spoke to an individual who started a computer software company in New England during the early 1980s. The company was very loosely and democratically organized; the only dress code was the unwritten rule: neckties were forbidden. After growing at a phenomenal rate in its early years, the company was successful in raising close to $1 million in venture capital. However, along with the funding came three new outside directors (one was a partner in the venture capital firm; the other two were executives recommended by the venture capital firm), each dressed in "typical banker's attire" when they visited the software company. This clash in culture had a very disrupting effect on the company. Moreover, as the founder told me,

> "The sad part of this is that we're stuck with them. At least, when I go to the bank for funding, I know that I can always get the banker off my back by paying off the note. It's just not the same with these guys."

Financial Arrangement.   Venture capitalists prefer to see a structured arrangement presented by the entrepreneurial team that describes the capital needs of the venture and that proposes a fair equity agreement for the parties involved. Although venture capitalists expect to see such a structured financial arrangement, the terms are generally subject to intense negotiation.

The effective business plan includes a provision for a specific dollar amount of capital needed for the business. Proposals for any amount of capital may be appropriate. However, for venture capitalists, proposals that are accepted are generally in the range of $100,000 to $2 million. Due to the cost of investigating any venture (several thousand dollars per venture proposal), it is not cost beneficial for venture capitalists to evaluate smaller proposals.

In addition, a properly developed business plan addresses the following financial issues:

- Acceptable return
- Provision for an exit
- Participation by other investors
- Structured deal

Acceptable Return.   Venture capitalists maintain a time horizon of approximately five years (or a range of from three to seven years) in which to realize their returns on their initial investment. During that time period, venture capitalists exepct their investment to increase in value by five- to fifteenfold, net of inflation.

Venture capitalists maintain a time horizon of approximately five years . . . in which to realize their returns on their initial investment.

Risk and return.   What dictates the return on investment expected by a typical investor? Essentially, it is based on the riskiness of the investment. Thus, the higher the riskiness of the investment is the greater the expected return for the investor.

Riskiness is generally based on two factors, which were discussed earlier: (1) the nature of the product or service, and, most importantly, (2) the quality of the management of the venture. Newly developed ideas are more risky than established products or services; investors generally wish to see products or services that are already being used and have been accepted by customers. (Having exclusive rights to a product or process via copyrights or trademarks, however, will make even a new product seem attractive in the eyes of the investor.) Similarly, individual entrepreneurs are seen as more risky than are established management teams.

Stanley Rich and David Gumpert have developed an evaluation system based on the two factors just noted.[13] The system identifies four levels to describe the status of the product or service and four levels to describe the status of management. In both cases, level 1 is the most risky type of venture and would, therefore, warrant the highest expected return by the investor, whereas level 4 is the least risky type of venture. The system is shown in Table 9-1.

Some venture capitalists would only invest in 4/4 (or possibly 4/3 and 3/4) ventures, whereas others would invest in riskier businesses. Regardless, as I mentioned earlier, the higher the risk is the higher the expected returns. Thus, venture capitalists would generally seek approximately four to five times their investment, net of inflation, in five years (or a 30% to 40% compounded annual return on investment) for a 4/4 company and would seek perhaps fifteen times their investment net of inflation (or a minimum of a 60% compounded annual return) for a 2/2 company.

Provision for an Exit.   The only way for any venture capitalist to realize a gain on an investment is to sell (at least part of) his or her ownership position. Before a venture capitalist invests in a business, he or she will often want to know what provisions for exit will be available five years down the road. At that time the investor will want to liquidate at least a portion of the holdings in the company in order to invest in other privately held growth business.

Participation by Other Investors.   An excellent way to attract venture capitalists is to demonstrate that other investors, and particularly, the existing top management team, have already invested in the company, thereby reducing the risk and exposure of the investor. There's the story of Frederick Smith, who in his quest for $90 million to launch Federal Express, used the tactic of asking *all* his potential investors for that "last million," rather than for the "first 89 million." Apparently, it worked, as such notable investors as Citicorp, Chase Manhattan, Prudential Insurance, and General Dynamics were insightful enough to back the venture in its early years.

[13]See S. Rich and D. Gumpert, *Business Plans That Win $$$*, Harper & Row, New York, 1985, p. 169

TABLE 9-1 Assessing the Riskiness of an Investment Opportunity

Level 4: Fully developed product/service. Established market. Satisfied users.	4/1	4/2	4/3	4/4
Level 3: Fully developed product/service. Few users as of yet. Market assumed.	3/1	3/2	3/3	3/4
Riskiest				
Level 2: Operable pilot or prototype. Not yet developed for production. Market assumed.	2/1	2/2	2/3	2/4
Level 1: Product/service idea. Not yet operable. Market assumed.	1/1	1/2	1/3	1/4
↓	Level 1: Individual founder— entrepreneur.	Level 2: Two founders. Other personnel not yet identified.	Level 3: Partial management team. Members identified to join company when funding is received.	Level 4: Fully staffed, experienced management team.

◄─────── Riskiest ───────

Similarly, but on a much smaller scale, consider Mark Ain of Kronos, Inc., in his quest for capital. Ain raised $45,000 to develop his idea for a computerized tracking system for hourly workers. He then sold nearly $.5 million in stock to finance the development of the prototype and another $600,000 (plus $200,000 more when that stage ran out of money) to finance its production. How did he do it? As Ain explains, "I would set a date for closing [each] offering; then I'd tell everyone, 'It looks like we're oversubscribed.' "[14] Kronos, Inc., is finally making money.

Structured Deal. As mentioned earlier, venture capitalists prefer to see a structured deal. Thus the answer to the following questions should be clearly stated in the business plan:

- Who is involved in the deal?
- How much money is needed?
- What is the minimum investment per investor?

[14]See *Inc.*, June 1989, p. 59.

- How is ownership translated into shares of common or preferred stock or convertible debentures or debt, and so on?
- What is the price per share of stock?
- What is the projected compounded annual return for the investor over the next 3–7 years?

Turning Venture Capitalists Off

In addition to understanding what turns venture capitalists on, it's important to know what turns them off. There are several key turnoffs, any one of which can set off a red flag that could undermine the reliability of the remainder of the plan, regardless of the quality of the product or service, the capabilities of the management team, or the terms of the financial arrangement. These include:

- A prepackaged package
- Product orientation
- Unrealistic financial projections
- Failure to deal with potential critical risks

Let's examine each of these.

Prepackaged Package.   The sterile standardized business plan packages that many consultants will sell to small business owners will often set off a red flag to the venture capitalist. Such packages use a common skeleton of a business plan, regardless of the nature of the company or of the industry, and substitute a few words and names in the plan as appropriate. They are often lacking in their analysis of the industry and incorrect in their financial projections. Often, they suffer from "Lotusitis." Although Lotus and the other impressive spread-sheet programs can develop neat, mathematically correct rows and columns of numbers, their end product often fails to meet the needs of the investors, who are generally more concerned with the assumptions surrounding these numbers than with the numbers themselves.

Product Orientation.   One of the greatest pitfalls of entrepreneurs is to focus on the product, rather than on the market for that product and on the competitors who are selling a similar product or service. Many inventors (or "tinkerers") fall prey to this pitfall. True, the product might be innovative and might have phenomenal features. The key issue, however, is, Will customers buy the product? And, will they buy the product from *you*, rather than from your competition?

For example, software entrepreneurs have developed numerous computer software packages priced at $200 to $400 that can do little more than already existing written directories priced at less than $20. Such software packages might be excellent products; yet venture capitalists, who generally have much stronger financial and/or marketing backgrounds than technology backgrounds, tend to shy away from entrepreneurs who are more enamored with the features of the product than with the market that must recognize the value of the product.

After all, satisfied customers, and not dazzling products, are the key to success in any business; all the successful businesses with which I've had contact are market driven, rather than product driven. The red flag for venture capitalists is when the business plan devotes more space to describing the product than to describing who will buy the product and how it will be marketed.

Unrealistic Financial Projections.   It's difficult to fool venture capitalists when it comes to the financial projections for the company. Specifically, entrepreneurs have a tendency of overestimating revenues or underestimating costs, which will result in a red flag being raised when the investor sees significant deviations from industry norms or questionable projections by companies in embryonic industries.

For example, projections of 50% growth rates and 60% gross profit margins by a company in an industry characterized by 10% growth and 25% gross margins would be questioned by an investor. Similarly, projections of 50% or 100% growth rates for a company that has developed a new, untested product would also be suspect.

It's important to avoid being overly optimistic in developing financial projections. Investors like to see a best case, a worst case, and a most likely case set of projections, thereby enhancing the believability of the entire business plan.

Failure to Examine Risks.   Undoubtedly, there will be numerous risks associated with the business. Recognizing that raising capital is the art of reducing risk (contrary to popular belief, venture capitalists tend to be risk adverse), it is imperative that the business plan address the critical risks and problems that may be encountered. Venture capitalists will generally be aware of some of these risks, so failure to address them will likely undermine the credibility of the entire plan. In addition, investors would rather fund entrepreneurs who demonstrate that they are "cautiously optimistic" than those who are "recklessly optimistic."

Addressing the risks will often turn a B or B+ plan into the A− range; turning those negatives into positives can raise it solidly into the A range.

A LOOK AHEAD

We've just presented some general guidelines used by venture capitalists in screening venture proposals or business plans. Although there are numerous differences among venture capitalists, they often use the same basic criteria with which to evaluate the investment potential of a company.

Venture capitalists tend to be turned on by proposals that demonstrate the following four features:

1. Clear definition of the business
2. Evidence of marketing capabilities
3. Evidence of management capabilities
4. Attractive financial arrangement

Furthermore, venture capitalists are generally turned off by proposals characterized by:

1. Prepackaged package
2. Product orientation
3. Unrealistic financial projections
4. Failure to deal with potential critical risks

By following these prescriptive guidelines, the entrepreneur will immeasurably increase his or her chances of obtaining venture capital funding. After the venture proposal is evaluated, the next phase of the process is the structuring of the venture deal, which is discussed in the next chapter.

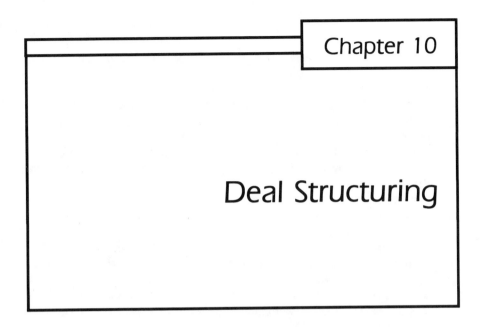

Chapter 10

Deal Structuring

HOW DEALS ARE STRUCTURED

The next stage of the venture review process is the negotiation of the equity positions (along with the debt provisions) for the entrepreneurial team and the venture capitalists. Although the *proposed* deal structure should be included in the business plan itself, the final arrangement is subject to negotiation.

Alternative Methods of Financing

Most ventures are funded from multiple sources, using a combination of self-funding, debt financing (loans), and equity financing (of which, venture capital is one form). The recent trend in the venture capital industry has been to use hybrid forms of financing—combinations of debt *and* equity—to fund ventures.

As is true with any type of investment, risk and return go together. Debt assumes a guaranteed repayment schedule and provides the lender with a prior claim to the assets of the company over that of an equity investor. Thus, the risk of providing a company with a loan is much less than it is in investing in shares of stock of that company; consequently, the potential returns for the lender are proportionately lower than they would be for an investor.

The most common debt and equity tools used to finance a business are as follows:

- *Common stock:* the purest form of equity in the company. Common stock holders receive no fixed or guaranteed return and have the lowest priority claim against assets in the case of liquidation of the company.

The risk (as well as the potential return) of common stock is the greatest of all debt and equity tools.

- *Preferred stock:* a special category of stock that has certain advantages, such as guaranteed dividends and prior rights in the case of liquidation, over common stock.
- *Debt with warrants:* a sweetened form of loan from the perspective of the investor. It allows the investor to purchase shares of common stock at a fixed price within a specified period while still collecting interest on the loan to the company.
- *Convertible debentures:* allows the creditor to convert any remaining outstanding debt into stock at a specified price. It differs from debt with warrants in that the creditor need not receive all the loan payments before purchasing the stock, whereas in the case of debt with warrants, the borrower must repay all the loan and the lender has the choice of whether or not to exercise the warrants.
- *Subordinated convertible debt:* similar to convertible debentures, except that the creditor has a lower claim to the assets in the case of liquidation or bankruptcy.
- *Straight loan:* a simple loan or a debenture, where the borrower is obliged to repay the loan at an agreed upon rate over an agreed upon time. Generally, such loans are secured with some type of collateral, either owned by the business or the entrepreneurs personally.

Founder's Stock.   Founder's stock is equity originally reserved for the originators of a company. Unlike stock options, it provides managers immediate ownership without having to spend money to buy options or wait to exercise them. Stock options are generally used to recruit managers.

Hybrid Forms of Financing

As noted earlier, the entrepreneur's objective is to enhance the potential return for the investor while reducing the downside risk as much as possible. Thus, the hybrid forms of financing—debt with warrants, convertible debentures, or some similar type of arrangement—have become very popular investment tools because they strike a balance between risk and return.

Debt with Warrants.   One of the most famous examples of the use of debt with warrants is when State Mutual Life Assurance Company, in the mid-1960s, loaned Ray Kroc's business $750,000 at an interest rate of 7.5%. As a sweetener, State Mutual received warrants to purchase 10% of the common stock of Kroc's company, McDonald's. About ten years later State Mutual earned approximately $12 million on the sale of its stock in McDonald's.

Equity Kicker Financing by Banks.   Several banks do "equity kicker financing." For example, Silicon Valley Bank, a small bank in San Jose, California, that specializes in working with technology companies, recently provided Sielox Systems of Sunnyvale, California, with a $200,000 line of credit at prime plus 3 points in exchange for 5,000 warrants (that is, 1.4% of the equity of the company), excercisable at $3 per share. When the company was acquired by Checkpoint Systems of Thorofare, New Jersey, for $6.50 per share, the bank earned a $13,000 profit on the warrants.

Stocks with Warrants. About 30 years ago, Allstate Venture Capital entered the venture business with an investment in Control Data Corp., then a start-up company in Minneapolis, begun by former employees of Univac. The venture capital firm's $350,000 investment in the form of preferred stock with warrants (which were later converted to common stock) in CDC grew to $50 million at one point.[1]

Venture Lessors

A recent trend in financing has been the emergence of venture lessors, who lease equipment to early-stage companies for a fee plus a percentage of the equity (usually less than 2%) in the venture. Venture leases have accounted for over $200 million in funding for ventures over the past two years. An average venture lease is less than $1 million.

A venture lease arrangement is attractive for the lessee (the entrepreneurial company) in that the company does not have to make a large cash outlay for equipment at such a critical stage in its development. It can also be attractive to the lessor (the leasing company) in that it recognizes a steady revenue stream, plus it has an opportunity to share in the success of the new venture as it grows.

The catch is that the venture lessor will usually only lease to companies that have already received venture capital funding. The venture lessor, therefore, lessens its downside risk by having the "due diligence" already performed by the venture capitalist.

Recently, Nationwide Remittance Centers (NRC), which uses an elaborate computer system to assist companies in speeding up collections on receivables, leased $500,000 worth of computer equipment from Dominion Ventures of San Francisco in such an arrangement. NRC, which had earlier raised $2 million in venture capital, wouldn't have been able to afford the computers otherwise.

Innovative Financing

There are numerous innovative approaches to finance business ventures. For example, in the early 1980s, Ken Diffenderfer, who had been selling fish from a roadside truck for three years, opened the Fisherman's Marketing Co. in Glen Echo, Maryland.[2] Diffenderfer had an innovative way to finance the

---

[1]See *Venture Capital Journal*, June 1988, p. 1.

[2]See Nora Goldstein, "Raising Outside Capital—Venture and Otherwise," *In Business*, November-December 1982, pp. 30–31.

venture. He offered his regular roadside customers a 10% lifetime discount on seafood in return for a $100 investment in his new company. He "hooked" seventy eager investors. After all, this is a financing approach where everybody benefits. The customers—investors got their money back within a year on just $20 of purchases per week; Diffenderfer not only received the necessary capital up front to start his business, but he was guaranteed a steady flow of customers.

THE ACTUAL STRUCTURING OF THE DEAL

Provisions of the Venture Agreement

The venture capitalist's investment can translate into an ownership position of anywhere from 10% (for established profitable companies) to 90% (for start-up or financially troubled companies). Ideally, the venture capitalists do not want to own more than 50% of the business in order to ensure that the new business is managed as an entrepreneurial concern by its current managers. However, there are some venture capitalists who, unfortunately, view this process purely as a "win/lose" financial negotiation, rather than as an active, long-standing, mutual relationship in which a stronger entrepreneurial company will emerge from the process.

Ideally, the venture capitalists do not want to own more than 50% of the business in order to ensure that the new business is managed as an entrepreneurial concern by its current managers.

Operational control would generally remain in the hands of the company's management team. However, the venture capitalists will generally ask for representation (and, occasionally, major representation which can, as illustrated earlier, adversely affect the company) on the board of directors of the entrepeneurial company in order to have some input in important strategic decisions that may alter the direction of the company.

There are two key concerns in structuring the deal:

1. Determining the value of the business
2. Determining the equity position for the investor, which is actually dictated by the value of the business

Thus, the venture capitalist is interested in seeing what the company will be worth three to seven years down the road (that is, at the time the investment will likely be liquidated through a corporate acquisition, an IPO, or other means) in order to determine how the investment will translate into a percentage of the ownership position of the company. The venture capital firm is, naturally, seeking to maximize its return; thus, the larger its ownership position is the greater the potential return.

What's the Business Worth?   The first piece of the puzzle is the valuation of the business. That is done generally by one of the following two methods:

1. By calculating the projected earnings (for example, in five years) and then multiplying that number by an appropriate multiple of earnings (referred to as its price/earnings, P/E, multiple). For example, if a development-stage company is expected to have earnings of $600,000 in year 5, and if similar companies are likely to be valued (for example, through an IPO) at a P/E of 8 (that is, eight times earnings), then the company is projected to be worth $4.8 million five years from now:

$$\$600,000 \times 8 = \$4.8 \text{ million}$$

2. Calculating the present value of the future stream of earnings of the business. For example, if we assume that the same company is likely to have earnings over years 1 to 5 of $200,000, $300,000, $400,000, $500,000, and $600,000,[3] respectively, and if we also assume that a rate of return of 20% (which takes into account the risk of such a venture) would be required for such an investment, then, as shown below, the company is projected to be worth approximately $1.1 million five years from now:

Year	Earnings Stream	Present Value Factor at 20% Rate of Return
1	$200,000	$166,670
2	300,000	208,330
3	400,000	231,480
4	500,000	241,130
5	600,000	241,130
	Totals	$1,088,740

It should be clear from this example that valuation is not an exact science. A valuation for a given business could vary significantly using the same data, but different methods of valuation.

[3] We've only considered the earnings for the next five years of the business. Obviously, if we were to project earnings over subsequent years, the valuation, using this method, would be considerably higher.

TABLE 10-1   Typical Returns Expected by Venture Capitalists

Stage of Business	Expected Annual Return on Investment	Expected Increase on Initial Investment
Idea stage/start-up business (seed capital; start-up capital)	60% +	10–15 × investment
New business (first-stage financing)	40%–60%	6–12 × investment
Development stage (second-stage financing)	30%–50%	4–8 × investment
Expansion stage (third-stage financing; bridge financing)	25%–40%	3–6 × investment
Turnaround situation	50% +	8–15 × investment

What's the Equity Position for the Venture Capitalist?   Once a value is established for the business, the next concern is to use that information to project an appropriate equity position for the venture capitalist, which is a function of the projected return on a given investment.

Typically, venture capitalists seek returns commensurate with the risks of their investments as shown in Table 10-1.

Thus, based on the previous example, in which the entire company would be worth $4.8 million, we can assume that a $400,000 investment in the company while it is in its development stage would translate into 50% of the equity of the business, as follows:

$400,000 × 6 times increase in investment = $2.4 million

$2.4 million/$4.8 million = 50% of the equity

Note that the figures in Table 10-1 are only general guidelines; each venture is evaluated on its own merit. Venture capitalists will often settle for a lower return on investment if:

- The company has sufficient capital.
- There is good cash flow.
- The original owners of the business have invested a sizable portion of their own funds in the business, thereby taking on a good deal of the risk themselves.

For example, if the original owners invest 10% of the total capital, then they can often expect to retain 40% to 50% of the ownership in the business; if they invest 30% of the capital, then they can often retain two-thirds or more of the ownership in the business.[4]

Certainly, the expected returns for the venture capitalist noted above are high. However, especially in recent years, during a period when blue-chip companies traded on the New York Stock Exchange, which are virtually risk free over the long term, have yielded compounded annual returns of 20%, 30%, or more, it is reasonable to assume that venture capitalists would be seeking double or triple those returns.

VCs Are VC

It's also important to understand the personality of the investor as it relates to risk and return. The initials VC can stand for venture capitalist. Yet, they can also stand for something else—*very conservative!* Venture capitalists are not just interested in making a lot of money. They are also interested in not losing the money that they have already invested in a company; they want to at least get their investment back. Thus, it is crucial to demonstrate to them how they "can't lose" on their investment.

To go one step further, a battle often develops between the entrepreneur and the venture capitalist. The entrepreneur argues for the upside potential of the business, whereas the venture capitalist states a case for its downside risk. In most cases, the venture capitalist has the leverage because (1) the venture capitalist is generally much more experienced in these battles than is the entrepreneur, and (2) the venture capitalist has something that the entrepreneur wants—*money!* Eventually, an agreement is reached that will, ideally, enable both parties to benefit. The important lesson is that the entrepreneur must understand the needs and risk preferences of the venture capitalist prior to presenting a plan for raising capital.

An Example

Let's look at an example to see how a venture capitalist's investment affects the equity position of a company. Suppose SUPERPROD Corporation, a one-year old company with excellent potential, is seeking venture capital. The company has developed a prototype but has not yet begun production due to its limited funds. Currently, the only persons working for the company are the two engineer–founders. Projected earnings for the company in five years are $3 million on $25 million in revenues. Let's assume that companies similar to SUPERPROD would be worth ten times their earnings, or $30 million in five years. Assume that SUPERPROD is now seeking $1 million to expand its production and marketing efforts. What percentage of ownership of the business would the venture capital company want in order to realize its expected return?

---

[4]Of course, these are very rough estimates; the venture capitalist will take into account all the factors discussed in Chapter 9 in structuring the deal.

Let's first examine the riskiness of this venture. Using the evaluation system described in Chapter 9, we would classify this venture as a 2/2 investment, from which venture capitalists would be seeking approximately a 50% + annual return or, let's say, ten times their investment in five years. Thus, assuming no inflation, the $1 million initial investment should be worth $10 million or approximately 33% ($10 million divided by $30 million) of the ownership in the business. When we adjust for inflation, the ownership position of SUPERPROD by the venture capital company would approach 40%.

Recognize that the current owners of SUPERPROD will be expected to give up nearly one-half of their ownership in the company at this early stage. Yet there might be two or three more rounds of venture financing necessary during the next five to ten years to enable the company to grow. Thus, if the owners will be giving up so much equity early on, it will be impossible for them to maintain a majority interest in the company as the business requires additional funding at a later time.

Do Venture Capitalists Want to Control the Business?

From the preceding example, it might appear as if venture capitalists want to become majority owners of a company. Although it will happen on occasion, this is not necessarily the case. Investors in small, growing, privately owned companies are just like any other investors, yet they have a specific objective of earning a 40% to 60% annual return on their investment, net of inflation; this return is very much in line with the riskiness of such an investment. Unlike investors in blue-chip companies, who expect a 10% to 20% annual return in less risky companies over a twenty- or thirty-year period, however, venture capitalists generally want to realize their returns within five years. Furthermore, in a typical venture capitalist's portfolio, there may be only one major success and three of four minor successes, with the remainder either losing money or failing completely. Thus, they expect higher than average returns to counterbalance the poor returns realized by many of their other high-risk investments. If they happen to secure a 51% ownership position in the company, it may be merely a reflection of the potential returns necessary to invest in the venture, rather than of the desire to control the company.

Negotiation

In 1982, Nubar Hagopian and Kenneth Foster of Magnetite, Inc., a Boston-based manufacturer of magnetic storm windows, were seeking $800,000 for their venture. EAB Venture Corp. offered to provide the funding, half in straight debt and the other half in convertible debentures, for 60% of the company. The entrepreneurs countered by offering just 40% of their stock, with the stipulation that they could earn back an additional 10% of their stock based on specific performance criteria. EAB compromised by sticking with its original 60% proposal, but with a 20% earn-back provision. The deal was finally accepted when the entrepreneurs agreed to EAB's terms, with the provision that they trade an extra seat on the board of directors to get the equity earn out up front. Consequently, the investors received majority control of the board, but only 40% of Magnetite.

Based on the agreement between the investors and the entrepreneurs, Magnetite was to have attained $1.9 million in pretax profits by November 1985 or the 60:40 ratio would be reversed in favor of the investors. When Hagopian and Foster realized they wouldn't achieve the stated objectives, the investors put in another $800,000, thereby increasing their equity stake to 60%.

Importance of the Deal

How important is the negotiation of the structure of the venture capital deal? It depends on whether you're speaking to the entrepreneur or the venture capitalist. To the entrepreneur, negotiation will often be of vital concern. Many venture capitalists, however, feel that *too* much emphasis is placed on such negotiation. After all, if the business succeeds, and the venture capital investment grows by twenty-, thirty-, or forty-fold, does it really matter if the venture capitalist owns 25%, as compared to 33%, of the company? In either case, the profits for both the entrepreneurial company and the venture capital firm are attractive.

According to Lucien Ruby, formerly a principal with Brentwood Associates and now a partner with Quest Ventures of San Francisco, the only time the structure of the deal matters is when the company fails, which occurs in only 10% to 20% of the deals financed by venture capital firms. At that time, the investor just wants to get *something* out of his or her investment.[5]

SECURITIES LAWS

Several complex federal and state securities laws must be taken into account when seeking equity funding for a business. Similar to tax laws, they become outdated with the passage of time. Thus the information provided here should only serve as a guide to the nature of securities laws.

Regulation D

Although private placement laws may vary somewhat from state to state, three important rules under Regulation D of the (federal) Securities Act should be considered in the case of private placements. The purpose of the rules, as outlined next, is to eliminate any unnecessary restrictions on the ability of small businesses to raise capital:

[5]See G. Kozmetsky and others, Financing and Managing Fast Growth Companies. The Venture Capital Process, D. C. Heath, Lexington, Mass., 1985.

- *Rule 504* is useful for companies interested in raising small amounts of capital from numerous investors. It allows the issuer to sell up to $500,000 of its securities during a twelve-month period regardless of the number or sophistication of the investors.
- *Rule 505* permits the sale of $5 million of a company's securities in any twelve-month period to any thirty-five investors and to an unlimited number of "accredited investors," which includes institutional investors such as banks, insurance companies, investment companies, certain employee benefit plans, directors, executive officers, general partners of the issuers, and certain wealthy individuals (based on net worth, income requirements, and so on).
- *Rule 506* permits the issuer to sell an unlimited amount of its securities only to certain investors. The issuer may sell its securities to any thirty-five "sophisticated investors" (that is, those that either individually or through a knowledgeable representative meet the requirements to be considered "sophisticated") and to an unlimited number of "accredited investors."

In addition, there are some general requirements common to all three of the above rules:

- The issuer has good reason to believe that each investor has the ability to evaluate the risks and the merits of the investment or is able to bear the economic risk of the investment.
- Each investor has access to the same information.
- The purchasers are not underwriters who will resell the stock.
- There is no general advertising of the offering.
- The securities are sold through direct communication between the issuer and purchaser.

1244 Stock

Certain tax laws can make a company a much more attractive investment than would otherwise be the case. One such law involves the manner in which stock is issued.

Prior to issuance of any shares of stock, the board of directors can issue 1244 stock under a section of the Internal Revenue Code (IRC 1244) that grants ordinary, rather than capital, treatment of losses on certain small business stock. If the losses were treated as capital losses, there would be a maximum annual deduction (presently $3,000) for them if they cannot be offset against capital gains. By treating the losses as ordinary losses, however, the entire amount can generally be written off in one year.

1244 stock allows shareholders in most new ventures to deduct up to $50,000 (or $100,000 on a joint return) of bankruptcy losses against ordinary income. The requirements (which are rather lenient) for qualification for section 1244 stock include the following:

- The stock must be common stock issued by a domestic corporation.
- The corporation must have over 50% of its gross receipts from other than passive sources (that is, investments) for five years before the losses.
- The stock must be issued by the corporation for money or other property pursuant to a written plan containing several limitations.
- There can be no other kind of prior stock offering outstanding.
- The amount of contribution received for the stock of the corporation must not exceed $1 million.
- Only individuals and partnerships qualify for 1244 benefits; corporations, trusts, and estates cannot claim 1244 treatment for stocks that they hold.
- The claimed losses cannot exceed the money or property given in exchange for the stock.
- The individuals receiving stock must be the original persons to whom the stock was issued. Therefore, to incorporate an existing partnership, in order to derive the benefits of 1244 stock, the company must take the following steps, in this order:
  1. Liquidate the partnership.
  2. Distribute the assets to the partners.
  3. Let the partners transfer the assets to the corporation in exchange for the 1244 stock.

The order is essential; if the company, instead, transfers the assets directly to the new corporation, it will not qualify for 1244 stock.

The advantage of 1244 stock is that it will "soften the blow" if the company does fail by allowing investors to deduct their losses in one year rather than over several years, which would be the case if the losses were treated as capital losses.

A LOOK AHEAD

An integral part of the venture capital process is the structuring of the debt and/or equity position(s) for the entrepreneur and the venture capitalist. Recently, there has been a trend toward hybrid forms of financing in order to address the risk and return preferences of the parties involved in the deal. The actual structuring of the deal should be viewed as a well thought out process in which the equity position of the venture capital firm is based on the future value of the company and on the expected return for a particular investment.

In the next chapter, we examine the final stage of the venture capital process, postinvestment activity.

Chapter 11

Postinvestment Activity

In Chapter 10, we discussed how venture capitalists actually make investment decisions. What happens next? Does the venture capitalist merely "sit around and wait" for something to happen? Obviously not. As mentioned earlier, a distinguishing feature of venture capital investments is that venture capitalists generally play an active role in assisting businesses in establishing and accomplishing their long-range goals; they're *venture catalysts*! Moreover, venture capitalists are often instrumental in assisting in the process by which they can cash out of their initial investment.

EXIT ROUTES

For securities traded on a national stock exchange, there is always a market in which to sell shares of stock. However, for privately held companies, the market is considerably more limited. There are four basic ways in which the investor can "exit" from the deal or get his or her money out of the company:

1. Buyback by the founders of the company (which is not generally the preferred alternative of the entrepreneurial team; why would the owners propose to pay 30% to 50% annual returns on money "borrowed" from investors when they could have borrowed at much lower rates from other sources earlier?)
2. Finding a new investor
3. Acquisition by a larger company
4. Going public via an initial public offering (IPO)

Going Public Versus Other Exit Routes

Going public is generally an attractive alternative from the standpoint of the venture capitalist because a ready market will then exist for them to get their original investment out of the business. It also can be a very profitable arrangement for investors, as has recently been evidenced by such IPOs as Lotus Development, Apple Computer, Compaq Computer, Microsoft, and Genentech, to name just a few.

We should not, however, overstate the importance of the IPO market as a means of cashing out. There are other exit routes for companies, most notably corporate acquisitions, which, in recent years, have been a more popular way to cash out than IPOs. Although the number of IPOs may have fluctuated significantly in recent years, depending on the climate of the public equity markets, acquisitions have grown steadily over the past decade.

INITIAL PUBLIC OFFERINGS

IPOs represent one of the most attractive means to exit from a venture capital deal. At the time of the IPO, venture capitalists will often liquidate a portion of their holdings of a particular investment. Typically, venture capitalists attempt to recoup their initial cash investment. For example, General Electric Venture Capital Corp. (GEVC) invested approximately $2 million in Nellcor, Inc., a Hayward, California, based manufacturer of patient monitoring systems. When the company went public in May 1987, GEVC sold 23% of its holdings for an amount equal to its initial investment.

Similarly, Noro-Mosely Partners (Atlanta, Georgia) for example, provided bridge financing of $3 million to One Price Clothing Stores (Duncan, South Carolina) in January 1987. When the company went public in May of that year, Noro-Mosely sold 25% of it shares at the IPO for $1.5 million, half of its initial investment.

Of course, venture capitalists will often retain their entire equity stakes at the time of an IPO, presumably because they feel that there will be significant stock appreciation after the company goes public. Such was evident with Compaq Computer, when Sevin Rosen, Kleiner Perkins Caufield & Byers, Humboldt Trust, and LF Rothshild retained *all* their stock in the company at the time the company went public. This certainly turned out to be an excellent decision for those venture capital firms, since Compaq's value has increased significantly ever since its IPO.

The Importance of Timing When Cashing Out

The choice for venture capitalists is to cash out at the time of the IPO or to wait a long time before completely exiting. SEC Rule 144 prohibits inside investors from publicly trading their stock that is unregistered for two years after

TABLE 11-1   IPO Volume

Year	$ Billions	Number of Offerings
1989	$13.8	245
1988	22.4	255
1987	23.8	533
1986	22.4	719
1985	5.6	531
1984	3.8	550
1983	12.6	888
1982	1.5	222
1981	3.2	448
1980	1.4	237
1979	0.5	81
1978	0.3	45
1977	0.2	40
1976	0.2	34
1975	0.3	15
1974	0.1	15
1973	0.3	100
1972	2.7	568

they purchased it if the company goes public during that time. For three years after the original date of purchase, insiders can only sell shares amounting to a small percentage of the average daily trading volume of the company.

With an IPO, however, the venture capital firm can sell its stock at an established return. This is a result of when the company registers with the SEC to offer its shares to the public; inside investors can piggyback the registration and have either all or a portion of their holdings become public shares as well.

The "Mad Rush" for IPOs

The tremendous success of the IPO of Apple Computer, which raised $110 million when it went public in 1980, demonstrated that the public equity markets could be receptive to new issues in technology stocks. This was confirmed by subsequent IPOs of Vector Graphic, Altos Computer, ASK Computer Systems, Pizza Time Theatre, and Cetus. Thus, venture capitalists realized that companies, especially those in high-tech industries, could receive ten or twenty times (or more) their initial investment from Wall Street investors in just two or three years, rather than the customary five to ten years. That prompted a stampede to the public equity markets during the 1980s, as shown by Table 11-1.

Between 1980 and 1983, the number of new issues nearly quadrupled, while the value of those IPOs increased by nine-fold. Even more dramatic is the number and value of IPOs from only a decade earlier. In 1974, there were only 15 IPOs, which raised a total of $100 million. In 1983, 888 IPOs raised $12.6 billion.

It was relatively easy to go public at that time. With the dramatic increase in quantity came a corresponding decrease in the quality of new issues. As noted by Benjamin M. Rosen of Sevin Rosen Management and one of the most astute venture capitalists in the nation, in referring to the dramatic increase in the number of issues going public in 1983,

> "that was a terrible period . . . we were all guilty. Anything that wiggled could either get venture capital or go public and did and a lot of people are paying the price for that. But the interesting thing about that is that quality did prevail."[1]

As noted by Burgess Jamieson, general partner of Sigma Partners in San Jose, California,

> "People say power corrupts, but I think it's money that does the trick. . . . We have the symptoms of the heightening of greed among venture capitalists and entrepreneurs. I suppose greed is okay up to a point, but it's like wine. A glass is pleasant, a bottle will have a different effect."[2]

One of the results of the dramatic growth of the IPO market was a tremendous influx of individuals in the venture capital industry who were more interested in "making a quick buck" than in building companies. For example, in 1979, Mark Richardson, a former Hewlett-Packard engineer, and three colleagues started Structural Measurement Systems (SMS), a San Jose, California, based company that develops software packages for diagnosing design-related problems like stress and noise. After it had reached the $1 million mark in sales, it sought additional capital for expansion. Richardson became disgusted with the venture capitalists that he approached, as their primary concern was with the prospects of the company going public within the very near future, rather than with how well the venture capitalists and the entrepreneurs could serve as partners to one another in building the company.

Failure Follows Success.   The euphoria finally came to an end in 1982 with the demise of Osborne Computer. On first look, it appears that the company had all the essential ingredients for success: a bright, articulate leader in Adam Osborne; an exciting, breakthrough product, in its portable computer; and an eager group of investors, which included Ken Oshman, founder of ROLM, and Jack Melchor, an experienced Silicon Valley venture capitalist. Yet the public offering that was to occur never did, as a result of problems in production, cash flow, and management. Eventually, the company filed for bankruptcy amid a battery of lawsuits.

Osborne was soon followed into the bankruptcy courts by such one-time highly regarded companies as Victor Technologies and Pizza Time Theatre.

[1]Louis Rukeyser, "Wall Street Week," February 8, 1985.

[2]See Joel Kotkin, "Why Smart Companies Are Saying No to Venture Capital," in *The Best of Inc.: Guide to Finding Capital*, Prentice Hall, Englewood Cliffs, N.J., 1988, p. 94.

Furthermore, other once successful companies, such as Fortune Systems, Diasonics, Vector Graphic, Xonics, and Evotek, which had each previously received several million dollars of venture capital, were struggling. These events were instrumental in not only destroying the IPO market in 1983–1984, especially for high-tech issues, but also in depressing the stock prices of already publicly held technology companies. Another important negative outcome was the failure of scores of smaller, newer venture capital firms.

The situation was quite similar to that of the late 1960s and early 1970s. That period had also witnessed a tremendous boom in emerging growth companies, many of which had well-publicized (and well-hyped) IPOs. Despite initial rises in their stock prices, many of these companies soon crashed as a result of their fundamental weaknesses. A significant potential problem is that, since there is a direct link between the public and private equity markets, episodes of unwarranted increases in the value of the stock of several corporations could have a dramatic negative impact on the venture capital industry and on entrepreneurial activity as a whole.

IPOs: The Pros and Cons

Of course, some companies have done exceedingly well after their IPOs, for example, Federal Express in overnight delivery; Compaq Computer in personal computers; Reebok and LA Gear in athletic shoes; Adobe Systems in computer systems; and Microsoft in computer software. Other companies, which were at one time the superstar growth companies in this country, have had dramatic declines in their stock prices after their IPOs, for example, Continuing Care, a marketer of home health care equipment; Home Shopping Network, a television retailer; and New World Pictures, a television and motion picture producer. Some, including Pizza Time Theatre, Wedtech, and Vector Graphic, have failed altogether.

IPOs have had some tremendous benefits. They have provided entrepreneurs with status as well as personal fortune, as has been the case with Bill Gates, Steve Jobs, Mitchell Kapor, and William Poduska. They have provided a source of capital, usually at a more attractive valuation to the entrepreneur than has generally been the case for more sophisticated private investors.

However, there have been some significant problems associated with IPOs. Specifically, they have generally resulted in a loss of control (in terms of percentage of stock ownership) of the venture for the entrepreneur. They have also been exceedingly time consuming (as well as expensive, with costs *starting* at $250,000 and increasing with the size of the offering), in terms of audits and reporting requirements. In addition, they have forced the company to carry out its business "in public," under the careful scrutiny of public investors, who often have a much shorter time horizon than the entrepreneur or the private investors. Nonetheless, companies will often be under pressure by venture capitalists to "go public" in order for the investors to cash out of their earlier investments.

The National Association of Securities Dealers (NASD) has recently called for stricter guidelines for listing a company on the national over-the-counter stock exchange. Because IPOs are a typical exit route for venture capital-backed companies, this can have a significant impact on the venture capital industry. As with any proposal to establish stricter guidelines, it is likely that this will differentiate more clearly the "winners" from the "losers." Thus, it will probably be negative for the marginal companies, which will not qualify for a listing; yet it will probably be positive for the higher-quality companies seeking a listing, which will appear that much stronger for "making the cut."

CORPORATE ACQUISITIONS

Although IPOs generally get the greatest publicity and are best known by the public, corporate acquisitions have been a far more common exit route for venture capital-backed companies. In fact, according to *Venture Economics*, there have been significantly more corporate acquisitions than IPOs for venture capital-backed companies in just about every year over the past decade (see Table 11-2).[3]

> Although IPOs generally get the greatest publicity and are best known by the public, corporate acquisitions have been a far more common exit route for venture capital-backed companies.

Recently, several prominent acquisitions of venture capital-backed companies have taken place. They include K Mart's $320 million purchase of PACE Membership Warehouse (Aurora, Colorado), an operator of discount warehouse clubs; Wal-Mart's purchase of Super Saver Warehouse Club, Inc., another operator of discount warehouse clubs; Reebok International's $180 million acquisition of its former rival, Avia Group International (Portland, Oregon); and Control Data Corp.'s acquisition of VTC, Inc. (Bloomington, Michigan), a manufacturer of high-performance integrated circuits.

Corporate Acquisitions in Biotechnology

In some industries, notably biotechnology, corporate acquisitions have increasingly become the norm. In 1988, for example, according to data provided by The Wilkerson Group, there were 344 acquisitions among medical and biotechnology companies, while there were only 29 IPOs in this industry.

[3]The number of IPOs in Table II-2 differs from the number of IPOs in Table II-1 since this table includes only the IPOs (as well as corporate acquisitions) used as exit routes for companies backed by selected venture capital companies, while the other chart includes *all* IPOs in a given year.

TABLE 11-2 Corporate Acquisitions of Venture
Capital-Backed Companies

Year	Number of Corporate Acquisitions	Number of IPOs
1988	133	36
1987	140	81
1986	120	96
1985	101	47
1984	86	53
1983	49	121
1982	40	27
1981	32	68
1980	28	27

What's responsible for this? Over the last decade, more than 200 bio-technology companies have gone public. Yet only a handful have made money for the public investors. Corporate acquisitions (by pharmaceutical companies and companies in related industries), however, have been successful, because the acquirers, which better understand the technology than the general public, have gained valuable technologies through this process. For example, Diamond BioSensors, of Ann Arbor, Michigan, which makes blood diagnostic products, was recently purchased by Mallinckrodt, Inc., a St. Louis-based chemical company, for $30.5 million. Five years earlier, the New York-based venture capital firm, CW Group, along with other investors, provided Diamond BioSensors with $9 million of funding.

CW Group, TA Associates, and other venture capital firms well versed in biotechnology have recognized that entrepreneurial companies that concentrate on developing a limited number of sharply focused products, which have already had some initial positive testing, will be prime candidates for corporate acquisition. In such a situation, everybody benefits: the entrepreneurial company receives the corporate funding to continue its product development and commercialization; the acquirer gains the new technology that can strengthen its existing product line; and the investors realize significant financial gains. This can be contrasted to the scores of upstart biotechnology companies, with poorly focused products at premature stages of development, that went public during the early 1980s. In those cases, just about everybody lost out; many have gone out of business, while others are still, ten years later, in the product development stage, with little chance of commercial success.

A LOOK AHEAD

The final stage of the venture capital process is postinvestment activity. It is during this stage that venture capitalists finally realize their returns on their initial investment in a venture; at that time, they can exist from or cash out of the deal, often through either an IPO or a corporate acquisition.

These last five chapters examined the venture capital process, from deal origination through exit, and presented prescriptive rules for entrepreneurs to follow throughout. The process is characterized by careful and critical screening of venture proposals and the subsequent negotiation for debt and equity positions.

What types of investments are favored by venture capitalists? In what industry and stages do they invest? How have these investments performed? These questions are addressed in Part IV.

PART IV

NATURE AND PERFORMANCE OF VENTURE CAPITAL INVESTMENTS

Chapter 12

Nature of Venture Capital Investments

PREFERRED INVESTMENTS BY VENTURE CAPITALISTS

1985 JEC Study

In 1985, the Joint Economic Committee (JEC) of the U.S. Congress conducted the first of its kind of study on the venture capital industry. Responses were gathered from 277, which was 47% (an extremely high rate) of the leading venture capital firms in the nation. Some of the significant findings of the study were as follows:

- Venture capital firms were highly specialized investors who, with other venture capital firms and investors, participated largely in seed, start-up, and early expansion investments.
- The majority of investments receiving venture capital support were in companies that use technology to expand the nation's economy into new products and processes that enhance productivity and the quality of life.
- Venture capitalists were hands-on investors who diversify their investments by region, stage of business development, and the like, and by coinvestment with other venture capital firms in order to minimize risk.
- The venture capital pool, although having grown significantly in recent years, was still in short supply.
- Venture capital firms anticipated a minimum rate of return of 30% per year on individual investments.
- Most proposals submitted by entrepreneurs went unfunded, partly because they couldn't meet the 30% per year rate of return standard.

- Approximately 50% of the deals funded by venture capitalists were antic-ipated to be "winners."[1]

Recent Trends in Venture Capital Investments

Several researchers have found support for the JEC study. For example, Professors Willard Carleton and Ian Cooper (among others) found that venture capitalists tend to invest in risky projects with high potential returns.[2] Moreover, these researchers found that venture capitalists prefer to fund ventures in which the entrepreneurs have already made a significant financial and time commit-ment and that they utilize complex financial packages—involving combinations of debt, equity, covertible debentures, and debt with warrants—to structure the financial arrangement between themselves and the entrepreneur.

One contradictory finding to the JEC study was that venture capitalists prefer not to fund start-ups. The contradiction is explained best by the time frame in which the studies were conducted. In the 1970s and early 1980s, upon which time period the JEC study was based, there was significant funding of early-stage ventures, especially those in high-tech industries, such as computers and related fields. Professor Jeffry Timmons, one of the nation's leading re-searchers in the areas of entrepreneurship and venture capital, and his asso-ciates found support for this.[3]

Over the past few years, there has been a trend among venture capitalists toward greater specialization.

However, since that time, there has been a fairly dramatic shift in the investment philosophies of venture capitalists. Over the past few years, there has been a trend among venture capitalists toward greater specialization, by geographic location, by industry, by stage of development, and, contrary to what the JEC study suggested in terms of funding technology-oriented ventures, two

---

[1] "A Study Prepared for the Use of the Joint Economic Committee of the U.S. Congress," *U.S. Government Printing Office*, Washington, D.C., 1985.

[2] For details of these studies, see W. R. Carleton, "Issues and Questions Involving Venture Capital," in G. Libecap (ed.), *Advances in the Study of Entrepreneurship, Innovation, and Economic Growth*, JAI Press, Greenwich, Conn., 1986, pp. 59–70; W. R. Carleton and I. A. Cooper, "Venture Capital Investment," in R. Crum and F. Derkinderen (eds.), *Strategies of Corporate Investment*, Pittman Publishing Co., Toronto, 1982.

[3] For details of these studies, see J. A. Timmons, "Venture Capital Investors in the U.S.: A Survey of the Most Active Investors," *Frontiers of Entrepreneurship Research, 1981*, Babson College, Wellesley, Mass., 1981, pp. 199–216; J. A. Timmons and others, "The Flow of Venture Capital to Highly Innovative Technological Ventures," *Proceedings: Babson Research Conference*, 1983, pp. 316–334.

of the emerging trends have been in low-tech industries as well as in leveraged buyouts [LBOs][4](although, as mentioned earlier, the investment community, as a whole, is less excited about LBOs today than it was during the mid-1980s). After all, if venture capitalists can obtain a ("relatively") fairly safe return of 35% to 50% on selected LBOs, why should they look for potential comparable returns in more risky start-ups?

Traditional Venture Capital?   E. M. Warburg, Pincus & Co.'s recent $1.2 billion venture capital limited partnership (which was formed in 1986) resulted in such notable investments as:

- $60 million investment in Westward Communications, an entertainment conglomerate based in London
- $83 million investment in Magna Copper Co., which spun off from Newmont Mining Corp.
- $125 million refinancing of Mellon Bank Corp. of Pittsburgh.

Such investments hardly seem like "traditional" venture capital investments. However, they are certainly investments that have the potential of strengthening these companies as well as of enhancing economic development.

Of course, Warburg, Pincus has numerous start-up and expansion stage ventures in its portfolio, for example, the $12 million investment in Cambridge NeuroScience Research (Cambridge, Massachusetts) and the $18 million expansion of the San Francisco Music Box Co. As noted earlier, the strategy of Warburg, Pincus has always been to maintain a balance of risk and return in its portfolio. As such, the company has invested perhaps 50% of its investment dollars in undervalued assets, although these investments only comprise 20% (in terms of number) of its deals. Alternatively, Warburg, Pincus has invested approximately 15% of its investment dollars in start-ups, although such investments represent approximately 50% (in terms of number) of its deals.

Similar to the investments of Warburg, Pincus, there has been—especially among the larger venture capital firms—a growing increase in the *sheer amount of dollars* invested in later-stage ventures. Although Warburg, Pincus's strategy has been fairly well established over the years (in fact, the firm has referred to

[4]For further details, see the following academically oriented articles: W. D. Bygrave, "Syndicated Investments of Venture Capital Firms: A Networking Perspective," *Journal of Business Venturing*, 1987, *2*, pp. 139–154; W. A. Carleton, "Issues and Questions Involving Venture Capital," in G. Libecap (ed.), *Advances in the Study of Entrepreneurship, Innovation, and Economic Growth*, Volume 1, JAI Press, Greenwich, Conn., 1986, pp. 59–70; G. D. Libecap, "The Dialogue on Venture Capital Markets," in G. Libecap (ed.), *Advances in the Study of Entrepreneurship, Innovation, and Economic Growth*, Volume 1, JAI Press, Greenwich, Conn., 1986, pp. 1–78; J. A. Timmons and W. D. Bygrave, "Venture Capital's Role in Financing Innovation for Economic Growth," *Journal of Business Venturing*, 1986, *1*, pp. 161–176. In addition, refer to the following practitioner-oriented articles: A. Deutschman, "A Case of Too Much Money," *Fortune*, November 7, 1988, pp. 94–104; E. L. James, "Desperate for Dollars," *Venture*, May 1988, pp. 57–60; M. J. Juilland. "What Do You Want from a Venture Capitalist?" *Venture*, August 1987, pp. 30–35; M. J. Juilland, "Strategies for a Time of Transition," *Venture*, June 1988, pp. 31–34.

itself as "venture bankers" ever since its inception twenty years ago), other large firms have actually shifted the percentage of their resources away from start-ups and toward established companies. As those venture capitalists have altered their investment strategy, they have also altered their philosophy and their role.

TREND TOWARD SPECIALIZATION

In Support of the JEC Study

The JEC Study (discussed earlier in this chapter) suggested that venture capitalists tend to diversify their investments. This is certainly still the case for many venture capital firms today. For example, U.S. Venture Partners, a $\$\frac{1}{4}$ billion Menlo Park, California, based venture capital firm has attempted to maintain a balanced portfolio of early- and late-stage investments, throughout the country, in such diverse areas as technology, specialty retailing, and consumer products. Consequently, they have invested in such companies as Applied Bio-systems, Inc., a manufacturer of analytical instruments for genetic engineering research (which went public in 1983); Sun Microsystems, a manufacturer of computer workstations (which went public in 1986); Home Club, a chain of warehouse-style home improvement retail stores (which was acquired by Zayre Corp. in 1986); Ross Stores, an off-price apparel retailer (which went public in 1985); and Avia Group International, a manufacturer of athletic footware and clothing (which was acquired by its rival, Reebok International, in 1987).

The Alternative View: Specialization

A Niche Economy.   More and more, however, we have evolved into a *niche* economy. For example, Information America (Atlanta, Georgia) provides on-line public record information and services to lawyers. Similarly, Roadshow Services (San Francisco) provides trucks and drivers for performers. And Back-roads Bicycle Touring (Berkeley, California) markets van-supported bicycle tours. Each of these companies was founded less than ten years ago and is now a multi-million dollar business. They represent a widespread emerging trend of carving out small, specialized niches and then filling them better than anyone else can.

The diversity of these niche-oriented businesses is startling. Among the most recent *Inc.* 500 listing of fast-growth private companies, in addition to the three companies just mentioned, which have grown by at least eight-fold over the last five years, there are other comparably successful companies in such specialized areas as archery equipment, handcrafted embroidery, Australian wines, parent education videos, and model racing cars.

A Niche Economy Results In Specialization Among Venture Capitalists. Therefore, just like the trend toward specialization among entrepreneurial companies, it should not be surprising that, contrary to the JEC study, there has been a dramatic trend toward *specialization* among venture capital firms. This has been one of the most significant recent developments in the venture capital industry. It has also been a very positive development for the industry and for entrepreneurs in that it has prompted venture capitalists to develop greater expertise in a given industry, thereby strengthening their role as *venture catalysts*. Oak Management Corp., of Westport, Connecticut, for example, has concentrated on three technology groups: computers, telecommunications, and biotechnology. Similarly, Battery Ventures, a Boston-based venture capital firm, concentrates on communications, information systems, and industry automation technology. They (along with Accel Partners and others) recently invested in Netlink, a Raleigh, North Carolina, based manufacturer of data communications processors for IBM networks.

MedVenture, a San Francisco-based venture capital firm, is even more specialized; it limits its investments to the life sciences (biotechnology, health services, medical instrumentation, and the like). Similarly, Julian Cole & Stein, of Los Angeles, generally limits its investments to high-tech manufacturing companies on the West Coast, as evidenced by their recent investments in LaserCom, a manufacturer of detectors and transceivers, and Advanced Power Technology, Inc., a manufacturer of MOS transistors.

As noted by David Brophy, professor of finance at the University of Michigan,

"There's an evolution going on in the structuring of the industry.... The old model, in which the venture capitalist was a generalist, confident that he could deal with any type of venture, is no longer possible. Because of the intense competition for money and deals, we're seeing much more targeting of specific areas of technology and growth."[5]

This has necessitated that venture capital firms become more specialized in their staffing needs and in the way that they raise funds from their own investors. Brophy adds,

"funds are tending to devote more people to specific areas of technology.... And there is an influx of people with operating backgrounds, people who have been successful in molding companies and getting products out the door."

Liberal Exception Policy

Even with specialization, many venture capitalists will deviate from their preferences. Some venture capitalists refer to this as their "liberal exception policy." For example, Brentwood Associates, a specialist in funding high-tech ventures, invested in Midway Airlines a few years ago. Why? Because, above all,

[5] See Lee Kravitz, "What Venture Capitalists Want," in *Venture's Guide to International Venture Capital*, Simon & Schuster, New York, 1985, p. 14.

the characteristics of the people involved in the venture are more important than the industry in which they operate.

◆◆◆◆◆◆◆◆◆◆◆◆◆

There is a misperception that early-stage high-technology companies in high-tech regions are the sole recipients of venture capital. As we will soon see, however, with increasing specialization, there has been a shift in venture capital commitments that has resulted in considerable funding to low-tech industries in low-tech regions at late stages of development.

SPECIALIZATION BY REGION

In general, venture capital firms are located in regions in which entrepreneurial activity is greatest. Specifically, the three leading states for *Inc.* 500 fast-growth private companies in this country in 1989 were California, New York, and Massachusetts; not surprisingly, these three states have the largest number of venture capital firms.

As noted earlier, venture capital firms, especially those in California, often concentrate their investments in their own region. For example, there are dozens of West Coast-based venture capital firms, such as Julian Cole & Stein (Los Angeles), MedVenture (San Francisco), and Menlo Ventures (Menlo Park, California), that invest in ventures primarily in California. Similarly, Boston is well endowed with venture capital firms that invest primarily in Boston and the surrounding area.

What about the other 90% of the land mass in the United States? Who invests in entrepreneurial companies in those areas, especially those in traditionally low tech, low growth regions?

Investing in Companies in Low-tech, Low-growth Regions

With less than 10% of all venture dollars raised going to businesses based in the Midwest, some venture capital companies have begun to concentrate on this particular market niche, thereby specializing by region, rather than by industry. One such venture capital firm is Marquette Ventures of Chicago, which was formed in 1987 when it raised $80 million from investors. Although its first two investments were specialty retailers from other regions (that's their "liberal exception policy"), an investment in Sports Authority, Inc., a sporting goods retailer based in Fort Lauderdale, and an investment in BizMart, a discount retailer of office supplies and furniture based in Arlington, Texas, the bulk of the $80 million is earmarked for Midwest companies, with the majority going to early-stage ventures.

Another regional investor in the same general location is Primus Venture Partners of Cleveland, Ohio. A majority of its investments have been in its home state of Ohio. For example, Primus's investments have included Ohio Business Machines (Cleveland), which distributes office equipment; Amerestate, Inc. (Cincinatti), a publisher of information on real estate transactions; and STERIS Corp. (Cleveland), a developer of sterilizers for the medical market.

Similar to Primus Venture Partners in its investment policy is Massey Burch, of Nashville, Tennessee, which is one of the oldest and largest venture capital firms in the country. Massey Burch has invested a sizable portion of its more than $100 million in paid in capital to growth companies in the Southeast. They have invested strongly, and wisely, in several companies in their own home town of Nashville, some of which have gone public, such as: Automotive Franchise Corp., which is involved in automotive service centers; Corrections Corp. of America, a private prison management company; Surgical Care Affiliates, which operates ambulatory surgical centers; and Southlife Holding Co., a life insurance holding company.

A smaller venture capital firm, which has concentrated on a specific region, is the Iowa Venture Capital Fund, a Cedar Rapids-based firm started by David R. Schroder in 1985. The firm's investments, which are generally in the range of $250,000 to $500,000, have included companies that have developed a connector used to insulate concrete walls and a fuel additive made from corn. One of the biggest problems faced by this venture capital firm is that it invests almost exclusively in seed and start-up companies in Iowa; that limits the ability of the entrepreneurial companies in which they have invested to secure additional rounds of financing. As noted earlier, venture investors often invest in companies in their region. With the bulk of the major venture capital firms located in New York, Boston, and San Francisco, it makes it difficult for companies initially backed by the Iowa Venture Capital Fund to secure later-stage funding from the more established venture capital firms.

Regional Economic Development

Venture capital firms that specialize by region often make a significant contribution to the economic development of that particular region. An extreme example is that of Kentucky Highlands Investment Corp., a small private non-profit venture fund that has attempted to nurture small business development in the poverty-ridden areas of the Appalachian Mountains. Kentucky Highlands has avoided the glamour investments in favor of small manufacturers and agricultural businesses. In so doing, this twenty-one-year-old venture capital firm has managed to generate acceptable returns for its investors while providing significant economic benefits to the region in which it invests. Kentucky Highlands, which invests in new ventures (it invested in a total of nineteen new ventures through 1989), has been responsible for the creation of 1,800 jobs, which are continuing to be created at the rate of 200 per year.

A characteristic investment of Kentucky Highlands was in a start-up plastics molding plant, started by Jack O. Touratsos, in Mt. Vernon, Kentucky.

Despite its low-tech nature, the company has been a real success story; it has generated 400 jobs, spun off three new machine shops, and been responsible for the significant success of its suppliers. When the company was sold recently, Kentucky Highlands made $3 million on the deal.

SPECIALIZATION BY INDUSTRY

A second trend in specialization has been by industry, either in high-or low-tech products. For example, Plant Resources Venture Fund, a Cambridge, Massachusetts, based venture capital firm, limits its investments to bioscience companies involved in agriculture, food, waste treatment, and health care. As such, they have recently invested in such companies as The Aqua Group (Tampa, Florida), which sells and distributes aquaculture-based seafood; AgriTech Systems, Inc. (Portland, Maine), a leading supplier of diagnostic kits for detection of disease in poultry, swine, cattle, and horses; and Sunseeds Genetics, Inc. (Hollister, California), a developer of improved vegetable seeds.

Computers and Office Automation

In recent years, approximately 30% to 40% of the *Inc.* 100 companies (the fastest growing small public companies in this country) have been in computers and related industries. More impressive than that is that over a dozen start-up companies in the computer industry have attained *Fortune* 500 status over the past twenty years. Such success stories, which include Intel, Apple, Tandem, Compaq, and Sun Microsystems, have been more than companies; they've been the emergence of industries. This has enhanced the impact that the computer industry has had on the venture capital industry.

The Decline of Investments in Computer Hardware.   The statistics just cited deal generally with ventures that were originally funded more than five years ago and have since gone public. More recently, the situation has changed dramatically. This will become evident in the *Inc.* 100 list for 1993 and beyond, since there is a lag of five years or so between the time that a company raises venture capital and the time it goes public. According to *Venture Economics*, there has been a steady decline in venture capital investments in the computer hardware industry, from 33% of the total capital invested in 1983 to 13% in 1988. This decline has continued over the past year. According to *Technologic Computer Letter*, a newsletter of the computer and electronic equipment industry, venture capital investments in this industry declined by more than 10% from 1988 to 1989.

Why has that occurred? Several case examples will illustrate this. Consider Symbolics, Inc., a Cambridge, Massachusetts, based manufacturer of artificial intelligence computers, which went public in 1984 at $6 per share. By 1986, the stock price increased to more than $15. The last three years, however, have been marked by losses and a restructuring. Consequently, the stock dropped to below $3 per share.

Perhaps the best recent example of companies in this industry not reaching their expected potential involves the formation of Stardent, a manufacturer of graphics workstations for scientists and engineers. Stardent is the result of the merger of two of the best financed, yet most disappointing, computer start-ups in history, Ardent Computer Corp., which, thanks in part to the backing of Kubota, Ltd. (Japan), raised $108 million, and its former rival, Steller Computer, Inc., which raised $60 million. A public offering for Stardent may still be far away.

There are several reasons for the declining level of investments in computer hardware. One problem in the computer hardware industry is that most of the niches are already filled; moreover, those niches that remain will probably not offer the explosive growth opportunities of such one-time early-stage niche players as Apple, Microsoft, or Compaq. In addition, the life-span of products has shortened dramatically. Consequently, computer companies are replacing product lines every one to two years, rather than every four to five years, as they had previously done.

Perhaps the biggest concern among venture capitalists is the risk and return balance of such investments. As was seen with Ardent Computer and with Stellar Computer, the start-up capital could be enormous—$20 million to $100 million or more. Once that's been invested, you don't even know if there will be a product; even if the company develops a product, the market can be uncertain and the competition can be fierce.

What's NeXT?   One of the biggest question marks in the computer industry is Steve Jobs's latest venture, NeXT, Inc. The company is well capitalized. Early-stage investment came from Jobs ($7 million), from Stanford University ($658,000), and from H. Ross Perot ($20 million). More recently, Canon, Inc., invested $100 million for 16% of the company (thus, giving NeXT a valuation of $625 million before it sold its first unit). Yet, at a meeting of a Technologic Partners Conference in 1988, a majority of the high-tech entrepreneurs and investors who were polled predicted that the company would not reach the $$\frac{1}{2}$$ billion mark in sales. It may be difficult to dispute the logic of their forecast; however, I certainly would not want to bet against the intellect, the vision, and the motivation of Jobs.

Health Care and Biotechnology

The health care and biotechnology areas have recently become prominent growth industries, as evidenced by the fact that 15% to 25% of the *Inc.* 100 companies have been in these areas over the last few years.

Health Care.   Recently, we have witnessed the tremendous growth of such health care procedures as electronic shock wave lithotripsy (ESWL) (for breaking up kidney stones), magnetic resonance imaging (MRI), cardiac catherization, coronary arteriography, phototherapy, and others. Consequently, several venture capital firms have been eager to invest in companies in such sectors of the health care industry as outpatient clinics, health maintenance, and medical diagnostics. This has been prompted by the successes of several companies in the health care field that have recently gone public.

Home Health Care.   One notable area of growth in health care and delivery has been in home health care, which has doubled in size over the last five years and, according to Frost & Sullivan, is expected to double again over the next five years. Home respiratory care is currently a $450 million industry that should generate nearly $900 million in 1993. The same growth rate is expected for diagnostic cardiac units (which is now a $70 million business), intravenous infusion systems (currently $26 million), and breathing monitors (currently $15 million).

One of the more interesting companies in this sector is MEDphone Corp. (Paramus, New Jersey), which manufactures a phone-linked computer system that enables health care professionals to make an "electronic house call." The cost to the patient is around $7,500 to purchase the unit and $300 to $500 per month to lease. The device, which is automatically connected via a telephone to a hospital or a physician's office, has electrodes that can be hooked to a patient's chest. Thus, the health professional can deliver an electronic volt directly to a patient over the telephone line. MEDphone is now developing a cellular telephone model that will be marketed to police, fire, and ambulance services.

Several other companies have developed (or are currently developing) similar home health care services. For example, MiniMed Technologies (Sylmar, California) and Infusaid, Inc. (Boston), will be marketing small insulin pumps that can be surgically implanted in patients and that dispense insulin in a controlled manner throughout the day. Tokos Medical Corp., which recently went public, has a product called Term Guard, which allows for home monitoring of uterine activity for pregnant women in danger of a premature delivery; the product costs the patient $75 a day, as compared to the $600 a day cost for monitoring in a hospital. Buddy Systems, Inc. (Northbrook, Illinois), rents computer consoles to postsurgical patients, at a cost of $30 a day, that monitor vital signs and transmit the information to the hospital via a telephone. All these companies provide products that allow patients to receive quality care at home, generally at a much lower cost than a typical hospital stay.

In the last few years, a number of small public companies in the health care field, which were founded in the early 1980s and are now generating more than $20 million in revenues, typify the companies in which venture capitalists like to make early-stage investments. They include New England Critical Care, Inc. (Marborough, Massachusetts), which is involved in home health care; HealthCare Compare Corp. (Downers Grove, Illinois), a medical care cost management company; H.M.S.S. (Houston, Texas), a home intravenous treatment company; Redicare (Newport Beach, California), an operator of outpatient medical centers; and HealthSouth Rehabilitation (Birmingham, Alabama), a company that develops and operates rehabilitation centers and has grown at a compounded annual rate of over 100% from 1985 to 1989.

Of course, not all ventures have achieved their expected level of success. An example is Diasonics, a medical imaging company, that manufactures nuclear magnetic resonance (NMR) machines, which was launched with the assistance of F. Eberstadt & Co., Hambrecht & Quist, and L. F. Rothschild Unterberg and Towbin. These venture capital firms paid approximately $1 per share for 800,000 shares of the company. The company went public in 1983 for $22 a share, raising over $100 million in the process. Within a few years, however, Diasonics ran into trouble and lost most of its value.

Nonetheless, the early successes of such companies in the health care field as mentioned above has prompted many venture capitalists to concentrate on that area. Due to the technical nature of the industry, several venture capital firms have become specialists in this industry—or in just one portion of this industry. For example, CW Group, a New York-based venture capital firm, specializes in health care and biological sciences. CW recently invested in Athena Neurosciences, Inc. (San Carlos, California), which is developing diagnostics and therapeutics for Alzheimer's disease and other disorders of the central nervous system, and National Rehabilitation Centers (Nashville, Tennessee), an operator of rehabilitation centers.

Similarly, American Health Capital Ventures, of Brentwood, Tennessee, specializes in emerging health care service companies. They have recently made investments in Integrated Health Services, Inc. (Hunt Valley, Maryland), which provides health services for the elderly; Russ Pharmaceuticals (Birmingham, Alabama), which formulates and markets branded generic pharmaceuticals; and Flying Nurses, Inc. (Brownsville, Texas), a supplemental nurse staffing company that provides its services to acute care hospitals. Also similar to the CW Group is Montgomery Medical Ventures, a San Francisco-based venture capital firm specializing in health care, which has invested in such companies as Applied Immune Sciences, which is developing treatments for immune-related disorders; and HiMedics, a drug delivery system company.

Biotechnology.   In the early 1980s, biotechnology was one of the glamour industries among private and public investors. Consider, for example, venture capitalists David and Isaac Blech, who have funded about a half-dozen biotech companies. Their biggest success among their biotech investments has been an investment in Genetic Systems of Seattle, a pioneer in the application of antibodies. In addition to the Blech's investment in the company, they helped raise $48.5 million in subsequent limited partnerships, private placements, and public offerings. Genetic Systems went public in 1981 for $1.25 per share. Five years later, Bristol Myers purchased the company for stock worth $10.50 per share, netting the Blech brothers $30 million.

In the early 1980s, biotech stocks also became "hot issues" on Wall Street. Genentech is the best known success story in this industry. On the day the company went public on October 14, 1980, its stock soared from an IPO price of $35 to $89. Soon, companies like Cetus, Biogen, Amgen, and Centocor were seen as attractive investment opportunities by public investors.

Shortly thereafter, there was a major consolidation in the biotechnology industry, with dozens of companies being acquired by larger chemical and pharmaceutical companies, for example, Genetic Systems by Bristol Myers, Hybritech by Eli Lilly & Co., and DNAX Research Institute by Schering-Plough. Many more failed to live up to their potential. Liposome Co., of Princeton, New Jersey, for example, was launched in 1981 to develop an effective drug delivery system using liposomes, which are water-filled, fatty membranes. The company, however, has spent $65 million and has not yet developed a marketable product.

The Current Situation in Biotechnology.   Today, there are about 1,100 companies in the biotech industry. According to a recent study by Ernst & Young, less than 25% of these companies are profitable. Most of them do not even have a product yet.

There is, however, tremendous promise in this industry. Today, sales of biotech-based drugs are nearly $1 billion; this should triple within the next 5 years. Yet the public sentiment has not been supportive of this industry, probably because of promises of too much, too soon. As noted recently by James Swartz, general partner of Accel Partners, a Princeton, New Jersey, based venture capital firm that has invested in this industry,

> "it took more than a decade before the transistor was embodied into any significant commercial product and another decade before transistor based circuits were applied to computers. Drugs and pharmaceuticals, even the non-biotech types, have a development cycle of ten to fifteen years."[6]

Consequently, venture capitalists, who, by nature, maintain a long-term perspective on their investments, have recently made significant investments in biotechnology. For example, Biosource Genetics Corp. of Vacaville, California, founded in 1987, creates complex chemicals through genetic engineering. Its first product is melanin, the pigment that gives human skin its color. The product has tremendous commercial applications in that it could be used in sunscreens to provide more effective protection against skin cancer. Biosource was backed by two scientists—venture capitalists, Helen Leong and David Berliner, who had earlier helped launch Advanced Polymer Systems of Redwood City, California.

One thing is clear about the newer biotech companies, as compared to those launched seven to ten years ago. Unlike the early 1980s, when start-up and early stage biotechnology companies were extremely diversified (for example, Cetus Corp. in its early years), the successful new biotech companies are narrowly focused. Applied Microbiology, Inc. (Brooklyn, New York), for example, which has focused on just two products, has had corporate sponsorship

---

[6]See Udayan Gupta, "Watching and Waiting," *Wall Street Journal,* November 13, 1989, p. R32.

from such American pharmaceutical giants as Pfizer and Merck. Applied Microbiology's alliance with Pfizer has enabled the smaller venture to develop a mouthwash with an antibacterial agent to help prevent and treat gum disease, which Pfizer will market.

The specialized nature of biotech companies has prompted many venture capital firms to become more specialized themselves. For example, Domain Associates, a $100 million venture capital firm based in Princeton, New Jersey, concentrates on commercial applications of molecular engineering. As such, they have invested in several dozen biotechnology companies, many of which have gone public over the last few years [for example, Amgen (Thousand Oaks, California), Applied Biosystems (Foster City, California), Genetic Systems Corp. (Seattle, Washington), Integrated Genetics (Framingham, Massachusetts), Immunex (Seattle, Washington), Genzyme (Boston), and Synergen (Boulder, Colorado)].

There is an important point related to the "cyclicality" of this industry. In industries such as biotechnology, which can quickly come into and go out of favor, timing is critical when it comes to raising capital. As noted by Ronald Cape, co-founder of Cetus Corp., "The time to take hors d'oeuvres is when they're passing them around."[7]

Telecommunications

The breakup of AT&T in 1984 and the dramatic growth of such sectors of the telecommunications industry as cellular communications and communications networks have been responsible for scores of successful companies in this industry. This is evidenced by recent IPOs of such emerging companies in the areas of cellular telephone systems, for example, Cellular Communications, Inc., a New York-based company with revenues of over $50 million in 1988; communications equipment for workstations, for example, Microcom, Inc., a comparably sized Norwood, Massachusetts, based company; multifunction communication networks, for example, Network Equipment Technologies, a $140 million Redwood, California, based business that was ranked number 1 on the 1990 *Inc.* 100 list, due to its 400% growth rate from 1985 to 1989; and pay telephones, for example, Intellicall, based in Carrolton, Texas. Each of these companies has been founded in the past ten years and is typical of the large number of telecommunications companies included in the *Inc.* 100.

Among privately held companies at an earlier stage of development, Intermedia Communications Inc., a three-year-old Tampa, Florida, based telecommunications company, which provides corporate customers with an alternative way to connect to long-distance carriers, received early-stage funding from Alan Patricof Associates (New York, New York), among others. The company has already set up fiber-optic networks throughout the state of Florida.

Specialization Among Venture Capital Firms.   Such successes have

[7]See Gary Slutsker, "Cloning Profits," *Forbes*, January 9, 1989, p. 152.

prompted several venture capital firms to invest in telecommunications companies; a few venture capital firms have become so specialized that they invest only in this industry. One such example is Communications Ventures, a venture capital firm in Menlo Park, California, which was started in 1987. The firm tends to limit its investments to telecommunications companies in the seed and start-up stages. Communications Ventures generally invests approximately $500,000 in such ventures, as it did with its recent investment in Pair Gain Technologies, Inc., a Torrance, California, based company that has created specialized digital communication lines for telephone companies.

Similarly, Accel Partners, of Princeton, New Jersey, has recently established a fund, Accel Telecommunications, that invests exclusively in such ventures. One such investment is International TeleManagement Corp., of Falls Church, Virginia, a provider of telecommunication system integration and facilities management services for mid-size companies and government agencies. Accel has had a very strong involvement in the telecommunications area for several years, as evidenced by their investments in over a dozen companies, including Ungermann-Bass, Vitalink, and Network Equipment Technologies.

Environmental Concerns

Another recent trend in venture capital investing has been in the area of environmental waste management, which has attracted over $100 million in venture funding over the last two years. Such entrepreneurial companies often have greater growth prospects and offer more controlled risks than other types of companies.

Demand for environmental products and services has grown as governmental regulations have become stricter. Consequently, venture capital firms have been eager to take part in the growth of these companies. For example, Burr Egan Deleage & Co. recently invested in Galson Remediation Corp., a Syracuse, New York, based company that has a patented chemical treatment technology to clean up dioxins and PCBs, which offers tremendous advantages to the alternative method of incineration. Similarly, In-Process Technologies, Inc., of Sunnyvale, California, a developer of a patented industrial waste-processing system that converts toxic gases to nontoxic materials, has received approximately $2 million in venture capital funding.

Some venture capitalists are cautious of investments in these areas, partly because of their lack of knowledge or experience in this industry and partly because of regulatory concerns. It's always dangerous to invest in an industry in which demand depends on government regulation; just as regulation has promoted the growth of environmental and waste management companies, so could regulatory changes negatively affect the long-term outlook for this industry.

Retailing

Some Success Stories in Retailing.   Retailing and consumer companies have become attractive investments since they tend to go from start-up to exit much more rapidly and with much less capital than do technology companies.

Expansion in the retail area can be done very efficiently, which is especially the case if retail stores work out attractive arrangements with the major national mall operators, such as the Rouse Company and DeBartollo. For example, The Limited's massive expansion in major malls over the past decade has not only made Leslie Wexner, its founder, a multibillionnaire, but it has served as the role model for other smaller retail stores looking to expand. It seems as though every upstart retailer wants to be "the next Limited" or "the next Gap" or "the next Toys 'R' Us." Several are, to some extent, already on their way, as is evidenced by Costco Wholesale Corp. (Kirkland, Washington), Price Club (San Diego, California), Office Depot (Boca Raton, Florida), Egghead, Inc. (Bothell, Washington), and One Price Clothing Stores (Duncan, South Carolina).

Costco, for example, which was founded in 1983, was initially capitalized with $7.5 million in venture capital; subsequently, it raised more than $200 million in private and public debt and equity. Costco's sales in its first full year of operation (1984) were comparable to that of Compaq Computer's incredible $111 million; Costco generated $101 million from seven stores. Within two years, Costco was a $\frac{3}{4}$ billion company with twenty-two stores. By 1988, its fifth year of operation, the company had more than $2 billion in sales from forty-three stores (and it had $3 billion in sales in 1989), making its growth pattern even more impressive than Compaq, Sun Microsystems, Apollo Computer, Businessland, Reebok, or any other company in history, be it high tech or low tech.

IPOs of Specialty Retailers.   A feature that makes specialty retailing an extremely attractive investment opportunity for venture capitalists is that several specialty retailers have recently gone public. For example, Egghead, Inc., of Bothell, Washington, went public four years after opening its first computer software retail store in 1984. During that time, it grew from a $5 million company to a $200 million company. Before its IPO, it had received venture capital funding from Citibank, Mellon Bank, Prudential Venture Capital, and T. Rowe Price Threshold Fund.

Belts and Bats.   The early success stories of specialty retailing companies have prompted U.S. Venture Partners, a venture capital firm in Menlo Park, California, to invest in The Icing, Inc., an Enfield, Connecticut, based upscale women's accessories store chain. Similarly, Bain Venture Capital, of Boston (as well as Bessemer Venture Partners, William Blair Venture Partners, Phillips-Smith Specialty Retail Group, Marquette Venture Partners, Security Pacific Capital Corp., and others) recently invested in The Sports Authority, a Fort Lauderdale, Florida, based chain of sporting goods stores.

The Sports Authority, which is one of the hottest retailing chains in the country, is a textbook example of how to properly launch a start-up. The company was started by Jack Smith, former chief operating officer of Herman's Inc., a national sporting goods chain. In December 1986, Smith was approached by venture capitalists who wanted to create a chain of warehouse-style sporting goods stores. Smith was interested in such a venture, but insisted that the company have more of an upscale, rather than a warehouse, image, and that it attempt to compete on selection, rather than on price. Such a focus, plus the experience of Smith and his quality management team, was enough to entice several venture capital firms to invest a total of $18 million in this venture over two early rounds of financing.

Another good example in the sporting goods industry is SportsTown, Inc., a discount sporting goods store based in Atlanta, founded in March 1987 by Tom Haas. Almost immediately, the company raised $7 million from a group of investors. This was followed by another $20 million within one year. At a time when funding for start-ups is so scarce, how did Haas "get his foot in the door"? He started out by doing everything right; he had a strong background in the field, a solid management team, and a business plan. In addition, Haas cultivated the necessary contacts to secure the financing. As he notes,

> "Anyone who has been in business for a few years winds up having friends in the business community. And some of them have ties to the capital markets. . . . Every time we visited a venture group, the circle widened because they had two or three people they wanted us to talk to."[8]

As a counterexample, Robert McNulty (who had earlier started HomeClub, which was bought by Zayre for $151 million in 1986) was far less successful in his venture into discount sporting goods. The investors in his SportsClub venture, which followed on the heels of HomeClub, lost $35 million on this venture after it filed for bankruptcy in 1988 and, subsequently, liquidated its assets.

Office Products.   One of the high-growth areas in specialty retailing is in office products, an industry that, including office furniture and computers as well as office supplies, generates over $100 billion annually in retail sales. There are three new players in this field, each of which is relatively new and has gone public over the last two years: Office Depot, of Boca Raton, Florida, which has stores throughout the south; Office Club, of Concord, California, which has stores throughout the West Coast; and Staples, of Newton, Massachusetts, which has stores in the Northeast. If their growth continues as expected, they will soon be closing in on one another's turf.

Staples, started in 1986, is the pioneer in the industry. It received its initial venture capital infusion from Adler & Co. and Bain Capital. All three of these office products companies, which generate a very appealing $450 to $500 per square foot in sales, were seen as relatively "safe" venture investments.

The growth of these companies is certainly startling. For example, Office Depot was started in 1986. In that year, the company generated $1.9 million in sales. It received its first round of funding (from such notable investors as Joe Pagano and Alan Patricof, as well as from Chemical Venture Partners, First Century Partners, and Oak Investment Partners, among others) in 1987 and

---

[8]See *Success*, January–February 1989, p. 53.

realized sales of $33 million in that year. The company went public in 1988, in a year in which sales quadrupled to $132 million. As a comparison, its chief rival in the southeast, WORKplace (St. Petersburg, Florida), which is a phenomenal success story itself, grew by twenty-fold over a two-year period, from a $2 million company in 1986 (comparable to Office Depot) to a $40 million company in 1988 (one-third the size of Office Depot).

Venture Capital Firms Investing in Retailing.   Several venture capital firms have begun to invest exclusively in retailing, with specialty retailing being a main focus of their investments. For example, the Phillips-Smith Specialty Retail Group in Dallas, a firm capitalized with about $20 million, has invested in BizMart, Inc., a chain of discount office product stores based in Arlington, Texas; STOR, a retailer of European furniture, which has recently gone public; Bookstop, an Austin-based "mega" bookstore; Festivities, a party items retailer; A Pea in the Pod, a retailer of high fashion maternity apparel; and The Sports Authority, a Fort Lauderdale, Florida, based sporting goods retailer. They have also invested in LBOs such as Revco, one of the nation's largest drug store chains. Unfortunately, Revco, which was in Chapter 11 bankruptcy in 1988, has not been as successful an investment as their other ones.

The two founders of this venture capital firm have excellent experience in the growth of retail stores. Donald J. Phillips and Cece Smith, formerly executives of Pearle Health Services, Inc., of Dallas, were largely responsible for Pearle's growth from 80 stores to 1,250 stores, at which time Pearle was purchased for $400 million by Grand Metropolitan Plc.

Franchising

Like retailing, which can grow dramatically as new stores open up nationwide, franchising has become a tremendous growth opportunity for the franchisors, which are the developers of the product or service concept, and for the franchisees, which operate the individual franchise units or locations; they pay royalties to the franchisors for marketing and technical support and for the use of their trade name.

Franchises represent a fairly low risk opportunity; only 3% of new franchises fail within their first year and only 5% fail within their eighth year. Consequently, venture capitalists have been interested in putting money into this $200 billion industry. They do so generally by investing in the franchisor.

Venture Capitalists Investing in Franchise Operations.   Allied Capital, of Washington, D.C., for example, one of the most established venture capital firms in this country, has recently invested in Petland, a Chillicothe, Ohio, based pet store franchise; Everything Yogurt, a Staten Island, New York, based frozen yogurt franchise; and the Great Frame Up, a do-it-yourself frame store franchise.

Profitable franchise operations have often been successful in raising venture capital from several sources. For example, Gymboree Corp., of Burlingame,

California, which provides developmental play programs for infants, toddlers, preschool children, and parents, has been funded by Walden Investors, U.S. Venture Partners, Chemical Venture Capital Association, and Aeneas Venture Capital Corp.

"Zoors" and "Zees."   Both the franchisors, which total over 2,000 in the United States, and the franchisees, which total nearly 400,000, have benefited from venture capital investments. For the franchisor, the returns can be extraordinary, as evidenced by the explosive growth of Domino's Pizza, Subway, and TCBY.

For the franchisee, it works a little differently. Franchisees are generally financed either through the franchisee's personal funds or through collateralized loans from the franchisor and/or bank. An individual franchisee is generally not an appropriate venture capital investment. However, many franchisors sell multiple units to investor groups, which may, therefore, control all franchise units in a state or city or county. For example, more than 24% of the NutriSystem franchises are owned by investor groups, which assemble a management team to run the business.

SPECIALIZATION BY STAGE OF DEVELOPMENT

Another trend in specialization has been in the stage of development of the venture being funded. Some venture capital firms invest solely or primarily in early-stage ventures, others invest in turnaround situations, while still others invest in leveraged buyouts (LPOs). For example, AMEV Venture Management of New York invests exclusively in late-stage and LBO deals. To illustrate, AMEV participated in the expansion financing of California Cafe Restaurant Corp., a San Francisco-based restaurant chain, as well as in the LBO of the Guarantee Products Division of DiGiorgio Corp. of City of Industry, California, which manufactures aluminum windows and doors.

One example of a company that does not follow this rule of specialization is Hambrecht & Quist of San Francisco. Hambrecht & Quist provides early-stage funding and then nurtures the company as it grows. Eventually, they will do the underwriting to bring the company public if it is appropriate to do so. For example, Hambrecht and Quist was an early-stage investor in Diasonics, which they eventually brought public in 1983. Moreover, when Diasonics had problems in 1984, Hambrecht & Quist got involved in the turnaround situation. However, as mentioned earlier, Hambrecht & Quist is one of the few exceptions. Most venture capital firms have become more specialized in their investment practices.

Seed Capital

In 1988, after just two phone calls, Judith L. Estrin and William N. Carrico raised $5 million in seed capital for their new venture, Network Computing Devices, Inc., of Mountain View, California. Of course, such a story will occur on occasion. However, the more likely story is the one of the entrepreneur who will spend one or two years in frustrating meetings with over one dozen venture capitalists, only to find that seed capital is more difficult to obtain than the entrepreneur had ever imagined. This is especially true for first-time and solo entrepreneurs, particularly if they have limited management experience. These entrepreneurs generally find that the quest for seed capital is exceedingly time consuming, and it usually leads to small amounts of capital, typically under $500,000.

Why, then, did Estrin and Carrico succeed in their search for seed capital with seemingly little effort? It was largely a result of their previous successful telecommunications start-up, Bridge Communications, Inc., which merged in 1987 with 3 Com Corp. Entrepreneurs in search of seed capital must recognize that management experience, especially in a related industry, is often a pre-requisite for securing funding. Thus, Estrin and Carrico's efforts were not in tracking down venture capitalists, but rather in building an earlier successful business.

Less Money Going into Seed Capital.   The amount invested just in seed capital, although having more than doubled over the last ten years, represents only 2% of the total of venture capital investments. Investors have been more attracted to later-stage investments, which offer quicker, safer returns. Due to declining returns realized by many venture capital firms over the past five years, there is increasing pressure for venture capital managers to limit their portfolios to lower-risk, quicker-return investments.

> Investors have been more attracted to later-stage investments, which offer quicker, safer returns.

Another problem facing entrepreneurs in search of seed capital is the lack of experienced professionals to assist them. Although the number of venture capital professionals has increased as the venture capital pool has expanded, this has not been the case for venture capitalists experienced in seed deals.

Risk and Return for Seed Investments.   Seed investments have the greatest potential returns, as was the case for Sevin Rosen Management's high-payoff investments in Lotus Development and Compaq Computer. However, to go along with the high potential returns of seed investments are significant risks, as was the case with Sevin Rosen's investment in Osborne Computer, which failed.

Generally, seed capitalists look for 50% to 100% higher returns on their investments than would the standard venture capital company. Moreover, funding is generally limited to $500,000 and, in many cases, much less. Therefore, "seed deals" represent a unique investment situation.

Some Successful Venture Capital Firms Still Target Early-Stage Ventures. Even in a period marked by specialization, especially in such low-tech industries as retailing and in later-stage investments and LBOs, some venture capital firms have still maintained a strategy of early-stage investments in glamour companies, with heavy emphasis in computers and electronics. This has been the strategy of Technology Venture Investors (TVI), a Menlo Park, California, based venture capital firm that, as its name implies, invests a sizable portion of its portfolio in early-stage, West Coast technology companies.

For example, in 1982, TVI invested $3 million for a 35% ownership position in Nellcor, which was then a one-year-old Hayward, California, based manufacturer of patient monitoring systems. Earlier, Nellcor raised $75,000 through self-funding and $1 million through private sources. In 1983, Nellcor's first product, the N-100, a pulse oximeter that monitors oxygen in a patient's arterial blood during surgery, was brought to market. Today, the N-100 is found in more than half the 7,000 hospitals in this country, which has resulted in Nellcor capturing about 70% of this $130 million industry, while growing at a compounded annual growth rate of over 160% from 1984 to 1988.

TVI has had other success stories over the past decade. With investments in Microsoft, which returned $100 million at the time of its IPO on TVI's $1 million investment in 1981, Sun Microsystems, and Linear Technology, it seems like TVI's strategy of investing in early-stage technology companies has paid off.

Similar to TVI in its investment philosophy is Alpha Partners, of Menlo Park, California, which has targeted high-tech start-ups such as Genelabs, which develops diagnostic and therapeutic biotechnology products; Mirus Corp., a manufacturer of computer hardware for 35mm slide production; and Analog Design Tools, a computer-aided engineering company. Similarly, Advanced Technology Ventures of Boston has invested primarily in high-tech start-ups such as VLSI Technology, which provides products and services for the design of VLSI circuits; Valid Logic Systems, a maker of computer-aided engineering systems; and Mosaic Systems, a manufacturer of electronically programmable interconnection devices.

Another example is Onset, a Silicon Valley-based venture capital firm that targets seed or start-up investments. Onset, like many of these other small "seed capital firms," affiliates itself with such major venture capital firms as Kleiner Perkins Caufield & Byers, Mayfield Fund, and New Enterprise Associates to ensure that additional funding will be available to the start-up companies when it is needed.

Role of the Smaller Venture Capital Firms.   For the entrepreneur in search of seed funding, the money often comes from the smaller funds that specialize in smaller investments to companies at earlier stages of development. There are a few large firms that devote a considerable portion of their portfolio to seed and start-up funding, for example, Aeneas Venture Corp. (Boston), New Enterprise Associates (Baltimore, Maryland), Clinton Capital Corp. (New York, New York), Merrill, Pickard, Anderson & Eyre (Palo Alto, California), and 3i Corp.

(Investors in Industry) (Boston). However, the trend has been for *some* of the smaller, specialized funds, those that invest less than $10 million per year, to have either a majority, or even *all*, of their portfolio in seed and start-up investments. They are, simply, in a better position to service start-ups than are the larger venture capital firms. Such smaller firms would include, in addition to TVI, Alpha Partners, and Onset (mentioned above), Technology Partners (Belvedere, California), Mohr, Davidow Ventures (Menlo Park, California), CommTech International Management Corp. (Menlo Park, California), Connecticut Seed Ventures (Avon, Connecticut), MedCorp Development Fund (Newport Beach, California), Zero Stage Capital (Cambridge, Massachusetts), Enterprise Partners (Newport Beach, California), Abacus Ventures (Greenwich, Connecticut), Capform Partners (Palo Alto, California), and Draper Associates (Menlo Park, California).[9]

As an example, Technology Partners, a venture capital firm managed by Bill Hart with about $20 million in paid in capital, has invested primarily in seed or start-up companies. The firm, which is probably best known for its investment in Amiga Computer, Inc., which increased four and a half fold in six months at the time Amiga was purchased by Commodore International, targets high-tech industries such as computers, telecommunications, and health care. Hart fits the mold of the classic venture capitalists who were interested in helping build companies from scratch. For example, after recently investing a total of $900,000, in two rounds, one of $300,000 and the other of $600,000 (this is a typical size investment of Technology Partners), in Tecxel Corp., a San Francisco-based software systems company, Hart met with the management of the company weekly to assist them with their strategy.

Feeder Funds.   One trend that has developed in seed capital is the concept of *feeder funds*, small venture capital firms that invest in start-ups, partly from capital raised from larger venture capital companies. The idea is that the large venture capital firms, which cannot afford to spend the countless hours assisting scientists with merely ideas launch a company, are very willing to invest in such seed deals, provided that a smaller feeder fund is working closely with the entrepreneur or entrepreneurial team. In return for the small investment in the early-stage venture, the large venture capital firms gets a "window" on early-stage deals that might make good investments at a later stage.

Avalon Ventures, a small San Diego-based feeder fund, managed by Kevin J. Kinsella, invests solely in seed ventures. This often involves recruiting scientists and management teams to build the companies. This was the case with NeoRx, a Seattle-based biotechnology company to which Kinsella lured thirteen scientists from the National Cancer Institute. Avalon has also invested in Athena Neurosciences (San Carlos, California), which is developing diagnostics and therapeutics for disorders of the central nervous system; FASTech (Waltham, Massachusetts),

---

[9]As you can see from this short list, start-up venture capital investors, which often fund early-stage high-tech ventures, are primarily located in the Silicon Valley area.

a developer of factory automation software; and Sonrisa Systems (Los Angeles), a maker of orthodontic diagnostic and monitoring equipment.

How have Avalon's investments performed? NeoRx went public in 1988, at a market capitalization of nearly $100 million. And an earlier investment in Network Switching Systems, Inc., an Andover, Massachusetts, based telecommunications company, resulted in a fortyfold return for Avalon. Because of Avalon's significant time involvement with the ventures in which they invest, it commands a premium return. Unlike most venture capital firms, which keep 20% to 25% of the profits, with the balance going to the limited partners who invest in the fund, Avalon has a 50/50 split with its investors, due to the significant time commitment the venture capital firm devotes to each company in which it invests.

Mezzanine Financing

Mezzanine (or *bridge*) financing is becoming an increasingly popular investment vehicle. It is designed for companies in the intermediate sales range ($5 million–$100 million in sales), which are considered intermediate-risk ventures; that is, they are somewhere between lower-risk senior debt financing situations and higher-risk equity financing situations. Typically, this is just the case for a fairly young company that has already received early-stage financing and is likely to go public within a year. The money invested by South Atlantic Venture Capital (of Tampa, Florida) into Silk Greenhouse (also of Tampa), a high-growth retailer of silk flowers and crafts, just about a year prior to its IPO is an example of mezzanine financing. South Atlantic (and its limited partners) managed a very attractive profit at the time the company went public. Subsequent (post-IPO) investors, however, have not necessarily done too well. Despite Silk Greenhouse's repeated showing on the *Inc.* 100 listing of fast-growth small public companies (it grew by a 150% compounded annual rate over the past 5 years), some of the investors in this $55 million company have experienced a 90% decline in its stock price, from a high of $24 per share to a low of less than $2 per share.

In most cases, mezzanine financing is either a combination of subordinated debt with warrants or convertible debt. Several venture capital firms, including AMEV Capital (New York, New York) and Investors in Industry [3i] (Boston), have established funds strictly for this purpose.

Turnaround Venture Capitalists

A recent trend in venture capital has been funding turnaround ventures. This is not for the 10% to 20% of venture capital-backed companies that have already failed; rather, it is for the approximately 10% to 20% of the companies that have not grown sufficiently to meet the expectations of their investors.

Typically, venture capitalists are not structured to deal with their own failures. Thus, the turnaround venture capitalists have found a very viable and significant niche for investments and involvement that has attracted both the large, established venture capital firms, such as Allstate Venture Capital (Chicago), and the smaller firms, such as Sunbelt Holdings (Phoenix, Arizona).

For the turnaround venture capital firm, it represents a high-risk, yet potentially a high-return investment. For the entrepreneur, it will often mean surrendering his or her total equity position in the venture in exchange for a cash payout and relief from debts.

The Nature of the Turnaround Deal.   A typical turnaround deal might work like this. Venture capital firm X approaches the ABC Company, a manufacturing business, owned 75% by the founder and president and 25% by its early-stage investor, venture capital firm Y. ABC has $20 million in assets and $30 million in liabilities; thus, ABC may have no market value and a negative net worth. Venture capital firm X offers to pay the entrepreneur and venture capital firm Y $500,000 for the business and prepares an earn-out arrangement so that the entrepreneur can stay on with the business. Venture capital firm X then offers to pay the creditors $10 million in cash (33 cents on the dollar) for the payables, which is far better than they might receive in the case of liquidation.

From where does the $10 million come? Like an LBO (which will be discussed in the next section of this chapter), perhaps $1 million (10%) might come from the venture capital fund, with the balance coming from a lender, secured by the $20 million in assets, which can be used as collateral. So, for a total up-front investment of $1.5 million, the fund can own the entire business.

The returns on such investments can be high, which is quite acceptable due to the high degree of risk. Of course, there are numerous ways to finance such deals, many of which use equity kickers to sweeten the arrangement for the lenders.

Recently, Reprise Capital Corp., of Garden City, New Jersey, organized a $25 million fund for turnarounds. Reprise has already invested in Mangood, a $70 million weighing systems manufacturer, which it brought "into the black" after Mangood had lost money for three straight years. Reprise also invested in PCA International, a $150 million national portrait photographer. In both of these cases, although top management was replaced, the workers' jobs were retained.

Leveraged Buy-outs

One of the most significant and, perhaps, controversial trends in venture capital over the past few years has been toward leveraged buy-out (LBO) deals. An attractive feature of LBOs is that they have fewer risks, yet comparable returns and a shorter time for maturation (exit) than traditional venture capital investments. Consequently, they have been viewed as a desirable type of investment, especially for large capital transactions. Thus, as noted earlier, LBO investments by the Venture Capital 100 amounted to over $1.3 billion in 1988, a fivefold increase in five years, or nearly 30% of the total investments by these venture capital firms.

LBO investments by the Venture Capital 100 amounted to over $1.3 billion in 1988, a fivefold increase in five years, or nearly 30% of the total investments by these venture capital firms.

It should be noted, however, that the investment banking community has recently begun to shift away from debt financing (for example, LBOs) in favor of equity financing. This could indicate that the growth of venture capital investments in LBOs may be stifled over the coming years.

An appealing feature of LBOs for the venture capital firms funding such deals is the way that they make their money. In addition to the annual management fee (which is generally 2% to 3% of the capital raised) and the share of the profits (which is usually 20%), the venture capital firms that arrange for the LBO often charge the acquired company a fee of approximately 1% of the total selling price for arranging and negotiating the transaction; they also often charge a divestiture fee as well as a directors fee. Obviously, the larger the transaction is the more money to be made. Kohlberg, Kravis & Roberts (KKR), for example, earned $75 million on its $25 billion buyout of RJR Nabisco, which was the largest financial deal in history. KKR also earned $60 million on its LBO of Safeway Stores, when it took the formerly public company private. Interestingly, KKR recently took Safeway public *again* in what may be indicative of a trend in our country of "deleveraging."

What Are LBOs?   LBOs are a means of either taking a public company private or putting a private company in the hands of management (thus, they are often referred to as management buy-outs, MBOs) or an investment group. Such deals use the assets and/or cash flow of the target company as collateral, without paying off immediately its existing unsecured creditors. LBOs, as a result of their high degree of debt or leverage (the debt to equity ratio will often be in the range of 10:1, which is similar to a mortgage in which the homebuyer makes a 10% down payment), can often secure a 30% + compounded annual return. This will be quite attractive to investors, especially since, unlike startups, they are generally characterized by stable management and an operating history.

Exit Vehicles for LBOs.   There are three routes to exit in LBO deals:

1. Sale of the company
2. IPO; a good example is Gibson Greeting Cards, in which the investor group, Wesray (which included former treasury secretary William E. Simon), purchased the company from RCA for $81 million, with all but $1 million coming from bank loans and real estate leasebacks. When

Gibson went public, the 50% interest held by Wesray's two principals was worth $140 million.

3. Another LBO, which is similar in concept to refinancing a house.

LBOs like specialty retailing and other low-tech investments, provide a faster, less risky route to exit than traditional venture capital investments, especially those in technology.

Types of LBOs.   Although there are some common features of most LBOs, we can distinguish between two general types of LBOs that are of interest to us: public LBOs (financing for publicly held corporations) and private (or venture) LBOs (financing for privately held companies).

Public LBOs.   Public LBOs, such as the purchase of RJR Nabisco, Beatrice Foods, and Safeway Stores by Kohlberg, Kravis & Roberts (KKR), have become extremely popular over the last decade. Since 1976, when KKR began with $3 million of its own funds to invest, it has acquired three dozen companies at a cost of over $60 billion. That would make KKR, which can be equated in size to IBM, the largest privately held company as well as the largest industrial conglomerate in the country. KKR oversees this empire with just five general partners and 14 associates.

Aside from KKR, other noted experts in the public LBO area have included: Forstmann Little & Co., Hicks & Haas, Wesray, Adler & Shaykin, and such well-known "corporate raiders" as Robert Campeau (who brought shock waves to the investment community as a result of the bankruptcies of two of his recent retailing acquisitions, Federated Department Stores and Allied Stores), the Haft family (Dart Group), Asher Edelman, Carl Icahn, Irwin Jacobs, and Saul Steinberg.

From where do the LBO experts get the money to pay the multibillion price tag for such companies as RJR Nabisco, Beatrice Foods, and Macy's? Much of the financing for public LBOs was arranged by the securities firm Drexel Burnham Lambert through the public sale of "junk bonds". Thanks to the keen insight of Michael Milken of this now defunct securities firm, investors came to realize that cash flow and management provide more credit-worthy assets than do traditional forms of collateral such as plant, equipment, accounts receivable, and inventory. It is not surprising that the collapse of Drexel Burnham Lambert, as well as the collapse of Michael Milken, has coincided with the recent general shift away from debt financing.

What is a typical public LBO? Let's take, for example, Robert Campeau's buyout of Allied Stores in December 1986. The purchase price was $3.6 billion, which was a 36% premium on the stock price from the month prior to the announcement of the LBO. So the previous stockholders, as of December 1986, made a good deal of money on their stock. The concern for Campeau after having his proposed purchase price accepted by the company was how to pay for the company. Since this was an LBO, the choice was quite clear: Campeau leveraged his investment. Almost immediately, however, Campeau sold off about $2.2 billion of assets of the company to minimize the debt. The result of this transaction was that over a two-year period, from the end of 1986 to the end of 1988, Allied's sales went from $4.2 billion to $3.3 billion; however, the company, which had lost over $50 million in 1986, was profitable in 1988. Employment went from 62,000 to 27,000. (People were not necessarily terminated; they simply joined a new company.) As a direct result of the LBO, however, debt more than doubled to over $350 million. Allied, which was plagued with problems ever since the LBO, filed for bankruptcy three years after the acquisition.

Sometimes a company is so "undervalued" when it is acquired through an LBO that the company can immediately sell off parts of the company for more than its total purchase price. For example, in April 1986, KKR acquired Beatrice for $6.2 billion, which was a 45% premium over its market value a month earlier. They then sold off $7 billion of Beatrice's assets (remember, they paid only $6.2 billion for the *entire* company). Consequently, sales dropped from $11.4 billion to $4.2 billion over the next two years. However, KKR must have sold off the unprofitable divisions, because profits increased almost fourfold, to nearly $1 billion. In addition, debt rose only slightly, from $300 million to $376 million, thanks to an infusion of capital from the large sell-off of assets.

In some instances, management attempts to keep the company intact, thereby avoiding a sell-off of assets to pay off the debt. That is exactly what happened in July 1986, when the management of Macy's purchased the company through an LBO for $3.5 billion. Over the next two years (unlike the last two examples), sales *increased* from $4.7 billion to $5.7 billion. However, profits declined from a gain of $200 million to a loss of approximately the same amount. In addition, the company piled up substantial interest, increasing from $98 million in 1986 to $570 million in 1988.

Private LBOs.   Private LBOs, which will be our focus, are quite similar to public LBOs in concept, but generally on a much smaller scale. Unlike larger LBOs, they are rarely financed by the public sale of junk bonds.

As an example, in November 1986, Charles Gallagher paid $100 million (80% borrowed) for Applied Industrial Materials (AIM) Corp. of Deerfield, Illinois, a producer of minerals, metals, and carbon, which had significant losses over the previous years. Almost immediately, Gallagher sold off divisions involved in oil service and quartz, which accounted for only 10% of the company's revenues. Yet he was able to sell these divisions for $45 million. Gallagher also used cost-cutting techniques wherever appropriate and began refocusing on the profitable segments of the business. Within a year, the company had paid off its $100 million debt and was showing a profit on $400 million of sales.

There is becoming less of a distinction between private LBOs and public LBOs as venture capital companies invest larger amounts in buy-outs. Recent examples would include the $6 million investment by Sequoia Capital (Menlo Park, California) in the buy-out of Microchip Technology, Inc., from General Instruments Corp.; and Primus Capital Fund's (Cleveland, Ohio) and Warburg, Pincus's (New York, New York) $50 million investment in LiTel Telecommunications Corp., a Worthington, Ohio, based provider of voice and data transmissions. Even larger was J. H. Whitney's $1.3 billion acquisition of Prime Computer.

Pros and Cons of LBOs.   There are, of course, positive and negative features of these (and other) LBOs. Many people feel that in the case of LBOs, although investors profit, they do little to provide any value added for the nation in terms of jobs, innovation, and productivity. However, many of the companies that are purchased through LBOs were previously in weak financial positions— in some cases, destined for failure. As a result of the LBOs, they have become more efficient and have often expanded their operations, thereby providing benefit to the economy.

More Jobs.   Despite the outcry against lost jobs, at a worst case, most of the venture capital LBOs have resulted in jobs being *retained*. Often, companies are revitalized and jobs are actually created as a result of an LBO. Thus, the term management buy-out (MBO) may be more appropriate for such acquisitions because it has a more positive connotation than the term LBO. For example, one of the first well-known LBOs was Victor Kiam's acquisition of Remington Products from Sperry Corp. Remington had lost more than $30 million over the previous four years when Kiam purchased it for $25 million, with about $750,000 as a down payment (including fees). Kiam gave job security to his workers and even created more than 400 new jobs during a recessionary period in the early 1980s, while doubling its market share. Despite the company being acquired through an LBO, it is generally referred to as one of the most innovative and best managed companies in the country. Of course, Remington might be considered the exception. After all, it is the *only* LBO listed in *The 100 Best Companies to Work for in America.*[10]

Economic Gain through Increased Taxes.   LBOs can have a positive impact on the economy as a whole. Specifically, LBOs provide more taxes to the economy through capital gains of the investors who are brought out by the LBO group, who will usually pay a premium of 30% to 40% of the existing stock price for the company. Ultimately, the company will work hard to reduce its debt and to become more profitable. The economic result of that will be more income taxes.

The loans themselves resulting from the LBO can have a positive effect. These loans represent new business for banks, the interest of which is taxable for them as interest income. Furthermore, the high level of interest payable by the acquired company can be beneficial in that it forces management to be cost conscious and to constantly improve productivity. According to recent research, the operating profit margins of companies two years after they were acquired by LBOs were not only higher than they had been previously, but they

[10]R. Levering, M. Moskowitz, and M. Katz. *The 100 Best Companies to Work for in America.* New York: Plume, 1985.

were 40% higher than their industry medians. Furthermore, post-LBO employment generally stayed the same as before the deal.[11]

Neutral Impact on R&D.   It has been argued that LBOs can hurt R&D efforts. However, because LBO groups are interested in "cash cows" that have significant assets and a steady cash flow, such as department stores, grocery stores, and consumer products companies, R&D companies would not even be good candidates for LBOs.

Problems with High Debt.   The problems associated with debt in LBOs should not be understated. Debt will limit the flexibility of the venture and may be devastating during recessionary periods. Clearly, the 1980s have been characterized as a period in which we've shifted away from equity financing in favor of debt financing. The result has been that U.S. financial companies have increased their debt by nearly $1 trillion, with interest payments consuming nearly 25% of their cash flows, as compared to about 17% in the late 1970s.

This may have prompted a movement toward "de-leveraging," as evidenced by recent public offering registrations of Safeway, The Rival Co., Mr. Coffee, and several other companies that were acquired by investor groups through LBOs and subsequently planned to go public (sometimes for the second time). In effect, the investment bankers, who were advocating debt financing during the 1980s, are now saying, "Maybe we goofed ... that was then, this is now ... debt is out, equity is in."

Downsizing Versus Consolidation.   Many of the larger, public LBOs (like the ones just discussed) have been characterized by a group of investors heavily leveraging a target company, followed by the investors breaking up the company by selling off parts of it to retire the debt. Consequently, these deals have often been referred to as "bust-ups."

For smaller, private LBOs, those of less than $200 million, for example, we have seen a trend toward consolidation, rather than toward downsizing or "bust-ups." For example, recently, Dubin Clark & Co., a Greenwich, Connecticut, based LBO firm, consolidated three of its acquisitions that manufacture metal buildings into Cortec Industries. Thanks to synergies in operation, Cortec, with sales of $100 million, is among the ten largest companies in its industry in the nation.

Similarly, in 1988 the Jordan Co., a New York-based LBO firm, consolidated six of its earlier acquisitions into one corporation, Jordan Industries. Rather than attempt to sell of parts of the company, as noted by John W. Jordan II, "our goal is to buy, improve, and build."[12]

Although the large LBOs have used downsizing to meet the debt demands of their investments and to be able to exit from the investments as quickly as possible—often without an attempt to build the company, but instead to "dress

---

[11]See John Paul Newport, Jr., "LBOs: Greed, Good Business—or Both?" *Fortune*, January 2, 1989, p. 67.

[12]See Edmund L. Andrews, "LBO Firms Meet Their Maker," *Venture*, February 1989, p. 48.

it up" for another investor—the small LBOs have used consolidation as a means to enhance economies of scale, raise capital more cheaply, and develop a purposeful expansion strategy. In addition, consolidation provides a means of attracting management talent. For example, Jordan Industries was able to lure Thomas Quinn, formerly an executive with Baxter Travenol Labs, with the prospect of building and partly owning a company. Thus, LBOs of smaller companies are particularly well suited to positively affect economic growth and development.

LBO Deals. Although, on the surface, LBOs appear quite different from traditional venture capital investments, there are some significant similarities between these two types of investments, especially in the case of the smaller-sized LBOs, as just noted above. The leader in LBOs (among venture capital firms) in recent years has been First Chicago Venture Capital, which has invested $\$\frac{1}{2}$ billion in LBOs over the past four years. Typical of their investments is Sterling, Inc., an Akron-based jewelry chain for which First Chicago and two other venture capital firms paid $21 million, financed through a combination of debt and equity, in 1985. Within a year, Sterling went public at a valuation of three times the 1985 purchase price. The following year, Sterling was purchased by Ratners Group Ltd., a British jewelry firm, for $205 million. From this deal, First Chicago realized a twenty-three-fold return from an original $2 million equity investment.

LBOs, which comprise more than two-thirds of First Chicago's investments, have turned out to be very attractive. First Chicago has a tremendous advantage in that, because it is a wholly owned subsidiary of First Chicago Corp., a bank with $40 billion in assets, it has direct access to large amounts of capital to structure large deals in a relatively short period of time. Furthermore, it allows the bank to use its expertise in debt financing.

Similarly, other venture capital firms and SBICs that are affiliated with large banks (for example, BancBoston Capital, Security Pacific Capital, Manufacturers Hanover Venture Capital Corp., Chemical Venture Partners, Morgan Capital Corp., Chase Manhattan Capital Corp., and CitiCorp Venture Capital) have been among the most active investors in LBOs over the past few years. Because the bank affiliates have substantial resources to invest, LBOs tend to be larger than typical venture capital investments. Such investments can be very attractive to investors, as it is easier to monitor one $10 million LBO deal than twenty $\$\frac{1}{2}$ million technology start-up deals.

Other venture capital firms, which have no bank affiliations, have also been involved in LBOs. For example, Greater Washington Investors, Inc., of Chevy Chase, Maryland, which invests heavily in early-stage technology companies, participated recently, along with Allied Capital Corp., Atlantic Venture Partners, Security Pacific Capital Corp., and the Sunwestern Investment Group, in a $26 million LBO of Raleighs-Garfinkel's, Inc., a Washington, D.C., based upscale retailer.

~~~~~~~~~~~~~~

The one unanswered question is, Should venture capital firms invest in LBO deals? As noted, LBOs are generally not viewed as the traditional type of venture capital investment and do not necessarily fit into the classic Doriot mode of building companies. On occasion, however, venture capital firms treat LBO investments just like any other typical venture capital investment and devote the appropriate attention to building or turning around these companies.

The danger sign is when venture capital firms become solely investors, rather than investors and advisors. That has already happened in some instances; however, there are numerous examples of when venture capitalists have assumed their traditional roles, with different and often more lucrative types of investments.

Of course, the financial rewards of such investments will cause some venture capitalists to lose sight of their former roles. Yet, for others, while the players and stakes have changed, the roles have remained essentially the same.

A LOOK AHEAD

An obvious development in the venture capital industry has been the trend toward specialization—by region, by industry, and/or by stage of development. In terms of its investment practices, recently, venture capitalists, as a whole, have generally shifted away from investments in technology into those in low-tech areas, such as retailing, and in LBOs. (As noted, however, due to the general movement by the investment community away from debt, it is questionable as to whether LBO deals will continue to be funded as aggressively by venture capital firms as they have been over the past few years.) These low-tech and late-stage investments have provided attractive returns for venture capitalists, without having the risks inherent in earlier-stage technology ventures in which R&D and production costs can be excessive.

How have individual venture capital investments performed? What returns have been characteristic of venture capital portfolios, given the risks of such investments? Have returns been in line with investor expectations? These questions are addressed in Chapter 13.

Performance
of Venture
Capital Investments

One of the most successful investment advisers in this country was recently asked for his formula for successful investing. After a moment's thought, he replied, "Buy low, sell high."

Obviously, financing a venture capital deal is a type of investment in which venture capitalists strive for a target return. Moreover, since venture capital firms invest in several deals, they must be concerned with the overall performance of their investment portfolio.

According to the JEC study cited earlier, venture capital firms anticipated a minimum rate of return of 30% per year on an individual venture investment. Is that a reasonable expectation? Do individual investments perform at or above that level? What returns can be expected for a portfolio of venture capital investments? In essence, do venture capitalists "buy low and sell high"?

PERFORMANCE OF SELECTED INVESTMENTS

There are numerous success stories of individual venture capital investments that give the appearance that venture capital funds, as a whole, perform remarkably well. For example, American Research and Development's (ARD) $70,000 investment in Digital Equipment Corporation (DEC) grew to over $\frac{1}{2}$ billion in about twelve years,[1] which translates into a compounded annual rate of return of over 100%.

---

[1]The amount of the investment in DEC and the returns for ARD vary somewhat, depending on your source of information; see G. Kozmetsky and others, *Financing and Managing Fast-Growth Companies: The Venture Capital Process,* D.C. Heath, Lexington, Mass., 1985; P. R. Liles, "Sustaining the Venture Capital Firm," Management Analysis Center, Inc., Cambridge, Mass., 1977; W. A. Wells, "Venture Capital Decision Making," unpublished doctoral dissertation, Carnegie-Mellon University, 1974.

Of course, some venture capitalists have a way of overstating the performance of companies in their investment portfolio. As one venture capitalist has noted:[2]

What They Say:	What They Mean:
Product's 90% complete	We've got a name for it
Leading-edge technology	We can't make it work
Limited downside	Things can't get much worse
Possibility of shortfall	We're 50% below plan
Proven technology	It nearly worked once before
We're repositioning the company	We're lost
Upside potential	It's stopped breathing

Nonetheless, the performance of several venture deals, as illustrated next, are noteworthy.

Success Stories of Venture Capital Firms . . .

The investments made by our leading venture capital firms read like a "who's who" of successful emerging growth businesses. Some of their success stories are as follows:

Kleiner Perkins Caufield & Byers.   Thomas Perkins got into the venture capital industry in 1966 with a $15,000 investment in University Laboratories, a Berkeley, California, based laser company. That investment grew to $2 million. In 1972, Perkins became a cofounder of the prominent San Francisco-based venture capital firm, Kleiner Perkins Caufield & Byers, which has invested in, among others, Genentech and Tandem Computer. Perkins has had an active involvement with his investments, having served as chairman of both Genentech and Tandem.

Sevin Rosen.   Sevin Rosen Management, a venture capital firm founded by Benjamin M. Rosen, one of the most notable venture investors over the past 20 years, and L. J. Sevin, founder of Mostek, a semiconductor manufacturer, invested $2.1 million in Lotus Development, a software manufacturer located in Cambridge, Massachusetts. That investment grew to $70 million when Lotus went public in 1983. Sevin Rosen also invested $2.5 million in Compaq Computer, a Houston-based company whose first product was a portable computer. When Compaq went public in 1983, that investment was worth $40 million.

Arthur Rock.   Arthur Rock's investments as a venture capitalist include Fairchild Semiconductor in 1957, a pioneer in silicon chips; Teledyne in 1960, a California conglomerate with sales today in excess of $4 billion; Intel in 1968,

2See *Inc.,* August 1989, p. 22.

a "chipmaker" that is an outgrowth of Fairchild Semiconductor; and Apple in 1978, a pioneer in the field of personal computers. Rock's investment in Apple grew from $57,400 to $13.2 million (a 200-fold increase) when Apple went public in 1980.

Allen & Co.   Allen & Company is best known for its investment in Syntex, a small pharmaceutical company, in the late 1950s. Within a decade, when Syntex became one of the leading manufacturers of birth control pills in the world, Allen's $800,000 investment grew to over $80 million. Allen & Company also invested in an early-stage venture, Digital Switch, a developer of micro switching telecommunications equipment. This technology enabled MCI to become a major competitor of AT&T in the long-distance telephone market.

Hambrecht & Quist.   Hambrecht & Quist, a venture capital firm that also provides such services as investment banking and underwriting of stock issues, is responsible for much of the growth of high-tech companies in Silicon Valley. Among the firm's notable investments are Apple Computer and VLSI Technology.

TA Associates.   TA Associates was formed by Peter Brooke, as the venture capital arm of Tucker Anthony and RL Day, a Boston-based investment banking firm. It eventually became an independent venture capital partnership and is now one of the largest venture capital firms in the country. TA Associates invested $1.7 million in Tandon Corp. between 1977 and 1980. By 1983, they had sold out their investment for $77 million. They also invested $171,000 in Biogen, a Boston-based biotechnology company. They subsequently sold out of this investment with over a $10 million profit.

Some Others.   Several other venture capital firms have had similar success stories. Sequoia Capital, for example, a Silicon Valley venture capital firm specializing in high-tech ventures, has invested in Atari, Apple, Tandem, Tandon, Altos Computer, LSI Logic, and 3 Com Corp. Burr Egan Deleage & Co., a Boston-based venture capital firm with $.25 billion paid in capital, has invested in Triad, Tandon, Genentech, Tandem, Federal Express, and Chiron. The Mayfield Fund, a comparably sized Menlo Park, California, based venture capital firm, has invested in Amgen, Atari, Businessland, Compaq Computer, Genentech, and 3 Com Corp. And, Institutional Venture Partners, also of Menlo Park, has invested a portion of its more than $200 million in committed capital to such companies as Borland International, Businessland, NBI, Seagate Technology, ROLM, Stratus Computer, and LSI Logic.

. . . And Failures

The most successful venture capital firms and venture capitalists have their share of failures. For example, in addition to its investments in Compaq Computer and Lotus Development, Sevin Rosen invested $400,000 in Osborne Computer Company, which later went bankrupt.

Franklin P. Johnson, who manages Asset Management Co., a Palo Alto, California, based venture capital fund with approximately $100 million in paid in capital, has realized tremendous returns from his early-stage investments in Amgen, Inc., a biotechnology firm based in Thousand Oaks, California, and Tandem Computer of Cupertino, California. However, even for one of Silicon Valley's most successful venture capitalists, there are significant risks that go along with the high potential returns of early-stage investments, as evidenced by his investment in VisiCorp, a San Jose, California, based software company that created the VisiCalc spreadsheet. Interestingly, it was VisiCorp (or, Daniel Bricklin, the founder of VisiCorp, who has since taken on the role of venture capitalist), and not Lotus, that pioneered the concept of the spreadsheet, which shows that being *first* is not necessarily the surefire road to success.

Similarly, Fred Adler's investments in Data General, Daisy Systems, Life Technologies, and Advanced Technology Labs have made him a "living legend" in venture capital circles. However, he was less successful in his investment in Tenet, a West Coast computer firm that ran into a major recession shortly after it started up in 1969.

One of Adler's investments has had a "roller coaster" history of success and failure. In 1970, Adler & Co. invested in Intersil, Inc., a semiconductor company. Intersil began to lose money in 1974. As a result, the board of directors took control of the company and cut the staff by 40%. Within months, the company became profitable again and began to beef up its sales effort and add staff. However, management failed to notice some of the negative signals of the economy and repeated many of its earlier mistakes. Several product lines were losing money on each item sold. The company was losing $700,000 per month by the fall of 1975, prompting the board to take control again. The board reassigned executive roles, reduced staff, and rid the company of unprofitable operations, thereby boosting profitability. Ultimately, the company was sold to General Electric after having reached the $100 million mark in sales.

Thus, even the best venture capital firms have had their share of failures. Osborne Computer, Fortune Systems, Pizza Time Theatre, Victor Technologies, Diasonics, and others, each had experienced, intelligent venture capitalists supporting them. Yet all these investments turned out to be losers for the venture capital firms that invested in them. The better venture capital firms try to limit their failures to one in ten—or, at worst, to two in ten. Their philosophy is that they cannot afford to have five or six losses that will be offset by one superstar performer.

THE PERFORMANCE OF THE PORTFOLIOS OF VENTURE CAPITAL FIRMS

Unfortunately, the investments in DEC, Lotus Development, Compaq Computer, Apple Computer, Syntex, and the like are not at all indicative of venture capital *portfolio* performance as a whole. For example, even with DEC in its portfolio, ARD's rate of return from 1946 to 1966 was only 14%.[3] (The investment in DEC had not reached its culmination by 1966. However, follow-up research, after DEC had been harvested, reports that ARD's return had fallen to below 10% by the late 1970's.)

Some researchers have reported extremely positive results of the performance of venture capital firms. For example, Professors J. D. Martin and J. W. Petty reported average rates of return of 27% for publicly traded venture capital companies from 1974 to 1979.[4] It should be noted, however, that these researchers studied the performance of the stock prices of the companies, rather than the performance of the ventures in which these firms had committed venture capital; the relationship of these two measures of performance is often misleading. Notwithstanding, a more recent study, using a similar methodology to Martin and Petty, reported that the average rate of return of publicly held venture capital companies from 1959 to 1985 was 16%.[5]

What Returns Have Been Realized by Venture Capital Firms?

Aside from ARD, studies have been made of the rates of return of the portfolios of other respected privately held and publicly held venture capital firms and SBICs. The rates of return for a sample of such investments over the 1960 and 1970s, after deducting management fees, ranged from approximately 12% to less than 20%.[6]

Comparative Returns Over Time. The returns of venture capital investments have varied somewhat over the last twenty years, both on an individual year basis and on a long-term (ten to fifteen year) basis. Industry-wide returns have rarely been better than 20% in any given year.

Individual Year Returns. Between the late 1970s and the early 1980s, venture investments reached their all-time individual-year highs in terms of annual returns for their investors—in excess of 30%. In the mid-1980s, returns were slightly above 20% per year. More recently (the late 1980s), portfolio returns have declined further to their current level of somewhere between less than 10% to as high as 15% to 20%, for a given year, depending on which data you believe.

[3]See W. Rotch, "The Pattern of Success in Venture Capital Financing," *Financial Analysis Journal,* September–October 1968, *24*, pp. 141–147.

[4]See J. D. Martin and J. W. Petty, "Analysis of the Performance of Publicly Traded Venture Capital Companies," *Journal of Financial and Quantitative Analysis,* 1983, *18*, pp. 401–410.

[5]See R. G. Ibbotson and G. P. Brinson, *Investment Markets,* McGraw-Hill, New York, 1987.

[6]For details of these studies, refer, for example, to B. Huntsman and J. P. Hoban, "Investments in New Enterprise: Some Empirical Observations on Risk, Return, and Market Structure," *Financial Management,* Summer 1980, *9*, pp. 44–51; J. B. Poindexter, "The Efficiency of Financial Markets: The Venture Capital Case," unpublished doctoral dissertation, New York University, New York, 1976.

Long-Term Returns. How have venture capital portfolios performed over the long term? A comparative analysis of long-term portfolio performance, which was reported in *Venture* magazine, showed annual compounded returns for venture capital firms for the 10- to 15-year period form the early 1970s to the mid-1980s of anywhere from 20% to 25%.[7] Other analyses have reported that annual returns have been around 20% for the period from the late 1970s to the late 1980s, or slightly less than the results reported in *Venture*.[8]

The reader should be cautioned, however, that anytime you have self-reports of the financial performance of privately held companies in a portfolio managed by privately held venture capital firms, there are bound to be discrepancies in the results from one study to another. Thus, the data just cited are meant to serve as approximate general ranges, rather than as absolute comparative measures of performance.

The Performance of Selected Venture Capital Firms. The top venture capital firms have performed rather well. (Again, be cautious of self-reported data, however.) As a few examples, Sequoia Capital has averaged annual returns of better than 50% since its inception in 1973; and TA Associates has been averaging returns of approximately 40% over the past 12 years.

Of course, there is a lack of data available on the portfolio performance of most venture capital firms. Some venture capital firms will not provide data because their investments either are at too early a stage of development to reflect their performance or, simply, have not performed as well as expected; other venture capital firms will not provide data because, as privately held venture capital firms investing in privately held companies, it is their policy to keep that information confidential.

A Related Concern. Regardless, an important concern of the industry is that, as portfolio performance industry wide has declined and as the number of venture capital funds and the capital being committed to those funds has increased so substantially (from $170 million in 1979 to $3.4 billion in 1983, a twenty-fold increase in four years), there may be a shortage of *experienced* venture capitalists and/or greater competition for good deals in which to invest. Thus, unlike years ago, when venture returns were generally higher, the industry

---

[7]Portfolio performance was as follows (see *Venture,* March 1985):

Study	Period of Study	Annual Compounded Returns (%)
First Chicago	1975–1984	24.5
Venture Economics	10 years	20–25
Harvard University	15 years	25
CIGNA	1970–1984	20+

[8]See Gregory F. Chiampou and Joel J. Kallett, "Risk/Return Profile of Venture Capital," *Journal of Business Venturing,* January 1989, pp. 1–10.

has become competitive, forcing venture capitalists to be more skillful in managing their portfolios.

≈≈≈≈≈≈≈≈≈≈≈

For the industry as a whole, although there are short-run booms, for example, in 1961, 1967–1969, 1972, 1980, 1983, in which venture capital funds realized returns of approximately 30% or more, the overall rates of return have been less than 20%. It is not surprising that these boom periods have coincided with favorable markets for IPOs since the new-issues market allows for liquidation of (privately held) venture capital investments.

Given the fact that venture capitalists invest in ventures with high-risk, high-return characteristics, the commonly held perception is that their portfolios would perform admirably. However, many of their investments have low or negative returns, while few have substantial returns, thereby reducing the returns of the entire portfolio.[9] Research suggests that, over the long term, 10% to 20% of the investments in a typical venture capital firm's portfolio are complete losses (compare these low failure rates to the 70% or 80% failure rate that is characteristic of new ventures throughout the population), 10% to 20% of the investments have annual rates of return of better than 40%, and less than 5% might be considered superstars, with annual rates of returns of greater than 80%.

What Affects Portfolio Returns?

A recent study was concerned with the factors affecting most favorably on portfolio returns. The researchers found that higher returns resulted from longer holding periods, later-stage funding of successful early-stage investments, and attractive pricing of the deal.[10] In addition, research suggests that over the past twenty years the more established funds significantly outperformed the newer funds.[11]

How Has the Performance of Venture Capital Funds Compared to That of Publicly Traded Companies?

About ten years ago, Alan Patricof, one of the leading venture capitalists in this country asserted that

"there are enough performance records from the earliest venture pools to provide ten-year comparisons that suggest almost without exception, that

[9]See W. Carleton, "Issues and Questions Involving Venture Capital," in G. Libecap (ed.), *Advances in the Study of Entrepreneurship, Innovation, and Economic Growth.* Greenwich, Conn., JAI Press, 1986; also, for further details of an empirical study related to this, see Huntsman and Hoban, op. cit.

[10]See H. Stevenson and others, "Venture Capital in Transition: A Monte Carlo Simulation of Changes in Investment Patterns," *Journal of Business Venturing,* 1987, 2, pp. 103–121.

[11]See Gregory F. Chiampou and Joel J. Kallett, "Risk/Return Profile of Venture Capital," *Journal of Business Venturing,* January 1989, pp. 1–10.

TABLE 13-1 Comparative Returns of Selected Investments

Type of Investment	Average Annual Return (%)	Standard Deviation of Average Return (%)
Venture capital:		
Funds 3+ years old	17.5	37.6
Funds 6+ years old	24.4	51.2
S&P 500 stocks	15.9	12.3
Small stocks	20.4	18.9
Long-term government bonds	10.5	16.2
Long-term corporate bonds	10.7	16.4

venture capital investing has outperformed almost every other market—not to mention most managed funds."[12]

There is limited support for Patricof's claim. For example, research conducted in the mid-1970s, using data from twenty-nine SBIC funds, reported a rate of return that was 63% higher than that of the S&P market index return (a sample of the largest American corporations).[13] There was, however, much greater variability of the individual investments in this portfolio. This would suggest that the improved returns are offset by greater risks.

As might be expected, however, the empirical support for Patricof's claim has never been overwhelming. For example, a study by Norman Fast reported that a large percentage of venture capital funds that were formed within ten years prior to his study were no longer in existence.[14]

More recently, as demonstrated by the data in Table 13-1, the average annual return for venture capital investments, which has been around 20% over the ten-year period from the late 1970s to the late 1980s, has been comparable to that of small stocks (a sample of small capitalization publicly held companies), but somewhat higher than that of the larger S&P 500 stocks.[15]

This provides some support for Patricof's earlier claim. Of course, along with the high potential returns of venture capital investments come higher levels of risk, as indicated by the larger deviations from average returns of those particular investments.

[12]See A. J. Patricof. "The New Role of Venture Capital," *Institutional Investor,* December 1979, p. 125.

[13]See J. B. Poindexter, "The Efficiency of Financial Markets: The Venture Capital Case," unpublished doctoral dissertation, New York University, 1976. Similar results were reported by Charles River Associates, "An Analysis of Venture Capital Market Imperfections," NTIS Report PB-254996, National Bureau of Standards, Washington, D.C., 1976.

[14]See N. D. Fast, "A Visit to the New Venture Graveyard," *Research Management,* March 1979, *22,* pp. 18–22.

[15]See Gregory F. Chiampou and Joel J. Kallett, "Risk/Return Profile of Venture Capital," *Journal of Business Venturing,* January 1989, p. 6; the study uses time-weighted, average annual returns for 1978–1987. Data on stock, treasury bill, government bond, and annual bond performance are from Ibbotson & Associates *SBBI 1988 Yearbook.*

If we examine the five-year period from the mid to late 1980s, as compared to the ten-year period just noted, we find some slightly different results. Between 1984 and 1988, the S&P 500 had an annual return of about 15%, which was about double the return for small company stocks (those with a market capitalization between $10 million and $85 million); however, the S&P returns were comparable to the returns of venture capital investments (see earlier section on the performance of venture capital portfolios). (It should be noted that during the 1970s and early 1980s the small stocks significantly outperformed their larger counterparts.)

There are many reasons for the improved performance of the S&P 500 stocks, including the stock market crash of 1987, the performance of LBOs, and the increased number of restructurings, all of which favor blue-chip stocks or other large, established companies.

Have Returns on Investment Been in Line with Investor Expectations?

The popular notion (which is consistent with the JEC study cited earlier) is that venture capitalists strive for a 25% to 40% return, that is, an increase of at least fivefold and, perhaps, up to fifteenfold, on their investments. Such returns are certainly possible for any given investment. However, the research cited suggests that the portfolios, as a whole, have not experienced such high returns.

It is also important to recognize that, as the venture capital funds have grown in size and as their portfolios have become larger and more diversified, it becomes more difficult to realize the 30% to 40% returns that were prevalent over the late 1970s and the early 1980s.

The Current Situation

It is getting tougher today to realize the traditional returns expected by venture capitalists. When Intel, currently a $3 billion company, was started in 1968, an initial investment of only $.5 million was all that was needed. Despite such a small investment, the returns to the investors were significant. Today, the situation is quite different. For example, in the mid-1980s, venture capitalists invested $21 million in Convex Computer, of Richardson, Texas. This is typical of high-tech start-ups; early-stage costs can often be $10 million to $50 million, with no guarantees of success. Convex was fortunate to have gone public in 1986 (before the stock market crash!), so we'll call it a success story. Despite the high risks involved with such a venture, the public offering only brought investors 7.5 times their original investment, despite a very strong IPO market. This is becoming more characteristic of the current venture capital market. It is becoming more and more difficult to expect a tenfold return on an initial investment, let alone a 100-fold or more return, as was the case with such companies as Syntex, DEC, Genentech, Apple Computer, and Tandem Computer.

A LOOK AHEAD

We have just examined the nature and performance of venture capital investments. It should be quite clear from this chapter that there are significant variances in the performance of venture capital investments—for one individual investment versus another individual investment; for individual investments versus portfolios of investments; for portfolios of investments of one venture capital firm versus those for another venture capital firm; for portfolios of investments over time.

In the final part of this book, we will explore some important current issues in the venture capital industry.

PART V

SELECTED TOPICS

Chapter 14

Foreign Venture Capital

As American industry has become more global, we find that venture capital is no longer exclusively an American phenomenon. Europe and the Far East, most notably, have become major players in the venture capital arena.

As noted by Ramon V. Reyes of Nazem & Co., a venture capital firm in New York, there is "An increasing awareness that venture capital plays a very real role in the economic development process."[1] Reyes has suggested further that

> "The European arena is particularly aware that it has been leapfrogged by the United States in terms of technology. . . . And now, in addition to forming alliances with U.S. firms, they are trying to develop a venture environment by cultivating a risk taking psychology in their own countries, which are traditionally conservative."

As entrepreneurial activity becomes more pronounced internationally, which is a trend that should continue through this decade, we are likely to see the further maturation of the venture capital industry throughout the world. Most countries are at an early stage of development, relative to the United States (refer to Chapter 2 for a discussion of the development of the venture capital industry in the United States). However, as we will soon see, several European and Asian countries, whose venture capital industry has paralleled that of the United States, have progressed significantly in recent years.

[1]See Lee Kravitz, "What Venture Capitalists Want," in *Venture's Guide to International Venture Capital*, Simon & Schuster, New York, 1985, p. 14.

VENTURE CAPITAL IN EUROPE

An Overview

For years, the Europeans have invested heavily in American venture capital limited partnerships. More recently, they have begun to form limited partnerships of their own, as well as in conjunction with American venture capital firms, to invest in European companies. These limited partnerships are quite regionalized; more than 80% of the investments are for companies based in the same country as the venture capital firm funding the deal.

The Size of the Venture Capital Industry in Europe.   Interestingly, according to the European Venture Capital Association (EVCA), which is the European equivalent of our National Venture Capital Association (NVCA), venture capital firms in Europe invested $5.5 billion in 1989 (a 24% increase from 1988), which was significantly more than was invested by venture capital firms in the United States.

An excellent indication of the growth of the venture capital industry in Europe is the growth of the EVCA itself, which was founded in Brussels in 1983. The EVCA is now comprised of close to 200 members throughout the continent, making it comparable in size to the NVCA, which was founded a decade earlier in the United States.

The Nature of the Venture Capital Industry in Europe.   Venture capital activity has only recently emerged as a major force in Europe.[2] Until a few years ago, industries were almost completely dominated by the state (as in the United Kingdom and France) or by the banks (as in Germany). In general, there was little entrepreneurial risk taking, since lifetime employment was seen as more valuable than entrepreneurism.

That situation has changed dramatically over the past decade, thanks to changes in public policy and the general business climates in those countries. Perhaps most important has been the creation of over-the-counter or secondary stock markets (analogous to our NASDAQ) in most European countries. These over-the-counter markets have relaxed regulations to allow smaller, newer companies contemplating an IPO to list their stocks at a fairly low cost.

In many ways, venture capital activity in Europe is very similar to that in the United States, only at an earlier stage of development. One key difference is the source of venture capital. Unlike in the United States, where the key investors in venture capital partnerships are pension funds, corporations, insurance companies, and the like, the major source of the funds in Europe is from banks, which provide approximately 20% of the capital (and a much greater percentage than that in Italy, France, and Denmark), which are followed

---

[2]The venture capital industry in Europe is basically confined to the Western part of the continent. As we will discuss shortly, it will probably take a few years before we see the development of a venture capital industry in Eastern Europe.

by government agencies, insurance companies, corporate investors, and pension funds. Only the United Kingdom is somewhat like the United States in this regard, in that 25% of the capital (as compared to about 50% in the United States) comes from pension funds.

Types of Investments.   The four industries that have received the greatest percentage of venture capital funding in Europe have been industrial products, consumer related, computer related, and other electronics related. Thus, there is a growing emphasis on high technology. This should not be surprising since there are major high-technology centers throughout Western Europe, which is known for its advanced stage of technological development. West Germany, the United Kingdom, and France, and, to a lesser degree, the Netherlands and Italy invest heavily in R&D and have a large number of scientists. The United States has its Silicon Valley; the United Kingdom has its Silicon Glen, a high-tech region in central Scotland where fifty U.S. companies have given birth to more than 300 electronics companies. Similar high-tech regions are found throughout Europe, such as in and around Cambridge, England; Berlin, West Germany; and Milano, Italy.

Syndication of deals has begun relatively recently (and on a limited basis) in such countries as Belgium, Germany, and France. However, an interesting recent development has been the formation of a pan-European network of venture capital firms by twelve large European corporations, including Bosch, Fiat, Olivetti, Petrofina, Philips, Pirelli, and Volvo. The network has invested the equivalent of $30 million (U.S.) in a holding company that invests in venture capital funds in Europe.

There are tremendous opportunities for the growth of the venture capital industry itself, as well as for the growth of entrepreneurial companies and the economy as a whole in Europe.

In Europe, venture capital activity has been greatest in the United Kingdom (which has about half of the total funds invested and about half of the total funds available for investment in Europe). The Netherlands and France are the next largest players in this industry, followed by Belgium and West Germany. However, more recently, most of the other countries in Western Europe have begun playing greater roles in this area, with exceptional growth being seen in Italy and Scandinavia, as well as in the other countries just mentioned.

This has strengthened significantly start-up activity in Europe. Interestingly, on a per capita basis, the number of start-ups in Western Europe is almost equal to that of the United States. The big difference is that the United States

TABLE 14-1   IPOs in the United Kingdom

Year	London Stock Exchange	Unlisted Stock Market	Nightingale Market
1987	22	10	4
1986	19	22	
1985	7	12	
1984	8	14	
1983	2	20	
1982	1	7	

has increased its start-up activity sixfold over the last ten years, while Europe has stayed relatively constant.

With a combined gross national product (in U.S. dollars) for the twelve member countries of the European Community (EC)[3] of over $4 trillion (which is approximately equal to that of the United States) and with a combined population of 320 million (which is approximately equal to that of the United States and Japan combined), we see that there are tremendous opportunities for the growth of the venture capital industry itself, as well as for the growth of entrepreneurial companies and the economy as a whole in Europe. This will be particularly pronounced as 1992 approaches, at which time the EC will remove most of the remaining barriers between member countries.

United Kingdom

Although the venture capital industry in the United Kingdom is relatively new, the industry has been helped significantly by recent efforts such as tax incentives and legislation permitting stock option plans, which have encouraged entrepreneurial activity. For example, Margaret Thatcher's administration developed the Business Start Up Scheme (which has since become the Business Expansion Scheme), which provides tax breaks to individuals investing in entrepreneurial companies.

Furthermore, the venture capital industry has been aided by a well-developed financial center that has two over-the-counter stock markets, the Unlisted Securities Market (USM), created in 1981 and affiliated with the London Stock Exchange; and the Nightingale Market, formed in 1987, which has even more relaxed requirements than the USM.

The result has been a dramatic increase in the number of venture capital-backed IPOs; see in Table 14-1.[4] These developments have prompted several prominent U.S. venture capital firms such as Citicorp, TA Associates, and Alan Patricof Associates to open offices in London.

Because the United Kingdom is an English-speaking country, it can easily

---

[3]The EC is comprised of Belgium, Denmark, France, Germany, Greece, Ireland, Italy, Luxembourg, the Netherlands, Portugal, Spain, and the United Kingdom.

[4]See Alan Patricof, "The Internationalization of Venture Capital," *Journal of Business Venturing*, July 1989, p. 229.

import U.S.-trained venture capitalists from the United States and can export employees of venture capital-backed companies for training to the United States. Moreover, the styles of business and the cultures of the United Kingdom and the United States are similar enough to allow for the exchange of professionals between the two countries. These factors can enhance the development of the venture capital industry in the United Kingdom, which is already the clear leader in terms of venture capital activity in Europe.

France

One of the first significant incentives to encourage venture capital activity in France came in 1971 with the creation of the Societes Financieres d'Innovation (SFIs; Innovation Financing Companies). Corporate investors in SFIs, the most notable of which is Sofinnova, can write off their investment for tax purposes. That, coupled with a 15% capital gains tax rate, provided the foundation for the current venture capital industry.

Venture capital activity in France began to take off in 1983 with the creation of the Seconde Marche, its over-the-counter market. That was followed shortly thereafter with the creation of the Societes de Capital Risque (SCRs; Venture Capital Companies) in 1985, which allowed private and corporate investors a write-off of their investments and applied a 15% capital gains tax rate to the distribution of dividends by SCRs to their shareholders.

This has resulted in approximately forty companies going public in a year, as compared to about two or three a decade ago. In addition, French venture capitalists have had considerable experience in U.S.-type venture capital investments. For example, Paribas, a leading French bank, has had venture capital funds in the United States and Japan for the past decade.

The biggest question mark, however, is whether there is the appropriate entrepreneurial climate in France, which is a country whose industry has traditionally been almost completely dominated by the state, to foster the growth of the venture capital industry there.

Germany

Germany, with a GNP of approximately $100 million, is Europe's richest country. Traditionally, Germany has had a "big business" orientation that requires a high degree of professional management experience; entrepreneurship had not been encouraged by the industry-dominated banks, which have strict requirements that discourage early-stage ventures, nor by public policy decisions. For that reason, venture capital activity has not been as strong in that country as it could be. Up until a few years ago, there were just a few, small venture capital firms in Germany, most of which were controlled by foreigners.

Since around 1986, that situation has begun to change. Consequently, the climate in Germany is becoming more appropriate for the development of the venture capital industry there. Germans have a high rate of savings (approximately 15% of their personal income), which can provide a large pool of venture capital. Moreover, tax laws are beginning to promote equity investments. In addition, in 1987, Germany established a new secondary market (Geregelter Markt) to allow for the exit of venture capital investments.

Traditionally, Germans have invested substantially in venture capital partnerships in the United States. With the development of the secondary market in Germany, we can only expect the venture capital industry in Germany to grow in the coming years.

Netherlands and Belgium

The Netherlands has one of the leading venture capital markets in Europe. This country possesses the necessary entrepreneurial environment as well as the appropriate strategic location to foster the continued growth of its venture capital industry. Moreover, the Netherlands has a strong secondary market, the Parallel Market, which has served as an exit route for venture capital investments since it was created in 1982.

The Belgian government created the *societe novatrice* (the "innovating company"), which provides such incentives to promote the growth of new, high-tech companies as reduced corporate income taxes, increased investment allowances, and exemptions from property taxes for the company. In addition, the government provides capital gains tax exemptions and personal tax allowances for the investors in those companies.

Belgium has a relatively small venture capital pool, but a high rate of investment, thanks largely to public policy activity and the incentives just discussed. In January 1985, a secondary market, with fairly relaxed requirements, was created in Belgium. Thus, the venture capital industry is very healthy there. It should be noted that this is just the opposite situation of Italy, which is just beginning to address some of these public policy issues.

Scandinavia

The leading Scandinavian country in the venture capital area has been Sweden, which has been expanding at approximately the same rate as the United Kingdom. The venture capital industry was rather dormant up until 1982, due to the disincentives (double taxation and extremely high tax rates, which have been as high as 85% for individuals) associated with any type of equity investment.

Currently, however, there are more favorable tax laws regarding investments, which has prompted the growth of the venture capital industry there. In addition, an over-the-counter market, which provides an avenue for exit, was established in 1983, thereby further supporting its growth.

Sweden has had an unusually high rate of entrepreneurship, as well as a highly educated population. These factors are likely to make Sweden even more attractive to venture capitalists in the years to come.

Some General Comments about Venture Capital in Europe

We can learn much about the venture capital industry in the United States by studying the developments in Europe, and vice versa. Some common elements in countries with a strong venture capital industry include:

- Liberal tax structure
- Strong over-the-counter market
- Flexible labor rules
- Deregulated industries
- Culture appropriate for entrepreneurship

The countries in Europe that best display these characteristics, for example, United Kingdom and the Netherlands, have fairly well developed venture capital industries. As other European countries progress along these dimensions, which is becoming more evident in such countries as Italy and Germany, there has been a corresponding expansion of venture capital activity. On the other hand, the countries in Eastern Europe, which do not generally display the above characteristics, seem to be several years away from developing a venture capital industry.

Overall, the outlook for the venture capital industry in Europe—and, again, we're referring to Western Europe, in particular—is extremely attractive. In addition, tremendous opportunities exist for syndication with American venture capital firms for investments in Europe and the United States.

VENTURE CAPITAL IN THE MIDDLE EAST

Israel

Venture capital in Israel does not really exist as a distinct industry as it does in the United States. Rather, the Israeli government, in keeping with its mission to promote high-technology industries, subsidizes the research and development efforts of small companies. Israel's Office of Chief Scientists, which is part of the Ministry of Industry and Trade, matches dollar for dollar a small company's investments in selected promising technology projects.

Funding is also available in the form of loans from the Israel–United States Binational Industrial Research and Development Foundation (usually referred to as BIRD F), which has been funded jointly by the United States and Israeli governments.

Some venture capital has become available, often in the form of debt, from some of the large banks in Israel: Israel Discount Bank, Bank Leumi, and Bank Hapoalim. In addition, an exit vehicle exists for venture capital-backed

Israeli companies, albeit in foreign countries. Already, over one dozen Israeli companies have been listed on the NASDAQ or American Stock Exchange. One of the most notable Israeli publicly traded companies is Elron Electronics Industries, Ltd., a high-tech company that is a special limited partner in Athena Venture Partners, a venture capital firm that invests in early-stage technology companies.

VENTURE CAPITAL IN THE FAR EAST

Japan

Japan is going through its second major venture capital boom. Its first, which occurred from 1973 to 1975, ended during the collapse of the Japanese over-the-counter market, which was partly a result of the oil price shock in 1974. The venture capital market picked up again in 1982, and in 1983, Japan's leading venture capital firm, the Japan Associated Finance Company (JAFCO) (affiliated with Nomura Securities, Japan's largest securities company) raised $23 billion yen (approximately $100 million).[5]

The leading venture capital firms in Japan are subsidiaries of either Japan's "Big 4" securities companies (Nomura, Daiwa, Nikko, and Yamaichi, which account for the vast majority of all transactions at the Tokyo Stock Exchange) or of its largest banks (for example, Sumitomo Bank, Mitsubishi Bank, and Mitsui Bank). (It should be noted that the nine largest banks in the world are located in Japan; the largest one, Dai-Ici Kangyo Bank, with assets of approximately $400 billion, is nearly twice the size of Citicorp, the largest bank in America.) Thus, there should be no shortage of financial resources for venture capital in Japan.

Nature of Investments.   Japanese venture capital firms invest in order to develop future business for the parent corporation. Typically, investments have been in ventures at later stages of development. Recently, however, there has been a greater tendency to fund newer ventures. This has been largely a result of the Ministry of International Trade and Industry (MITI) establishing a guarantee program for start-ups.

Because capital gains are not taxed in Japan, private investors have an incentive to invest their money in venture capital funds. (The same incentive does not exist for corporations, whose capital gains are taxed at the rate of 50%.) However, the venture capital industry in Japan has not taken off like it has in the United States, which is largely attributable to the Japanese attitude of risk aversion. This explains why Japanese pension fund managers invest a large majority of their assets in blue-chip companies. Moreover, the risk-averse

---

[5]See "Japan: Smoothing the Way for Venture Capital—Again," *Business Week*, October 11, 1982, p. 53.

attitude affects the formation of management teams in newer, smaller ventures. It is often difficult for such ventures to recruit quality management and personnel from established companies due to the country's strong emphasis on lifetime employment.

Another major impediment to venture capital investing in Japan has traditionally been the lack of an exit vehicle, in the form of a new issues market or a mergers and acquisitions market. Recently, however, thanks to the efforts of MITI, Japan established its new over-the-counter market, with requirements similar to the analogous stock market for such securities in the United States, the National Association of Stock Dealers Automated Quotation (NASDAQ). There were nineteen IPOs in 1987 and about double that many the following year. Despite its liberalization in 1984, however, the over-the-counter market has not been a preferred investment vehicle for Japanese investors. Therefore, it is difficult to take a company public.

Despite these obstacles, it is likely that the situation will improve. MITI has made several steps in the right direction. In addition, several U.S. investment banking houses, such as Citicorp and Salomon Brothers, have recently established offices in Tokyo. This can provide the venture capital industry in Japan with the appropriate exit vehicles to foster its growth.

Investing in U.S. and European Companies.   The venture capital industry in Japan has undergone some significant changes. Thanks to a 1980 law in Japan, which enabled the free flow of capital between Japan and foreign countries, Japan has become actively involved in the venture capital market, primarily in the United States and secondarily in Europe. This has resulted in direct investments in corporations, as well as investments in U.S. venture capital pools. Currently, according to *Venture Economics*, Japanese corporations are investing at the rate of nearly $.5 billion annually in minority positions in U.S. companies. This is a dramatic increase of Japanese investments from just a few years ago—a threefold increase from 1987 and a tenfold increase from 1985.

Japanese corporations are investing at the rate of nearly $.5 billion annually in minority positions in U.S. companies.

As an example, in December 1987, Mitsubishi invested $500,000 in Suprex Corp., a Pittsburgh-based maker of analytical instrumentation for chemical analysis. Similarly, Nomura Securities recently invested $4.5 million (in an R&D limited partnership and a direct equity investment) in Plant Genetics, a Davis, California, based agricultural biotechnology company. Also, Mitsui & Co. recently invested in Candela Laser Corp., a Wayland, Massachusetts, based manufacturer of high-tech medical devices. As for European investments, Sumitomo Corp. and Nippon Investment Finance recently invested in Euroventures BV, a venture capital consortium formed by seven major European companies.

Direct investments have not just been made by Mitsubishi, Mitsui, and the other multibillion dollar Japanese conglomerates, which are known for their technology products. The old-line Japanese industrial companies are also investing in foreign companies. Interestingly, they, too, are investing in high tech. For example, Kubota, a $4 billion Japanese diversified agricultural machinery conglomerate, which manufactures tractors, has invested in MIPS Computer Systems (Sunnyvale, California), a maker of reduced instruction set computing (RISC) chips, one of the latest developments in the computer industry, while Nippon Steel has invested heavily in Silicon Valley companies. The Japanese companies gain a window on technology, while the American companies gain manufacturing knowledge and access to international markets.

Interpore International (Irvine, California), which makes a bone graft substitute used in oral surgery, recently linked up with Tokuyama Soda Co., a billion dollar Japanese company with a dental products division, that had an interest in Interpore's technology. Consequently, Tokuyama Soda invested more than $1 million in Interpore and provided the company with an international market in exchange for the distribution rights in Japan.

Joint Venture Activity.   In addition to direct investments by Japanese companies, there have also been several joint ventures of Japanese and American investors. For example, Mitsui, one of the giant Japanese trading companies (or *sogo shossha*, as they are called), and Vista Ventures, a venture capital firm based in New Canaan, Connecticut, recently teamed up to launch Orien, a fund that has invested in Sigma Circuits, of Santa Clara, California. Sigma gains access to the Japanese market, while Mitsui is provided an opportunity to diversify into the distribution of certain high-tech products worldwide.

Similarly, Kubota invested $20 million in the Sunnyvale, California, based Dana Computer (which became Ardent Computer and has since merged with Stellar Computer to form Stardent Computer), a maker of graphics computers, in exchange for 25% of the equity of Dana. Kubota was granted the exclusive rights to market the product throughout Asia, while Dana gained access to Kubota's manufacturing expertise as well as its ability to obtain electronic components at greatly reduced prices from Far Eastern manufacturers. Certainly, one of the most appealing features of this investment for Kubota was Dana's founder, Allen H. Michels, who had earlier founded Convergent Technologies, a leading supplier of network minicomputer systems.

The Japanese corporations have been and will continue to be major forces in funding early-stage American companies in need of venture financing. In many ways, this has been the "perfect marriage." Thanks to a strong yen, the Japanese have been able to "purchase" American technology, thereby enabling them to diversity into the high-technology areas that will keep them competitive in the world markets. At the same time, the American companies are quite happy to have a relationship with their investors that also provides manufacturing expertise and access to foreign markets.

However, in addition to the Japanese trading and manufacturing companies investing directly in high-technology companies in the United States, they have played a key role in the American venture capital industry. This has been accomplished either in the form of direct venture capital investments, in such firms as Adler & Company, Kleiner Perkins Caufield & Byers, Concord Partners, Vista Ventures, Montgomery Securities, and Hambro International, or through networks or strategic alliances (discussed later).

The "Four Tigers"

In recent years, we've seen the tremendous economic growth of the "four tiger nations" of Asia: Hong Kong, Taiwan, Singapore, and South Korea. Combined, the exports of these four nations is about 80% of those of Japan. Moreover, there is the tremendous economic potential of other Asian countries such as Thailand and, to a lesser extent, Malaysia, the Philippines, Indonesia, and the People's Republic of China. This entire region could very easily account for more than one-quarter of the world's total GNP by the year 2000 (versus 20% today), as compared to that of North America, which will likely account for less than 30% of the world's GNP, as it does today.

The notion of venture capital, however, has been slow to catch on in these countries. One reason is that it is difficult to cash out via public offerings. For example, to list a stock on the Hong Kong exchange, realistically, it takes three years of profitability, with the expectation that the company will soon be generating $10 million to $15 million (in U.S. dollars) in profits annually.

Nonetheless, there is a Hong Kong Venture Capital Association, as well as several venture capital firms, some of which have explored joint venture opportunities with American venture capital firms. For example, Techno-Ventures (Hong Kong) Ltd. is affiliated with Advent International of Boston, a billion dollar network of venture capital firms. As a related example, in Singapore, the government-owned Singapore Technology Corp. recently invested $5 million in Sierra Semiconductor, a California start-up, which has a proprietary technology for custom chips. This eventually led to a $40 million joint venture in Singapore.

Thus, there seems to be several opportunities, albeit limited at this time, for the growth of the venture capital industry in certain Asian countries, particularly in the "four tiger nations."

NETWORKS

Global Networks: A Developing Trend

A recent trend in the global venture capital area has been that of *networks*, sometimes referred to as *strategic alliances*. These are linkages between U.S. venture capital companies and their counterparts around the world, most notably in Europe and Japan. The networks create pools by raising money from pension funds, insurance companies, banks, corporations, and wealthy individuals in much the same way that traditional American venture capital firms do and then invest those funds in ventures throughout the world.

The result is a global information exchange and joint venture relationships among American, European, Australian, and Asian companies. In addition, we see the beginnings of small firms growing on a multinational level as a result of their global linkages. As noted by Arthur Spinner, general partner of the Hambro International Venture Fund, one of the leading players in this arena, "Rather than establishing bases in each U.S. market, we encourage companies to establish hubs here and then think globally, looking at big centres abroad which are just as easily reached through today's technology."[6]

Obviously, financial returns are an important stated objective of such networks. Although these networks are still in their infancy, we've seen evidence of strong financial returns that have resulted in corporate acquisitions and public offerings of several of the venture capital-backed companies.

The Key Players and Their Investments

Advent International is the largest multinational venture capital network, which draws capital and distributes funds throughout the world. Advent has more than one dozen globally managed funds.

Other networks, although much smaller than Advent, include Baring Brothers Hambrecht & Quist, which funds European ventures; Orange-Nassau Group, a Dutch-incorporated, French-owned venture capital firm that has invested some of the money that it has raised from American, European, and Japanese investors in Hong Kong and China; Vista Ventures, of New Canaan, Connecticut, which has invested in Europe and Japan; Alan Patricof Associates, which invests primarily in mature companies and a few high-tech ventures in Europe; and KKI-Hambro International Venture Fund, which has also invested in Europe and Japan.

An example of such an investment is KKI-Hambro's recent funding of Kyokuto Security Systems, a 20-year old company, which is Japan's ninth largest building security company. The KKI-Hambro Fund I was capitalized with $26 million, mostly from Japanese investors, including several large banks and trading companies. Hambro has also invested in Corporate Software, Komag, Inc., and Telematics International, all of which recently went public.

A LOOK AHEAD

In a relatively short period of time, the venture capital industry has expanded to a global industry in which entrepreneurial companies and their investors are located throughout the world. As seen in our examples of Japanese

---

[6]See *Times of London*, April 6, 1987.

investments in venture capital companies, this has resulted in beneficial mutual relationships for all parties involved.

Perhaps the most significant development in the area of international venture capital is the formation of international venture capital networks. Such networks have enhanced and will likely continue to enhance global informational exchanges and joint ventures throughout the world.

The next chapter will address some critical current issues affecting the venture capital industry.

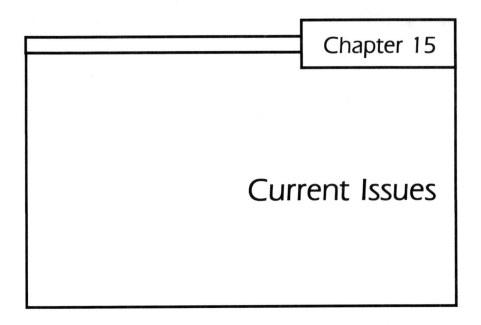

Chapter 15

Current Issues

ECONOMIC AND PUBLIC POLICY ISSUES

The venture capital industry has experienced tremendous success over recent years. The pool of venture capital has increased by tenfold from its $3 billion to $4 billion level of a decade ago. This has been attributed largely to two significant public policy developments:

1. Removal of the impediments to pension funds investing in venture capital pools
2. Successful lobbying to reduce the capital gains tax

In Chapter 6, we discussed the issues involved in pension fund investments as they relate to venture capital. Let's now examine the impact of the capital gains tax on venture capital activity.

Capital Gains Tax Rate and Tax Reform

The Generally Accepted Relationship Between Tax Rates and Venture Capital. A public policy issue of particular interest is the relationship between the capital gains tax rate and the flow of venture capital. What prompted this was the realization that increased flows of venture capital during the period from 1979 to 1984 coincided with a decline in the maximum capital gains tax rate (from 50% to 20%); furthermore, the Tax Reform Act of 1986, which resulted in an increase in the maximum capital gains tax rate for individuals (from 20% to 28% and, in some cases, to 33%) brought fear to venture capitalists that the venture capital pool might be adversely affected.

As noted by Franklin P. Johnson, Jr., partner of the Asset Management Company, a venture capital firm in Palo Alto, California,

> "The most important single element of a strong entrepreneurial environment is the opportunity for individuals to make and keep money ... but the ability to keep it, once earned, is primarily dependent upon tax rates. ... For the entrepreneur and his backers, very low or no taxes on gains from the realization of increases in capital value are a vital condition."[1]

What accounts for this perception? After a near doubling of the capital gains tax rate in 1969, venture capital investments fell from approximately $\frac{1}{2}$ billion annually in the late 1960s to approximately $10 million in 1975. The result was a concern on the part of Congress about the decline of new business formation. This prompted the passage of the Steiger amendment in 1978, which reduced the capital gains tax rate. By the late 1970s, the flow of venture capital began to increase dramatically. The general consensus was that this was a direct result of the lowered tax rates. The venture capital industry was so delighted with this that, in 1979, the National Venture Capital Association (NVCA) established the Steiger Award to be presented annually to "one or more public servants who ... have contributed outstanding service to the nation."[2]

In 1981, Congress reduced further the maximum capital gains tax rate from 28% to 20% (after having lowered it from 49% to 28% in 1979). Not surprisingly, the venture capital industry benefited significantly. According to *Venture Economics*, the total venture capital pool in the United States increased from $3 billion to $6 billion from 1977 to 1981.

In 1984, the Joint Economic Committee (JEC) of Congress reported that, in a survey given to venture capital firms, venture capitalists felt that change in the capital gains tax rate was the *most* important public policy decision affecting the flow of venture capital.[3]

That year, the Treasury Department proposed an increase in the capital

[1]Franklin P. Johnson, Jr., "Making and Keeping Money," *Harvard Colloquium on Entrepreneurship,* July 1983, p. 91.

[2]Previous recipients of the Steiger Award have been:

1989   Congressman Ed Jenkins; Senator Rudy Boschwitz
1988   Vice-President George Bush
1987   Secretary of Labor William E. Brock
1986   Congressman Ed Zschau; Senator Daniel Moynihan
1985   Senator Lloyd Bentsen
1984   Congressman William Fenzel
1983   Senator Bob Packwood
1982   President Ronald Reagan
1981   Congressman James Broyhill; Senator Russell Long
1980   Congressman Barber Conable; Senator Allan Cranston
1979   Congressman James Jones; Senator Clifford Hansen

[3]U.S. Congress, Joint Economic Committee, *Venture Capital and Innovation,* December 1984.

gains tax rates. The response from the venture capital community was summed up well in its most highly regarded journal:

> "Now that the initial shock of the Treasury Department's proposed tax reform program [increases in the capital gains tax rate] has abated, it is time to analyze its effect on the business development process. That is easy. In a word: disaster!"[4]

Small business lobbyists have argued for a a reduction in the capital gains tax, as this will likely encourage capital formation for small business creation. I feel, however, that we must go one step beyond that—to develop a "venture capital gains tax," which would provide tax incentives for typical venture capital investments. Otherwise, it is likely that the incentives derived from a decrease in the capital gains tax will be targeted for larger, established, less risky corporations.

Opposing Viewpoints.   Does the capital gains tax matter that much? Apparently, not everybody believes it does. In 1985, Michael Barker, editor of *Politics and Markets,* reported that he could not find any correlation between the inflows of venture capital and the capital gains tax rate.[5] However, Stanley Pratt, publisher of *Venture Capital Journal* and one of the most respected members of the venture capital community worldwide, argued against Barker's findings, which he attributed to "number crunching." Pratt noted

> "Since *Venture Capital [Journal]'s* first editorial on the Treasury's capital gains tax proposal, there have been a number of rationalizations that this tax change will not adversely affect the venture capital industry and new business development. Most of this thinking has been based on simplistic statistical analyses which display a lack of understanding of the critical role played by the entrepreneur."[6]

The next significant change in our tax structure came in 1986, when the capital gains tax was increased. The result was not a decrease, but an *increase* in the flows of venture capital to a record level in 1987. This was followed by a dramatic *decrease* the following year.

What is happening? Is there a delayed effect? Recently, Professors William Bygraves and Joel Shulman of Babson College sought answers to these questions. They reported that, consistent with Barker's earlier findings, there was no direct correlation between the changes in the capital gains tax rate and the flow of money into the venture capital industry and into businesses funded by venture

---

[4]*Venture Capital Journal,* December 1984.

[5]See *Business Week,* "Do Venture Capitalists Really Need a Tax Break?" April 8, 1985, p. 100.

[6]See *Venture Capital Journal,* March 1985.

capital firms between 1969 and 1987.[7] The study suggested, instead, that the most important predictor of the flow of venture capital was a healthy over-the-counter market.

Of course, it can be argued that Mr. Pratt's earlier quote can be applied to this study as well. However, there is some support for the Bygraves and Shulman study from the global venture capital markets. Particularly, it should be noted that two of the strongest venture capital markets outside of the United States are found in the United Kingdom, which has one of the highest capital gains tax rates, and the Netherlands, which has no capital gains tax. These two countries, like the United States, have a strong secondary market that facilitates initial public offerings.

What can be said about the results? The generally accepted notion, especially within the venture capital industry itself, suggests that the industry is strongest when the capital gains tax rate is lowest. That seems reasonable. However, the research studies have not provided unequivocal support for this contention. Perhaps this is because other important factors, in addition to the capital gains tax rate, strongly affect the amount of venture capital raised. For example, over the last few years there has been more pension fund money in the venture capital pool than at earlier times. Yet pension funds are not taxed. Thus, the capital gains tax rate might have little impact on the investments made by the pension funds, which account for about half the money raised by venture capital firms. On the other hand, the capital gains tax rate might significantly affect the portion of the venture capital pool raised from wealthy individual investors. Interestingly, the studies cited above do not take into account perhaps the largest pool of investment capital (in the United States) for private companies: investments by friends, family, and associates of the entrepreneur, as well as other sources on informal venture capital, which are taxable. In addition, as just suggested, other factors might affect the venture capital pool. For example, the sharp decline in the amount of venture capital raised in 1988 was more likely due to the stock market crash of October 1987 (which is discussed later in this chapter) than to the capital gains tax rate.

The Current Situation and Future Prospects.   Where do we stand now? Beginning in 1988, the maximum capital gains rate was increased from its 1981–1987 rate of 20% to 33% (including the 5% surcharge rate). Concurrently, ordinary income tax rates have declined. The effect of dropping the ordinary tax rates and raising the capital gains tax rate is likely to encourage investors to seek out more secure investments, rather than to tie up money for several years in higher-risk start-up ventures.

Impact on Entrepreneurship and Economic Development.   These developments could have a negative impact, not only on the venture capital industry, but for the economy as a whole. As noted earlier, if the flow of funds to venture

[7]See William D. Bygrave and Joel M. Shulman, "Capital Gains Tax: Bane or Boon for Venture Capital?" in B.A. Kirchoff and others (eds.), *Frontiers of Entrepreneurship Research*, Babson College, Wellesley, Mass., 1988.

capital deals declines, the result is fewer start-ups and expansions, fewer innovative ideas, fewer jobs created, and fewer taxes generated. Venture capital, by itself, will not hurt the entrepreneurial characteristics that are vital to new business formation. However, because venture capital is the catalyst for business development, the effects could be harmful to our entrepreneurial economy.

There are some indirect effects of the capital gains tax increase in entre-preneurship. As the (maximum) rate increases, entrepreneurs with established companies are less inclined to leave secure positions to start new ventures. According to many venture capitalists, the result has been that the pool of talent for venture capital firms has begun to dry up.

Impact on Recruitment and Equity-based Compensation. Another major drawback to the higher capital gains tax is that equity-based compen-sation enhancements are less attractive in attempting to recruit good managers for an entrepreneurial team. It becomes less enticing for a manager to give up a guaranteed, attractive salary at an established company to join an emerging growth venture that offers an equity arrangement to the manager, when the capital gains on the stock, if any, will be taxed the same as ordinary income. The early indicators suggest that, to compensate for this, starting salaries for top-notch managers have risen significantly, which can result in a cash strain for a young business. Consequently, some companies have begun tying ex-ecutive compensation more to profits than to stock. Of course, the capital gains tax rate may be an overstated obstacle if the primary motivation for a manager joining an upstart company is the challenge and intrinsic reward associated with such ventures.

Is the Impact Overstated?   How much of an impact will this have? Most likely, it will not destroy the venture capital industry, but it can have a significant impact. As noted by Patricia Cloherty, general Manager of Tessler & Cloherty, a New York-based venture capital firm, the new law is "A dampener, not a killer."[8]

Many people feel that the effects will be rather insignificant, particularly because pension funds and other large institutional investors, which provide such a large percentage of the pool of money to venture capital firms, are exempt from taxation. In fact, it is reasonable to assume that pension funds will play a greater role in the venture capital process, since they have increased their commitments to venture capital funds from approximately 30% of the total annual commitments to about 50% of the total annual commitments over the past few years. Of course, that percentage increase may be due, in part, to the weakening dollar, which helped to diminish the portion of capital derived from foreign investors.

Some Other Effects of Tax Reform.   There have been several other effects, both positive and negative, of recent tax legislation. A positive result of

---

[8]See Joan C. Szabo, "Raising Venture Capital Now," *Nation's Business,* February 1987, p. 32.

tax reform is that, now that investors have been effectively shut off from investing in nonproductive tax shelters, the venture capital market provides an attractive alternative for their investments.

Another effect of tax reform is the way in which deals are structured. Because current income and capital gains are taxed equally, guaranteed interest income, therefore, becomes more important to some investors than *possible* capital gains on an investment five or seven years down the road. Consequently, this favors structuring investments using a debt–equity structure (that is, debt with warrants, convertible debentures, and the like), rather than one involving straight equity. This has already begun to take place in the industry, partly due to such arrangements satisfying the risk–return preferences of investors.

What will be the ultimate impact of tax reform on the entrepreneurial companies seeking funding? As suggested by Russell French, general partner in the Atlanta-based venture capital firm, Noro-Moseley,

> "The good investment opportunities will get funded on basically the same economic terms as before. Companies with an upside potential will be able to attract management in the same way as before. Compensation structures will be different, but stock options still remain viable. Tax reform is not going to change the basics."[9]

This supports the idea of the long-term orientation of venture capital activity.

OTHER RELATED ISSUES

Venture Capital After the Crash

We know that there is a strong link between the private venture capital market and the public equity markets. This is based on a somewhat cyclical rationale: During bull markets, there is an increase in the number of companies going public; for example, the number of IPOs increased by about fourfold from 1982 to 1983, as the bull market began to take off.

As more emerging growth companies go public, venture capitalists are able to liquidate (at least a portion of) their equity positions in those companies, thereby freeing up capital to invest in similar emerging growth ventures. Thus, as long as the stock market stays strong—and this is generally accompanied by, or follows, a strong IPO market—venture capital is generally abundant, and new business development thrives.

IPOs Before and After the Crash. What happened during the stock market crash of October 1987? We should first examine what happened right before the crash. Throughout the summer of 1987, with the Dow Jones In-

---

[9]See Joan C. Szabo, "Raising Venture Capital Now," *Nation's Business*, February 1987, p. 34.

dustrial Average reaching new highs almost daily, as expected, there was a tremendous increase in the number of IPOs; between May and September, there was an average of approximately sixty IPOs per month.[10] More important, these IPOs were at incredibly overpriced valuations. Start-ups with *no* operating history, which had no reason to go public, filed for their IPOs, with inflated valuations in the millions (or tens of millions) of dollars.

Then, on October 19, 1987, the market crashed. The number of IPOs immediately dropped to less than ten per month. For the first six months of 1988, there were only 132 IPOs, which raised $12.8 billion, as compared to 317 IPOs, which raised $14.9 billion during the same period the previous year. The result was that since companies were not going public and thus venture capitalists were not able to exit from their existing investments, the funds earmarked for investing in private companies temporarily dried up as well.

Positive Developments.   Was disaster inevitable? Actually, it was not. There were several positive outcomes that developed from the events on an around October 19, 1987. First and foremost, we realized that the established venture capital firms are truly interested in the long term. Thus, day-to-day (or month-to-month) fluctuations in the market, which are short-term reactions, prompted largely by greed and fear, will have little bearing on the long-term strategies of venture capitalists. As noted by Donald Valentine, general partner of the San Francisco-based Sequoia Capital,

> "I would say it's a little distressing, but it will have no bearing on whether we invest or not. . . . The venture capital community now is the only group of long term investors, and I see no reason to change our stance simply because some computers in New York run amok. The source of the problem isn't in the fundamental performance of our companies, it's the lack of investors who buy *companies.* Instead, they buy indexes, and they buy options on indexes. Computers keep track of everything, and they end up buying and selling in an unconscionable way."[11]

William Hambrecht, president of Hambrecht & Quist, of San Francisco, one of the largest venture capital firms in the country, adds

> "When emotions clear, the market will catch up with performance. If you build a growth company, the market will recognize it. . . . The market will get back to earnings. The rational question is, is the company making money and is the earnings power growing?"[12]

Although the crash had a devastating short-term effect on the world's

[10]This does not include IPOs priced at less than $1 per share or those that did not have an underwriter.

[11]See Rober A. Mamis, "Venture Capital after the Fall," *Inc.*, December 1987, pp. 187–188.

[12]Ibid.

public equity markets, where values declined by 25% to 35%, the impact was not nearly as severe for venture capital portfolios, which are not as affected by the psychology of the marketplace.

There is strong evidence to support this notion when we examine cases of solid, well-managed companies that have succeeded in raising capital despite the state of the public equity markets. For example, despite it being the "wrong time to start a company," Federal Express was started in 1971 and Tandem Computers in 1974. This suggests that, over the long term, quality companies prevail, regardless of the short-term economic climate of the country.

Impact on the Entrepreneurial Companies.   The effect on the entrepreneur can be more significant than it is on the venture capital community. I am familiar with an entrepreneur who was about to take his computer hardware company public in October 1987. The proposed offering price was $10 per share, which seemed fair in comparison to similar companies that had recently gone public. Then the crash came. The entrepreneur was then told by the underwriters that he would be "lucky" to get $4 per share for the company. Ultimately, he withdrew the offering.

For a stock that has a precrash price of $10 per share to lose 60% or 70% of its value in a few days, when *nothing* has happened to the fundamentals of the company, suggests that the public markets do not necessarily indicate a true "value" for the company. (Venture capitalists are much better than public investors at arriving at an appropriate *long-term* value.) Either the stock was overpriced at $10 or it was underpriced at $4. The important issue is that nothing in the fundamentals of the company had changed, so the prices of the stock, both at the high level and the low level, are more likely to be emotional responses to market conditions than an understanding of the long-term qualities of the company, which is what stock prices are *supposed* to indicate.

For the entrepreneur, this will probably mean that he or she will receive less capital and/or give up more ownership than before. (And such an effect may carry over to the private placement market as well.) In most cases, this will be a better situation. We'll have more realistic valuations and better quality companies going public.

Some Examples.   Some companies have sought other means of financing. For example, MediVision, Inc., a Boston-based operator of eye surgery centers, was a week away from filing its $30 million IPO at the time of the October 19, 1987, crash. Rather than accepting a lower valuation in an IPO, however, the company opted for a private debt financing package, which was arranged by Piper, Jaffray & Hopwood, a Minneapolis-based investment banking firm. Also, as noted in Chapter 11, corporate acquisitions became a very popular exit route even more popular for venture capital-backed companies than IPOs.

Of course, other companies went ahead with their planned IPOs, but at much lower valuations than originally expected. For example, Conner Peripherals, a Dallas-based maker of disk drives (which has since joined the ranks of the *Fortune* 500), and Maxim Integrated Products, a Sunnyvale, California, based manufacturer of analog circuits, went public during that time. A few companies, such as Octel Communications Corp. (Milpitas, California), Vitalink Communications Corp. (Freemont, California), and Silk Greenhouse, Inc. (Tampa, Florida), that went public in early 1988 actually did quite well in the immediate aftermarket for their stock. (Eventually, Silk Greenhouse did a dramatic turn for the worse, losing 90% of its value from its highest price.) The initial success of these companies prompted several other early stage companies, such as Egghead, Inc. (Bothell, Washington), Dell Computer (Dallas, Texas), and Office Depot (Boca Raton, Florida), to file for IPOs within the following months.

The important issue, however, is that the private equity market consists of sophisticated investors with an excellent understanding of valuation techniques for emerging growth ventures. This is not necessarily the case for the public equity markets. Thus, the venture capital industry might be affected temporarily by short-term economic conditions. However, over the long term, quality is the driving force behind the value and the valuation of emerging growth ventures.

A LOOK AHEAD

This chapter has addressed some of the current public policy and economic issues affecting the venture capital industry. In particular, we examined the impact of the capital gains tax rate and the stock market crash on venture capital activity.

To some extent, these issues are similar in that "conventional wisdom" suggests something that is not necessarily supported by empirical research studies. There has been considerable debate regarding the capital gains tax rate. It may very well be that, regardless of what the research suggests, it will be difficult to convince the venture capital industry that they should not be concerned if the capital gains tax is increased.

As far as the stock market crash of 1987 is concerned, it happened so suddenly that there is little research available to provide us with much needed answers. Nonetheless, it is probably best to view it as a once in a lifetime event that had a significant short-term effect, but a negligible long-term effect on the venture capital industry.

Chapter 16

Some Closing Thoughts

This book has been an attempt to provide the reader with an understanding of the nature of venture capital and its impact on entrepreneurial companies in terms of growth, profitability, and the like, and on the economy as a whole in terms of revenues and taxes generated, jobs created, and more. The book has been *descriptive*, in its emphasis on the role of *venture catalysts* in entrepreneurial growth and economic development, and has been *prescriptive*, in providing guidelines to assist the entrepreneur in his or her search for venture funding.

Although the material presented throughout this book has resulted from several years of research and experience in the area of venture capital, I feel that we have barely uncovered the "tip of the iceberg" on this subject. Numerous issues should be addressed in the coming years to broaden our knowledge base.

<hr/>

Early on in this book, I presented several examples that illustrate the role of *venture catalysts* and that reinforce their strong positive impact on building companies and on making the entrepreneurial dream a reality. It is important to continually examine this premise over time and to determine how the role of the venture capitalist has changed and is likely to change over the coming years. It is also important to examine how the role compares from one venture capital firm to another. Perhaps, most important, we need to continue to examine case studies that describe *both* the positive ("dream maker") and negative ("deal breaker") aspects of venture capital.

Throughout this book, I have cited examples of how venture capitalists have assisted companies in their growth as well as counterexamples of how venture capitalists have provided little, if anything, to such companies. We can draw a few preliminary conclusions from these examples. One important conclusion is that the venture capital industry is made up of professionals, the quality of whom varies considerably. While the better ones have acted in the traditional venture capital role of building companies, there are others who have treated venture capital investments just like any other passive investment. An even greater concern regarding the professionals in this industry is the influx of "quick-buck artists," who have tainted the image of this industry. This would suggest that stronger, consistent standards should be established to promote the integrity of the venture capital industry in order to protect the interests of both the venture capital firms and the entrepreneurial companies in which they invest.

Another conclusion that we can draw from the case examples presented in this book is that, *theoretically*, the relationship between the venture capitalist and the company being funded should be beneficial for both parties; moreover, the venture capitalist should play an active role in assisting the company on matters related to its long-term direction, and the entrepreneurial company should take control over day-to-day operations. Unfortunately, these roles do not necessarily take effect in the manner in which they were intended. Often, an adversarial relationship develops between the two parties. Why? As discussed earlier, this is often indicative of selected individuals in the profession, rather than of the industry as a whole. Thus, it is important that entrepreneurs be selective in choosing investors, just like venture capitalists are selective in choosing companies in which to invest. Second, there are times when venture capitalists *should* and *do* take a more active role in the venture, even if it means taking on greater control than was originally expected. After all, the venture capitalists have a lot of money at risk in a given venture capital deal and are accountable to their limited partners for the performance of such investments.

〰〰〰〰〰〰〰

It is also important that we examine the impact of venture capital not just for selected companies, but for the broader economy. The GAO study that was discussed in Chapter 3 gave us a useful, but limited, understanding of the impact of venture capital on economic development. Such a study should be carried out on an annual basis to help us better understand and appreciate the economic impact of venture capital activity.

It is also important to understand the impact of *informal* risk capital investments on entrepreneurial companies and on the economy. What can be done to encourage further informal as well as formal venture capital activity? This information has dramatic implications for public policy decisions and on regulations affecting the venture capital industry.

We have a basic understanding of the key players involved in the venture funding process, the venture capitalists, the investors in the venture capital funds, and the "investees," as well as of the relationships among the key players. However, our knowledge is limited. For example, what are the specific activities in which venture capitalists get involved with an entrepreneurial company after funding the deal? What role do venture capitalists play on boards of directors? What differences exist from one venture capital firm to another? We must conduct the necessary case studies that follow up the activities of venture capital firms *after* an investment is made by them in a given company.

We also have a basic understanding of the venture capital funding process. However, there are still several unanswered questions: How does the screening process compare from one venture capital firm to another? How are decisions made regarding initial funding by a venture capital firm as compared to follow-up funding by the same firm? How are risk and return evaluated? How are investments monitored? How is the evaluation of investments conducted? What can be done to improve the venture capital process?

We also have data (although limited) on the short- and long-term performance of selected venture capital investments as well as of venture capital portfolios as a whole. It is important to monitor the performance of venture capital firms on a regular basis and to compare those results to the performance of other available investments. In addition, more attention needs to be devoted to the performance of LBOs and later-stage investments, which have taken on an increasingly greater portion of the portfolios of major venture capital firms.

◄◄◄◄◄◄◄◄►►►►►►►►

In summary, we have developed a basic understanding of selected aspects of venture capital activity and of the key players involved in the process. Our quest for new knowledge in this field should be carried out on a continual basis.

Although the venture capital industry itself has been a rather recent development in this country, we have presented numerous examples, both positive and negative, of the impact of this industry on selected companies and on the economy as a whole. Despite the problems encountered by some entrepreneurs in dealing with venture capitalists, overall the cases presented throughout this book illustrate how *venture catalysts* can fuel entrepreneurial growth in this country. Consequently, entrepreneurial companies have benefited, investors have profited, and the economy has prospered.

Index of Companies and Entrepreneurs*

*Includes top managers, entrepreneurial companies, large corporations, officers, and directors

Index of Venture Capitalists*

*Includes venture capital firms, incubators, banks, investment banking firms, investors, and other related companies

Subject Index